Proclaim Liberty

Proclaim Liberty

Essays on Freedom and the Future of America

Edited by Jamin Hübner

Hills Publishing Group • Rapid City, South Dakota

Proclaim Liberty
Copyright ©2016 Jamin Hübner
All Rights Reserved.
Printed in the United States of America

Hills Publishing Group
Rapid City, South Dakota
hillspublishinggroup@protonmail.com

ISBN-10: 0-9905943-2-7
ISBN-13: 978-0-9905943-2-1

CONTENTS

Contributors...xii

Editor's Preface xiv

Jamin Hübner

Part I: Essays on Liberty

1. The Magna Carta, Then and Now 18

   Debra Shattuck

2. Religion, *Logos*, and Freedom: An Interdisciplinary Approach ...26

   Bret Saunders

3. Enrichment versus Job-Training: An Answer to the Forces of

   Educational Disruption...55

   Hunter Baker

4. Nullification: The Rightful Remedy...73

   Michael Maharrey

5. Fake Money and Fraudulent Banking: The Greatest Threats to

   American Liberty 94

   Jamin Hübner

6. Christian Reflections on Privacy Rights

   and the Surveillance State 170

   Jamin Hübner

Part II: Obergefell vs. Hodges

7. Reflections on Religious Liberty in Light of the Current Crisis .. 194
   Hunter Baker
8. Gay Marriage and the Fourteenth Amendment 212
   Debra Shattuck
9. Fundamental Differences: How the Legal Lineage of *Obergefell*
   Can Help Us Frame a Response to it 230
   Donald Roth

CONTRIBUTORS

Hunter Baker is University Fellow and Associate Professor of Political Science at Union University in Jackson, Tennessee. He is a graduate of Florida State University (BS), University of Houston Law Center (JD), University of Georgia (MPA), and Baylor University (PhD). He is the author of *The End of Secularism, Political Thought* and *The System Has a Soul*.

Jamin Hübner is the Director of Institutional Effectiveness and Founding Chair of Christian Studies at John Witherspoon College in the Black Hills. He is a graduate of Dordt College (BA Theology), Reformed Theological Seminary (MA Religion), the University of South Africa (ThD Theology), and is currently finishing an MS in Applied Economics from Southern New Hampshire University. He is the author of *Mishandling the Word of Truth* and other books.

Michael Maharrey is the National Communications Director for the Tenth Amendment Center. He is a graduate of the University of South Florida St. Petersburg (BA Mass Communications) and the University of Kentucky (BA Accounting). In addition to having written for several major newspapers, he is the author of *Our Last Hope: Rediscovering the Lost Path to Liberty*, *Smashing Myths: Understanding Madison's Notes on Nullification*, and *Nullification Objections: Dismantling the Opposition*.

Donald Roth is Assistant Professor of Criminal Justice and Business Administrator at Dordt College in Sioux Center, IA. He is a graduate of Dordt College (BA History), and Georgetown University (JD, LLM Taxation). He is a member of the State Bar of California and is the author of *Building a House in the Sand*.

Bret Saunders is Associate Professor of Humanities and Director of Learning Resources at John Witherspoon College in the Black Hills. He is a graduate of New Saint Andrews College (BA Liberal Arts and Culture), and the University of Dallas (MA, PhD Philosophy), and was selected to participate in the 2014 National Endowment for the Humanities seminar at the University of Chicago.

Debra Shattuck is Provost and Associate Professor of History at John Witherspoon College in the Black Hills. In addition to being a retired Air Force Colonel, she is a graduate of Lorain County Community college (AA), Cedarville University (BA History and Secondary Ed.), Brown University (MA History), Industrial College of the Armed Forces (MS Strategic Resource Management), and the University of Iowa (PhD, History). She is author of *Bloomer Girls: Women Baseball Pioneers*.

Editor's Preface

Jamin Hübner

2015 marked the 800th anniversary of the *Magna Carta*. In commemoration of the event, various universities and organizations around the world hosted conferences, conventions, and publishing projects relating to liberty and civil freedoms. In fall of the year, John Witherspoon College hosted the public conference entitled *Proclaim Liberty: Freedom and the Future of America* in Rapid City, South Dakota. This volume represents the proceedings from the conference.

As it turned out, 2015 also marked the year of a legal milestone in the topic of religious and civil freedom: *Obergefell vs. Hodges,* where the Supreme Court ruled 5-4 in favor of recognizing gay marriage as a "fundamental right." Naturally, the gathering in the Black Hills included a number of presentations surrounding this controversial decision. As the conference Director, it became clear that the contemporary hubbub had the potential to transform the event into "The Gay Marriage Conference," which would hardly be desirable. (On second thought, perhaps we might have had more attendance with this title!). To diversify the offerings, I invited Michael Maharrey of the Tenth Amendment Center to give an introduction to "nullification," and gave a talk myself on central banking and the meaning of money. While this helped balance the selection of topics, the overall effect was still a little lopsided.

It naturally became a priority to include additional contributions in the present volume. I was able to get my colleague Dr. Bret Saunders to write on freedom and the human person, addressing the need for a more penetrating, philosophical discussion. After a long search, I was unable to obtain a contribution on privacy rights and the discoveries of Edward Snowden—an important topic on American freedom if there ever was one. I contacted the Cato Institute, Mises Institute, Acton Institute, Institute for Justice, Heritage Foundation, and a number of individual scholars who might be able to locate someone to write on the topic. The answer was always the same: "not my area" or "don't have time."

I cannot bring myself to publish a volume on freedom in America without addressing privacy rights. Contemporary government surveillance is too important of a topic to ignore. If that means writing an essay on it myself, then so be it. (And that's what happened.)

The final result is hopefully a most enlightening symposium divided into two main categories (outlined above in the Table of Contents). It goes without saying that readers will find some essays more beneficial than others, and that the contributors do not all necessarily agree with each other on the matters they discuss. All, however, share basic Christian convictions and a common concern about the liberties of the nation in which we all live.

Some essays also have a roundabout way of addressing this topic, while others confront matters head-on. Some are more academic in tone, while others colloquial and conversational. Some are very upfront about their Christian and political convictions, while others are not. All of this is to a reader's benefit, who will undoubtedly find something for their particular interest and appetite.

Where editorial remarks proved useful, I inserted footnotes prefaced with "Ed.:" to identify where those insertions occur. Otherwise, I have generally avoided trying to "improve" upon the work of each author.

In the end, may this work be edifying to those who read it and catalyze intelligent discussion about freedom and the future of America.

Jamin Hübner
Black Hills
July, 2016

Proclaim Liberty

1

The Magna Carta, Then and Now

Debra Shattuck

Good afternoon everyone. Let me add my welcome to those you have already heard. We at JWC are delighted that you could join us for this conference and we hope that you come away from it with a renewed sense of appreciation for the ideals of liberty and freedom that have been at the foundation of U.S. civil life for over 200 years.

Before I begin the formal portion of my talk I want to introduce a special guest who has joined us today.[1] John Wilkinson is a former Royal Air Force Flight Lieutenant who spent his formative years during World War II in the cockpit of British Spitfires defending the freedoms we celebrate today. In 1940, the 17-year-old John watched the Battle of Britain from the ground and was forced to climb through rubble and between burning buildings in London to get to work each day. When he turned 18, John volunteered for flight training, graduating with honors as the best flying cadet in his class. He was soon pressed into service flying bomber escort missions deep into Germany. John eventually flew over 1,000 hours, many of them in combat.

---

[1] Ed.: Because of health issues, Wilkinson was not able to actually attend the conference.

He shot down three German FW-190s and indirectly destroyed a fourth. He also destroyed 80 ground vehicles and targets. John had many close calls during World War II, including six in-flight engine failures. Wow! John credits the "hand of the Lord" for preserving his life during the war, but it was not until 1968 that he gave his life to Christ and was "born again." I had the opportunity to hear John tell his wartime story in September at a meeting of the Black Hills Veterans Writer's Group. I was delighted when he mentioned that, as a boy, he had attended school in a castle where the Magna Carta had spent the night before being presented to King John at Runnymede. I knew then that we had to invite John to attend our conference. I am so pleased he could join us. John is a living link to two important historical events, separated by seven hundred years. His presence reminds us that the past is always present. We can directly trace the events of our day to those of the distant past. And, more importantly, we are reminded that historical events are *human* events, shaped by the decisions and actions of individuals like John. Please join me in welcoming Flight Lieutenant John Wilkinson to our conference.

~

The ideals of liberty and freedom are not unique to the United States nor did they originate with the Enlightenment thinkers of the eighteenth century who inspired a generation of American colonists to integrate them into the new form of government they created for the United States in 1787. Though we tend to think of liberty and freedom as *political* ideals, first planted (some would say) in the soil of a place called Runnymede in 1215, they are in fact *spiritual* ideals placed into the heart of man by God Himself. In the Old Testament, we learn that God instituted the celebration of Jubilee—a time when His people were to free their servants and to return home to property and clans. In the New Testament, we hear Christ's proclamation that He had been sent (in fulfillment of Isaiah's prophecy) to "proclaim liberty to the captives" and to "set at liberty those who are oppressed,"[2] God has taught man to value liberty and freedom. These ideals lie at the heart of Christianity. Paul reminded Galatian believers: "For freedom Christ has set us free; stand firm therefore, and do not submit again to a yoke of slavery."[3]

Though Christ and Paul were speaking of liberty and freedom from a spiritual perspective, those who heard them must certainly have hoped that their words applied also to their political status; the Jews and Christians of first century Palestine were, after all, suffering under the sometimes brutal rule of the polytheistic Romans. But, for over 1,200 years following the birth of Christianity, there was little indication that the ideals of liberty and freedom would ever cross over into the political realm. Across the globe, men and women lived and died under the self-proclaimed authority of absolute monarchs, local petty dictators, and power brokers of every stripe—ecclesiastical and secular. Until the late eighteenth century, individuals had few political or human rights the way we understand them today. Most human beings were not citizens in the modern sense of the word; they were subjects—subordinated to the whims and the will of those who ruled over them—rulers who not only made the law, but considered themselves above the law.

Many scholars trace the origins of modern civil liberties to 1215 when rebellious British barons forced their king to affirm a set of demands they had inscribed on a sheet of parchment. Over time, individuals began referring to this document, sealed by King John at Runnymede, as the "Magna Carta." This is technically incorrect. The "Magna Carta" did not exist by that name until November 1217 when England's regent, William Marshall, issued a revised version of the Runnymede treaty on behalf of the 11-year-old monarch, King Henry III. This "Charter of Liberties" was issued along with another document called "The Charter of the Forest." Because the Charter of Liberties was written on a larger piece of parchment than the Charter of

---

[2] Lk 4:18 and Is 61:1 (ESV).

[3] Gal 5:1 (ESV).

the Forest, it became known as the "Great Charter" or "Magna Carta" in Latin.

The other thing you should know about the "Great Charter" (the Magna Carta) is that, while it does include statements relating to individual rights that subsequent generations would elevate to the level of political holy grail, these statements were *not* the centerpiece of the document; they comprise only a few of the over 60 clauses in the original agreement. You will not find overt statements about inalienable human rights (like life, liberty, and the pursuit of happiness) in the Magna Carta, but you will glimpse these ideals in their natal form. Over subsequent centuries, the Magna Carta inspired millions of men and women across the globe to assert their rights as human beings to freedom and to equal treatment under the law. Thus, it is really the legacy of the Magna Carta, more so than the original document itself, that we celebrate today.

So what sparked the creation of the Magna Carta in the first place? For the next ten minutes or so, I am going to describe the historical context that birthed the Magna Carta. The document that evolved into the Magna Carta of 1217 was a peace treaty negotiated between King John and his barons during a civil war in England. The treaty consisted of 4,000 words, divided into 63 clauses that had been hammered out during tense negotiations over the previous weeks. Renounced by Pope Innocent III as invalid and void just three months later, that treaty did nothing to end the civil war. In fact, as scholar Nicholas Vincent notes, "nearly one-third of its words were either dropped or substantially rewritten within the first ten years of its existence" and over the subsequent centuries, "all but four" of the treaty's original clauses were declared obsolete and erased from British statute books.[4]

The peace treaty sealed at Runnymede in June 1215 culminated years of tension between John and his barons. John had come to power in 1199 at the age of 32 when his much beloved older brother, King Richard I (also known

---

[4] Nicholas Vincent, *Magna Carta: A Very Short Introduction* (New York: Oxford University Press, 2012), 3-4. Kindle edition.

as Richard the Lionheart) died of wounds sustained in battle. John quickly alienated many of his barons and church officials by his heavy-handed policies, particularly those related to raising revenue. In medieval kingdoms it was assumed that monarchs owned all the lands in their kingdoms. They used these lands to garner favor from supporters and to raise revenue. Monarchs deeded land to wealthy subjects in exchange for vows of fidelity and a share of the wealth produced on those lands. One of the primary responsibilities of any kingdom's landed aristocracy was to raise the armies that protected monarchs from foreign and domestic attacks and that fought whatever wars the monarchs decided were necessary.

There was always a delicate balancing act that played out between monarchs and their landed aristocrats when it came to exercising power and distributing revenues. One of the ways monarchs raised money was to levy a tax on families to retain lands given to their now-deceased patriarchs. If families wanted to inherit the lands—they had to pay a price. Monarchs also charged money to their barons who wanted to marry; in some cases, they charged the barons money to authorize the marriage of sons or daughters. Monarchs charged barons fees known as "scutage taxes" if they chose to send a substitute in their place when called upon to join a military campaign. All of these fees and taxes were tolerated by Europe's landed aristocracy as a necessary evil. John, however, took fundraising to an extreme that alienated his barons and caused them to rebel. Within a few years of assuming the British crown in 1199, John lost almost all of the provinces in France that had been part of his realm. Determined to regain this lost territory, John spent millions of pounds funding several unsuccessful invasions of France. To raise money for these campaigns, John began charging his barons exorbitant sums for inheritance taxes, scutage, and marriage fees. In 1214, for example, he demanded over £13,000 from one of his barons who was seeking permission to marry. In addition to his usurious fiscal policies, John also gained a reputation as a brutal and lecherous ruler who condemned political enemies and their families to dungeons and who regularly attempted to seduce the wives of his barons. Many believed he had murdered his own nephew in 1203 to prevent disloyal subjects from elevating him to the monarchy.[5]

By the summer of 1214, after John led yet another failed attempt to recapture his lost lands in France, many of his barons had had enough. They began conspiring to overthrow him and proceeded over the next year to rally support for their cause and to capture London. Their actions led directly to the meeting at Runnymede where John put his royal seal to the wax on the treaty, symbolizing his agreement with its contents. The clauses within the charter were wide-ranging, addressing numerous issues of contention:

- In clause 1, John confirmed that he and his "heirs in perpetuity" would respect the fact that "the English Church is to be free and have its rights in whole and its liberties unimpaired." (This clause was a result of a major conflict between John and Pope Innocent III between 1207 and 1213 over the right of the Pope to appoint archbishops within England. When John had stubbornly refused to agree, Pope Innocent had placed the entire country of England under interdict—forbidding the sacraments to British subjects.)

- Clauses 2-8 addressed the issue of inheritance taxes and fees for marriages, stipulating that these would be fair and that the widows of barons would not be forced to remarry against their will.

- Clause 13 promised to restore free commerce "by land and water" to London and other "cities, boroughs, towns, and ports." The related clause 33 stated that "Henceforth all fish-weirs will be completely removed from the Thames and the Medway and throughout all England, except on the sea coast." (These large wooden or masonry fish traps, placed on behalf of the monarchy, had been hindering river traffic for years.)

---

[5] Dan Jones, "The Mad King & Magna Carta," *Smithsonian* 46:4 (Jul/Aug 2015): 50-57.

- Other clauses promised that fines and taxes would be reasonable and would be negotiated.

- A number of clauses dealt with the right of individuals to protection of the law and trial by their peers. Clause 38 ensured that "Henceforth, no baliff will put anyone on trial by his own unsupported allegation, without bringing credible witnesses to the charge." Clause 39 stated: "No free man will be taken or imprisoned or disseized [deprived of his property or land] or outlawed or exiled in any way ruined, nor shall we go or send against him, save by the lawful judgement of his peers and by the law of the land." And Clause 40 promised, "to no one shall we deny or delay right or justice."

You can hear, in those last few clauses, the prelude to our cherished civil rights regarding protection from unlawful search and seizure, trial by jury, and equal protection under the law. Among the other concessions John was forced to make was to stop bringing foreign mercenaries to England, to give up huge swaths of forest he had claimed for the exclusive use of the crown, and to restore all the "lands, castles, liberties" and rights he had taken from his political enemies and to refund them any excessive fees he had collected. John promised to allow the barons to select a panel of 25 of their peers who would advise him on matters and help adjudicate disagreements between him and his barons.

It should come as no surprise that the words on the document King John sealed under duress at Runnymede in June 1215 did little to change him. The royal charter did not end the armed conflict. The panel of 25 barons never materialized. Instead, John immediately turned to his former enemy, Pope Innocent III who, three months later, granted John's request to declare the charter null and void. Once again the subjects of Britain found themselves facing papal censure. In 1216, some of John's rebellious barons invited France's Prince Louis to Britain and pledged their allegiance to him as their future king. In October 1216, events took another turn when the hated King

John died of dysentery and was replaced by his 9-year-old son, Henry. England's barons immediately withdrew their support from Louis and pledged fidelity to the boy king. It was thus the coronation of Henry III, not the treaty of Runnymede, that ended the military standoff between monarch and barons.

Yet, the treaty of Runnymede lived on. It became a powerful symbol of the ideals of liberty and the rule of law down through the centuries. After 1217, British monarchs reissued new versions of the Magna Carta whenever they needed to quell revolts. It was the Magna Carta of 1297, issued by Henry III's son, King Edward I, that was officially entered into British statute roles, thus becoming the law of the land. Once it gained this status, the king could no longer change it unilaterally—it could only be amended by parliament. The Magna Carta inspired numerous modifications to English law, including the Habeas Corpus Act of 1679 and the Bill of Rights passed under William and Mary in 1689. As early as the 1630s, phrases from the Magna Carta appeared in statutes published in the English colonies in North America. You can hear echoes of the Magna Carta in the clauses of the U.S. Declaration of Independence that condemn King George III for "imposing taxes on us without our consent" and for "transporting large armies of foreign mercenaries to complete the works of death, desolation and tyranny." In December 1948, when Eleanor Roosevelt unveiled the U.N. Declaration of Human Rights she had helped to write, she called it, "a Magna Carta for all mankind."[6]

The past is always present and, today, we are the beneficiaries of the determination of courageous men to assert their right to be treated fairly by their monarch. Though these men never intended to usher in new forms of political governance or to socially uplift the millions of commoners in realms across Europe and the world, their actions inspired generations of men and women to do just that. The spirit of Magna Carta lives on.

---

[6] "The Story of Magna Carta," Documentary by Guy Fox Historical Projects, Ltd., 2015. www.bl.uk/magna-carta/videos/what-is-magna-carta."

2

Religion, *Logos,* and Freedom:
An Interdisciplinary Approach

Bret Saunders

Introduction

These are hard times for religion. Although people in power—whether political, popular, or academic—are happy to pay lip service to religion and its importance, few other institutions are being so radically misinterpreted and attacked. Religion was once considered the architecture of life. The term "religion" used to refer to a relationship with a transcendent being, beliefs about that being, and liturgical practices—all of which were supposed to shape an individual's thoughts, words, and deeds. Not so today.

In the West the main attack on religion is coming from the "New Atheists" claim that "religion poisons everything"[1] and that we must recognize "the absurdity of most of our religious beliefs."[2] For them religion

---

[1] Christopher Hitchens, *God Is Not Great: How Religion Poisons Everything* (New York: Hachette Book Group, 2007).

[2] Sam Harris, *The End of Religion* (New York: W. W. Norton & Company, 2005), 48.

is dangerous, not just in public but in principle. You never know what evil may spread among true believers, because at root all religions are "radical." Religion threatens the very essence of liberal society.

There is, however, another view that is more dangerous because it is both more widespread and more "tolerant." According to this view, "religion" refers to little more than a hobby, a relaxing pastime fully compatible with a liberal society. That is why Michelle Obama can speak of "freedom of worship" instead of the Constitution's "free exercise of religion" in public life.[3] Now religion may be a very meaningful hobby; it is nonetheless one hobby among others. It may offer meaningful friendships; they are still one community among others. Whether undertaken for diversion, comfort, or companionship, religious "activities" do not unite life as a whole because they occupy separate departments of life and are woven into life by something else.[4]

Where does the religion-as-hobby version come from?

It may be surprising to hear that "religion," in the sense of "a system of beliefs in a supreme being," was an invention of early modern philosophers and theologians. In the Middle Ages the term *religio* appeared rarely but usually referred to "the liturgical practices of the church" or to "a virtue…,

---

[3] See Ross Douthat, "Defining Religious Liberty Down," http://www.nytimes.com/2012/07/29/opinion/sunday/douthat-defining-religious-liberty-down.html?_r=0 (accessed 2/26/16).

[4] In one of the greatest sentences in recent Christian writing, David Bentley Hart lampoons "consumerist" religion: "[O]ne may cultivate a private atmosphere of 'spirituality' as undemanding and therapeutically comforting as one likes simply by purchasing a dream catcher, a few pretty crystals, some books on the goddess, a Tibetan prayer wheel, a volume of Joseph Campbell or Carl Jung or Robert Graves, a Nataraja figurine, a purse of tiles engraved with runes, a scattering of Pre-Raphaelite prints drenched in Celtic twilight, an Andean flute, and so forth, until this mounting congeries of string, worthless quartz, cheap joss sticks, baked clay, kitsch, borrowed iconography, and fraudulent scholarship reaches that mysterious point of saturation at which religion has become indistinguishable from interior decorating." *Atheist Delusions* (New Haven & London: Yale University Press, 2009), 24.

[a] knowledge embodied in the disciplined actions of the Christian."[5] It was the concrete and definite shape by which one's relationship to the divine expressed itself in action. It was how obedience to the first commandment expressed itself in the second. It was both the extent to which we fulfill our covenantal obligations to Yahweh and the extent to which we fulfill our obligations to our neighbors (Mt. 25:40). Religion was what God does for us in worship, what we do for God in worship, and what we do for others as an extension of our worship. Prior to the modern period, therefore, *religio* denoted a specific personal relationship to a divine being, a relationship expressed in specific, concrete acts of worship—indeed, in a way of life.

Then came modernity and the degradation of religion from its culturally incarnate form into Deism and then atheism.[6] "The rise of the concept 'religion' is in some ways correlated with a decline in the practice of religion itself."[7] Some thinkers in the 15th century began referring to "religion" as a generic impulse of human nature that could be expressed in any number of specific and valid forms, none of which are comprehended by the concept itself. For others, "Religion move[d] from a virtue to a set of propositions."[8] Various "religions" might differ in propositional content, but all their members could peacefully coexist in a modern nation-state. Religion might claim authority over the private sphere of the heart, but the political sovereign ruled the body and regulated whatever concrete liturgies it might engage in. Thus Spinoza distinguished between "external and inward religion" to show "that the Right over matters spiritual lies wholly with the Sovereign, and that the outward forms of religion should be in accordance with Public Peace, if

---

[5] William T. Cavanaugh, "A Fire Strong Enough to Consume the House: The Wars of Religion and the Rise of the State," *Modern Theology* 11:4, October 1995, 397-420; here 404.

[6] See John Milbank, *Theology and Social Theory* (Oxford: Blackwell, 2006); Michael J. Buckley, *At the Origins of Modern Atheism* (New Haven & London: Yale University Press, 1996).

[7] Cavanaugh, "Fire," 404, quoting Wilfred Cantrell Smith, *The Meaning and End of Religion* (New York: The Macmillan Company, 1962), 19.

[8] Cavanaugh, "Fire," 404.

we would worship God aright."[9] Although in Spinoza's modern state "every man may think what he likes, and say what he thinks,"[10] that does not mean that he may act as he believes. Spinoza grants "religion" an outward form, but only if it is separated from any doctrinal roots.

The Early Modern period set the stage for the broader privatization of religion in the Enlightenment. Although a few thinkers continued to try to rationalize religion, it migrated further into the Romantic realm of private emotion, where the Second Great Awakening found it. Whereas "in past centuries religion had been the integrating factor of Western culture[,] in the eighteenth century it was forced to the sidelines."[11]

In his "Farewell Address," George Washington named morality based on religion as one of the "twin pillars" of democracy. The New Atheists would reject that claim, but to those of us who agree with Washington, the current misunderstanding about and animosity toward religion is deeply worrisome. Many of our own allies are clueless about what has happened to "religion;" how familiar words are chirped by politicians with very different meanings; how religion is being systematically banished from public life by "tolerance" and soft despotism. Therefore, what is desperately needed is religion—full-bodied, public, political religion. Only "deep" religion quenches our deepest thirsts and fulfills our highest hopes. Why can it do that? Not because of "the religious impulse at the core of our nature" but because religion just is our nature, as I will argue further on.

But before we begin this recovery of the genuine meaning of religion, we need to introduce its companion concept—freedom. Notice how freedom is central to the attack on religion today: although the liberal left wants us free for our private cult practices, they agree with the New Atheists that a robust public religion threatens freedom—the freedom of individual choice,

---

[9] Benedict de Spinoza, *A Theologico-Political Treatise*, trans. R. H. M. Elwes (New York: Dover, 1951), 245.

[10] Spinoza, *Treatise*, 257.

[11] Louis Duprè, *The Enlightenment and the Intellectual Foundations of Modern Culture* (New Haven & London: Yale University Press, 2004), 229.

democratic process, science, reason, and liberal institutions devoted to the public good (whatever that is; usually "as determined by experts"). Religion *restricts*; religion persecutes the Galileos of every age.

The problem with this "critique" of religion is that it often depends on a flawed notion of freedom. Thinkers throughout the Western tradition have long recognized the difference between negative and positive freedom— between freedom *from* and freedom *for*.[12] The authors of the First Amendment were protecting an external, negative freedom, a freedom from restraint or compulsion in the areas of speech, conscience, assembly, and the press. This kind of freedom gets more attention both in the Constitution and the Declaration of Independence: all men have a right to "liberty," which is the freedom to "pursue happiness" within the proper bounds of representative governments.

However, we need to recognize another, complementary sense of freedom: the internal freedom that consists in our capacity to think, act, function or be in any way. This is what the classical tradition called "excellence" or "virtue." For example, in playing the guitar I am free to play songs within the range of my limited abilities. I am not (now) free to play "Blackbird" by the Beatles or a tune by Bach. Think of these two senses of freedom like the forces at work on a moving car. External freedom means the e-brake is off, the car is in drive, there is no concrete barrier, red light, etc. Internal freedom means it has fuel and the engine is running. These two senses of freedom are important because, as the American Founders recognized, our external freedoms are only valid and good if driven by internal freedom, i.e. if practiced by people are free from vice and free for acts of virtue. As Washington said, "Human rights can only be assured among a virtuous people." Clearly, freedom *for*, internal freedom, is increasingly neglected today because freedom tends to mean something more like "uninhibited total self-determination."

---

[12] The most eloquent recent statement of this distinction is Isaiah Berlin, "Two Concepts of Liberty," in *Four Essays on Liberty* (New York: Oxford University Press, 1984).

So, because the attack and misunderstanding of religion intertwines with a misunderstood notion of freedom, in what follows I am attempting a double search-and-rescue: although I will be searching explicitly for religion, I expect to grapple with the deeper meaning of freedom too and how it interlaces with religion. My argument, in short, is that the concepts of religion and freedom are co-determinative and therefore mutually reinforcing. In other words, in as much as religion is realized, so much is freedom realized. Conversely: so much liberty, so much religion. Freedom rings if and only if a worshipper sings.

To advance this argument, I will first draw on historical and philosophical resources to develop a working definition of religion as "constant binding." Then I will explore the ways in which the religious qualities of human beings are rooted in their deeper nature as *logos*. I will argue that *logos* and its religious expressions liberate, paradoxically, *through* bondage. In concluding I will argue that the American zeitgeist undermines *logos* and thereby freedom.

Religio as "Constant Binding"

It may seem misguided to start by excavating the word-roots of "religion." Don't we risk committing the dreaded "etymological fallacy"? Yes, but it's worth the risk. C. S. Lewis once commented, "of course language is not an infallible guide, but it contains, with all its defects, a good deal of stored insight and experience."[13]

The word religion derives from the Latin prefix *re-* ("again") and the verb *ligare*, "to bind." *Re-* can mean simply "again" or "a second time," as in "review," but it can also mean "again and again." We find *ligare* in "ligament," "ligature," "obligation," "oblige," "allegiance". Thus the Latin noun *religio*, speaking strictly etymologically, means "constant binding," the constant link,

---

[13] Introduction to *The Four Loves*, in *The Beloved Works of C. S. Lewis* (Edison: Inspirational Press, 2004), 213.

bond, or band. Religion binds human beings in two directions. It binds horizontally in that it makes the lives of human beings cohere by threading their thoughts, actions, and relationships together throughout the days and years. It restricts the hopes, options, or choices of the believer. It places restrictions on all the circumstances pertaining to actions—on timing, means, purpose, place, etc. For example, it tells the unmarried that sexual relations are good, but not now. It says that worship of the divine is good but not just in any way or anywhere.

On the other hand, it binds vertically because this thread is or indicates an ultimate value, idea, or person. Whatever motivates you to get up in the morning, whatever gives you energy and fulfillment, whatever is the end for which all else is a mean—that is your religion. Religion is the primary integrating factor in the lives of individuals and cultures, even where they do not "worship" a personal being or even admit its existence. Etymologically, the word does not presuppose either theism or "organized" religion.

Some might dispute the reality of religion in this sense. Is there really an ultimate binding principle and force on people's lives, or do some people adhere to multiple values, purposes, or "gods"? The answer is yes and no. Many do not recognize what drives them at the deepest level. If they honestly searched their hearts, they might indeed find a single, fundamental motivation. What is the ultimate reason for making the decisions you make—especially the weightier decisions? Most ends are means for further ends, but what is that final end? You went to college (primarily) so you could get a job so you could pursue your gifts and provide for children, so that….what? Some people pretend to live in the moment of separate desires. "I pursued Taekwondo because I wanted to; then I joined the tennis club because I was into tennis; then I took up poker. I do what feels good; I live for pleasure." This sort of talk expresses the mistaken idea that one may live without religion, without a single binding force on one's life. But such a life reduces to pleasure, which in turn reduces to Self. What is supposed to unify their lives is selfishness, but this bond hasn't the conceptual fullness and energy to accomplish the task assigned it. To the extent that a person or people has multiple "ultimates" (other than Self), their lives and culture will lack integration and achievement—unless hypocrisy intervenes.[14] But *something* always lurks behind our plans and choices. We are striving to become something, even if we do not acknowledge the effort.

Far from being an artificial construction from etymology, religion as "constant binding" fits "religious" events recorded in the literature of archaic societies. We will look at two moments—from the Old Testament and Homer's Iliad—in which an agreement binding human parties is sealed by a vertical appeal to the deities.

In Genesis 31:44-54 Jacob and Laban reconcile by making a covenant. The meeting occurs on a mountain, the usual meeting place of Yahweh with his people. Yahweh's presence "between" the hostile parties is symbolized by a monument they raise toward heaven. A cooperative liturgy enacts the covenant: the senior Laban initiates verbally, Jacob physically. The monument is built and a meal is shared. Either during or right after the meal, the "same" monument is named differently by each man. Laban's statement of covenantal obligations (vs. 50-2) shows that the stone's witness represents God's own witness. It both divides and unites the covenanters; it separates their ill-will while uniting them in benevolence; it restricts their freedom for doing evil but frees them from the fear of suffering it. Most importantly, the pillar of rock, stream of words, and pillar of sacrificial smoke forge a bond between the reconciled parties—with Yahweh over, between, and through them. It is just because Yahweh overshadows them that he can enforce their obligations to each other.

The late Bronze-Age heroic society of Homer's *Iliad* exhibits a similar pattern. In the third book warring Trojans and Achaians call for a truce so that their champions can fight in winner-take-all mortal combat. This truce requires an oath and a ritual enactment: "cutting oaths of faith and

---

[14] It is possible to read India this way. Although polytheism prevails in "religion," the rising middle class grows more resistant to traditional doctrine and practice as they assume the worldview, ideas, and attitudes of Western, industrial liberalism.

friendship" (3.73; 256). This metaphor for covenant making, which exactly matches its Old Testament counterpart, refers to the cutting of the sacrificial victim that replaces the division between the two parties. The victim receives the violence that the two sides meant for each other. Moreover, insofar as the best parts of the animal are burnt and ascend to the gods in a single fire, and insofar as the divided animal is shared by the newly reconciled community, the division of the victim ("cut off" from its life) forms the basis of a new unity and peace. What interests us, finally, is the sharing in the animal's death, the promise that "the same be done" to whomever breaks the oath, and, most importantly, the invocations of the gods to stand over and between the parties as witnesses to their covenant (3.271-301).

These are two definitive mythic examples of the vertical certification of a horizontal bond. The complete definition of this bond or covenant is a solemn blood-bond, sovereignly administered, with attendant (sometimes implied) blessings for fidelity and curses for infidelity.[15] The pervasiveness of covenants within "religion"—whether for marriage, peace, or dedication—attests to the "binding" action at religion's center.

Such is the clearest evidence that religion means "constant binding," but there is more. In the Judeo-Christian imagination, God's initial creative acts are envisaged as the imposition of bounds on a preexistent material (Gen. 1:2-10). Like an artist sketches bare shapes before filling them with paint, Yahweh articulates the regions of the cosmos before filling them with other creatures (Gen 1:11-25). Few in the Christian literary and theological traditions have imagined this creative binding as vividly as the seventeenth-century English poet, John Milton. At the moment of creation the Son and Spirit go forth to view Chaos, formless and void, "outrageous as a sea, dark, wasteful and wild" (7.212).[16] Echoing the command of Jesus to the storm on

---

[15] After O. Palmer Robertson, *The Christ of the Covenants* (Phillipsburg, NJ: Presbyterian and Reformed Publishing, 1980), esp. ch. 1. He defines covenant as "a bond in blood sovereignly administered" (4).

[16] Milton in *Paradise Lost*, Gordon Teskey, ed. (New York & London: W. W. Norton, 2005).

Galilee, Milton has the Son say, "Silence, ye troubled waves and thou, deep, peace!...Your discord end!" (216-17). Then,

> He took the golden compasses prepared
> In God's eternal store to circumscribe
> This universe and all created things.
> One foot he centered and the other turned
> Round through the vast profundity obscure
> And said, "Thus far extend, thus far thy bounds,
> This be thy just circumference, O world! (225-31)

The Son is imagined as an architect, although he himself is the "golden compass." Milton has in the background of these verses the tradition of the "golden mean," the ratio (Grk. *logos*) at the heart of created reality and beauty. From his metaphorical "stance" the Son draws the boundaries of the cosmos, carving it like an island out of Chaos. This action is reinforced by a verbal command that obliges reality to stay in the bounds that the Creator himself is.[17] Such pairing of speech and action is common to the representations of the Son in Paradise Lost. It is Milton's way of accommodating theology to the demands of drama, while insisting that they are the same thing, that the Son, in other words, operates through speech-acts. The Son's stance just is his speech/self.

Milton's representation of creative binding might seem overly fanciful, not to say mildly heterodox. But in fact it harmonizes with the rest of the biblical metaphorics of creation. In Proverbs the personified Wisdom declares she was present "before the mountains were settled, ...when [God] set a compass upon the face of the depth,...when he gave to the sea his decree, that the waters should not pass his commandment" (Prov. 9: 25, 27, 29). Likewise Isaiah declares that "[God] hath measured the waters in the

---

[17] Milton often pairs action with speech when depicting the Son in Paradise Lost. It is his way of accommodating his theology to the demands of drama, while insisting that they are the same thing, that the Son, in other words, operates through speech-acts.

hollow of his hand, and meted out heaven with the span, and comprehended the dust of the earth in a measure, and weighted the mountains in scales, and the hills in a balance" (Is. 40:12; cf. Job 28:24-26; Ps. 19:4b). To be sure, this latter passage shifts the image from geometry to arithmetic, but nevertheless reproduces the link between the metrics of the cosmos and the being of God. God measures out and imposes a region for the sea and sky. Yahweh sets, says, and is, the boundary.

We can go further still by recognizing a specific role for the Son in creation-as-boundary-making. We are familiar with the Son's role as the logos through which all things were spoken into being and remain in being (Gen. 1:3 ["God said"]; Jn. 1:3, 10; Col. 1:16-17; Heb. 1:3). But less familiar is the Son's role as the metaphysical boundary of all things—their *arche* and *telos* (Rev. 1:8, 22:13). "[*Arche*] means 'source of power or meaning,' 'first principle,' 'creative initiative,' indicating priority in time and rank."[18] To understand how the eternal creating *logos* functions as the *arche* or source of creation, we need to recognize a meaning of *logos* veiled by the usual translation: *logos* can mean "proportion." It is not just that the Son's power holds creatures together. More than that, his archetypal structuring unifies, balances, and harmonizes the vast play of forces in the guts of being.[19] The precise balance of particles and forces in an atom; the proportion of size to heat to distance that funds life on earth; the structural intricacies of crystals— all this is comprehended in the semantic range of *logos* as Aristotle and the Apostle John understood it.[20] *Logos* is the energy that maintains things as what

---

18 N. T. Wright, *Colossians and Philemon*, TNTC (Grand Rapids: Eerdmans, 1986), 74.

19 In his *The Triune Creator* (Grand Rapids: Eerdmans, 1998), Colin Gunton "conceive(s) providence chiefly in terms of two models: the Son as the giver of structure, and the Holy Spirit as the one who gives the world space to become within but not apart from that structuring" (192; italics added).

20 Cf. Aristotle, *De Anima*. 416a 16: "all things put together by nature have a limit (*telos*) and proportion of size (*logos tou megethou*) and growth, and this belongs to the soul (*psuche*)." Notice that the *logos* is the structuring energy of the soul, which determines the "limit" or bounds of the creature.

they are. The Son sets and is the limits for what they can and should be. But the Son is also the ontological *telos* of creation; he receives the fruit of the Father's creative and recreative plans ("all things were created…for him" [Heb. 1:16; cf. Matt. 28:19-20]) and he announces the end of sin's reign on the cross.[21] Most importantly, he is the "beginner and ender" (*archegon…teleioten*; Heb. 12:2) of the *new* creation.

Such are the vertical bounds that obtain between God and creation. But we must also, though briefly, consider the horizontal binding that Man imposes on creation as he imitates his Maker. This subcreation works by *restricting* the material it redesigns. It was the blind but brilliant Milton who saw this too. He describes Edenic nature as a "wilderness . . . with thicket overgrown, grotesque and wild" (4.135-37). Later we again find

A wilderness of sweets, for Nature here
Wantoned as in her prime and played at will
Her virgin fancies pouring forth more sweet,
Wild above rule or art, enormous bliss" (5. 294-97)

In these lines we hear the attributes of Chaos, though on a different level. Although Yahweh has formed Chaos into the shape of earth, trees, hills, brooks, sunlight, etc., these forms now require the additional boundaries of culture. Strikingly, Milton imagines this curtailing or bounding of a relatively disordered Eden in terms of marriage:

On to their morning's rural work they haste
Among sweet dews and flow'rs; where any row
Of fruit trees over-woody reached too far

---

[21] In his crucifixion account (19:28, 30), John employs several verb forms stemming from *teleioō* ("bring to completion"), which in turn stems from *telos*, "end." Altering the KJV, a literal translation would run as follows: "After this, Jesus, knowing that all things were now at their end (*tetelestai*), that the scripture might be brought to its end (*teleiōthē*), saith . . . [all things] are now at their end (*tetelestai*)."

Their pampered boughs, and needed hands to check
Fruitless embraces: or they led the vine
To wed her elm; she spoused about him twines
Her marriageable arms, and with her brings
Her dow'r the adopted clusters, to adorn
His barren leaves…. (5. 211-19)

Adam's and Eve's work is twofold. First they prune the excesses of the garden in the way one prunes fruit trees today to yield more stable and uniform growth and higher-quality fruit. They also beautify the garden by "marrying" various plants to each other—for example, the weak trailing vine to the strong upright tree-trunk. The tree's authority and guidance strengthens and stabilizes the vine, whereas the vine's large leaves and pliancy embellish the tree. Obviously the picture encodes Milton's view of marriage. More importantly, for our purposes, it reveals that human subcreation imitates divine creation as limiting or checking of chaos (garden plants must be monogamous, cannot trail off wherever they wish). It reveals that the primary way humans imitate the creator (placing bonds on Nature) is also the most sacred and solemn bond between themselves.

Human Being as *Logos*, the Binding that Frees

I have been arguing that human beings live religiously. Whether they acknowledge it or not, humans work, play, speak, or otherwise act in terms of a single ultimate principle or person. This binding force ties individuals to itself, unifies their lives, and ties them together into communities of various extents. This constant binding is paradoxical in nature, because through restriction it also liberates. It liberates the individual *from* chaos and *for* subcreation. It gives the individual, in the best instances, a secure context of mutual obligations and resources wherein she can flourish. We also noted that restricted-yet-free subcreation in turn binds and frees the natural world.

These observations raise the question: why do human beings display these rites, customs, traditions, and stories? Why are they religious?

Let's put that question off for a moment to consider a problem with the account thus far, a problem that raises a related question. We began by noting some evidence—anecdotal, common-sense, and textual—for the ubiquity of religion as "constant binding." But then, without announcing the move, we offered the Christian religion as the archetype of constant binding. If someone agrees that human beings are religious and (against the New Atheists) *should* be religious, then our move raises this question: why should human beings choose the constant binding offered by Christianity instead of any other religion?

What I will try to do now is answer both of these questions with the same argument. My claims in what follows are these: that *logos* (speech, ratio, relation), the essential attribute of human nature, is the binding that frees; that *logos*, in the sense of word, text, and personal relation, is the common ground of religion and freedom; and that freedom is undermined insofar as *logos* is undermined. These claims will clearly address the first question. They will also address the second, though less clearly, Logos is more deeply embedded in Christianity—in its rites, customs, doctrines, and stories—than in any other religion. So, if it is agreed that human beings have a longing for religion, then Christianity is the best choice simply because it is the most religious religion.

Logos as Gathering

In both Platonic and Christian cosmology, *logos* is the divine attribute and cosmic property that structures creation. (The difference being that in Christianity the *logos* is personal.) It was Aristotle, however, who supposedly and famously defined human beings (*anthropos*) as ζῶν ἔχων λόγον, "living being having *logos*" as an essential attribute.[22] An essential attribute is the quality that distinguishes members of a species from the rest of a genus. The

---

[22] To my knowledge, Aristotle never actually put it this way. But other comments of his amount to the same doctrine. See *Pol.* 1253 a1-19 and *De Anima* 432a 30-b 2.

Christian teaching that man is the image of the incarnate *logos* Jesus Christ agrees with Aristotle.[23]

It seems rather distant and mysterious to think that our nature *is logos*, unless *logos* just means "speech" or "language." And translations of St. John 1:1 seem to confirm that by saying "in the beginning was the *word*." However, "word" and "speech" are barely the tip of the semantic iceberg that is *logos*. Unless we hear the polysemy in this term we will miss much of our own nature as well as the deep-rootedness of religion in it.

Logos comes from the verb *legein*, which meant "say, speak, tell" but originally "pick out, gather, pick up, choose."[24] Excavating the concrete physical action in the etymology, Martin Heidegger interpreted *logos* as "the gathering"—of perceptions into words, words into sentences, and sentences into discourse.[25] *Logos* is the fundamental power of gathering up and sorting out the elements of the world through symbols. It is the power of relating, of relation. It is therefore the underlying capacity of both speech and arithmetic, because both of these skills "gather" the world symbolically. *Logos* can mean "ratio" or mathematical proportion, as well as "expression," "articulation," "sentence," "argument," "judgment," "discourse."[26] In what follows we will observe *logos* in its paradoxical action as the "gathering" that separates, the "binding" that frees.

---

[23] In a passage that bristles with condemnation, St. Peter calls certain false teachers *aloga zoa*, "brute beasts, made to be taken and destroyed, [who] speak evil of things they understand not; [who] shall utterly perish in their own corruption" (II Peter 2:12). The point is that sin dehumanizes.

[24] Liddell and Scott, *An Intermediate Greek-English Lexicon* (Oxford: Clarendon Press, 1889), s. v. "legō."

[25] *Introduction to Metaphysics*, trans. Gregory Fried and Richard Polt (New Haven and London: Yale University Press, 2000), 135-44. See also *Fundamental Concepts of Metaphysics*, trans. William McNeill and Nicholas Walker (Bloomington, IN: Indiana University Press, 1995), 305-26.

[26] Liddell and Scott, *An Intermediate Greek-English Lexicon* (Oxford: Clarendon Press, 1889), s. v. "logos." This list clarifies why "Word" is a poor translation for logos in Jn. 1:1, as Beza recognized when he substituted Lat. *sermo* for the *verbum* of Jerome's Vulgate: "in the beginning was the *discourse*."

First and rather obviously, the "common noun" gathers together a class of beings under a single title or a quality. When you say, "there's a dog over there," the term "dog" assembles the attributes of dog and refers them to the short-haired Irish setter standing there in the lawn outside the post office. For average folks in the domain of ordinary speech, the ensemble of qualities is morphological, whereas for biologists it is genetic or phylogenetic. That is why for most of us a wolf is just a big wild dog and a Malamute is just a tame wolf. In either case, though, qualities are assembled in the term and referred to the object. But notice something else. You didn't know the dog was a Irish setter; and I couldn't identity most of the trees I've seen in my life; just like many people can't tell the difference between a ten and fifty-dollar bottle of wine. To those of us lacking the expert's refined eye and lexicon, an Irish setter is "just a dog" and Chateau Latour Pauillac is "just a nice wine." In falling so short, our speech is restricting the reach of our knowledge into the object. That means that insofar as the object is matter of concern (relation) to us, our *logos* (our power of relating) binds the object itself, mutes the display of its full reality. The more common the noun, the more it blocks the phenomenon. Before we mourn this restriction, we should note a corresponding release. In one way, the veiling of a thing's depth reality allows us to focus on something else, just we miss much of the scenery we drive by but partake more fully of our destination. In another way, the common boundaries placed on an object just are the conduits of its deeper reality. Isn't that the way of most edifying conversations? They begin in the murk of conventional description, even cliché, but proceed to new vistas of specificity—textures and fine colors filling in the silhouette.

That last remark suggests that adjectives and other descriptives extend the gathering power of a noun. Someone describes, explains, and names a Begonia ("Heron's Pirouette"). Henceforth it will never be "just a pretty flower" to me. Rather, all the rich depth of that conversation will be included in the phrase "that flower" or "Begonia" (if I'm lucky to remember the name). But for adjectivals in general there is a similar binding-freeing as for nouns. Imagine the color red. Did you imagine "cherry" red or "ruby" red or "rosy" red? What is *red*, after all? Apart from the precision of a chromatograph, which has no bearing on ordinary experience, it is a rough average of all the gradations of that color in our experience. The word "red" blocks that variety, keeps it behind bars. That is the word's job. But the wonderful thing about prison doors is that they can be opened. Imagine me "setting the scene" for a story I am telling you. I describe a weathered grey cabin in woods of deep evergreen. Now the magic of my words is that they allow your imagination to shape, shade, brighten, and texture the world of my story with your own colors. The indeterminacy of the description (not "ruby red" but "red," etc.) liberates your creativity *within the limits* of my story-world. Of course this also happens with nouns. When I said "cabin," did you add a shingle roof? Vine-covered walls?

All these powers of *logos*, these layers of closure and opening, operate at a more complex level in the sentence. In a sentence the speaker takes hold of something "as" something, gathering subject and predicate together, binding the subject to the terms laid down by the predicate. The speaker chooses a limitation to be placed on the subject. (*Legein*, remember, means "picking out" or "choosing.") Because no sentence can say everything, every speaking (*legomenon*) is a certain choice of words. Notice that we do not say someone "chose his words" but that he chose them "carefully," implying that the choosing is constant. For instance, the sentence "Steve is a carpenter" gathers together a thing with a quality so that we discover something about Steve or focus on something we already know to deepen it. In this case we select his occupation out of all the other things we could have said about Steve, such as that his hair is brown and that he was born in Texas. *Logos* is this gathering, but a gathering that separates, a binding that frees. For the sentence also holds subject and predicate apart, preventing their complete fusion. Language binds things to qualities, categories, descriptives; yet at the same time it frees them for further predication, such as we see in analogies. In *Miracles*, for example, C. S. Lewis writes that death is the chess move whereby Satan takes God's piece but loses the match several moves later. Here the power of *logos* frees the "mere game" of chess from its normal semantic domain and lets it range in the vastest of theological realms. Thus, it is in and through *logos* that we do our most powerful subcreating.

Logos as Perception

We have seen how the gathering-binding-freeing of *logos* operates in language. However, *logos* pervades our being in other less noticeable ways. Its pervasiveness appears in our constant striving toward adventure and discovery, our desire to uncover new experiences and to express their uniqueness ("that gimpy red rooster that hates me…) and their universality, (…is a bird in such-and-such family of domestic fowls"). This gathering-discovery appears at a deeper level in our perception. Here are several examples:

Suppose you are walking in the woods, "taking in the scenery." With your gaze you lazily sweep the brushy hillsides near the trail. Suddenly a flash of color catches your eye. Is it a leaf turning in the breeze? A dragonfly? A squirrel? But the movement was too purposeful for a leaf; it was certainly living movement. The chirping that finally reaches your ears signals the presence of "some bird;" then another moment of squinting reveals a cardinal. Were you to map the epistemological route to this identification, you would pass through a series of "wholes" or "categories" (something there—what's that? > flying thing > living thing > bird > red bird) before final reaching—"specifying"—the cardinal.[27] I am not saying that you necessarily hear yourself think "bird > cardinal." Probably we would hear even our quickest intuitions if we really listened; and we fast-lane moderns rarely do. But you cannot miss the gathering energy of *logos* in the cardinal's emergence. First the "thing" is taken as "something alive," held together with that category. But that is just a momentary placeholder: immediately a more specific term is introduced, and then another until you reach the most specific and likely "name" in your knowledge. Each layer excludes certain options

---

[27] This analysis is phenomenological rather than neuro-physiological.

(leaves, twigs, bears, etc) but also frees the process for further thought. Thus our initial perception becomes less "common," more precise, the more deeply it is layered in these classes.

A second example, now from social life, shows a similar thought-process. You arrive at a party apprehensively. As if lost, you sweep the room with your gaze, "taking it all in." The "all" is the party in general—the decorations, music, the food, the vibe. Of course you are most concerned with the people, so you look around to see who is there. You are looking for someone we know who might notice you, someone facing in your direction and not too deeply engaged in conversation. There—in the corner you discover a good friend laughing comfortably with another partygoer. Happily you head over there when your friend beckons; you are relieved, perhaps unconsciously, because you may stop looking awkward on the "outside" of the party. Your friend will introduce you to other people, and things will roll on smoothly from there. You were "taking in" the whole but sorting out the identities of and possibilities for relationship with the various individuals and groups your gaze encountered (Who are they? > Too fancy for my set > Too engaged in conversation > He's being too serious > What's that? Do not want to discuss Trump over there! > who *is* she? > Oh, there's Bob! . . .). But also again, the recognition of barriers to partying just is your freedom to (finally) party. Here again we are confronted with the gathering-separation, the binding-freeing, of *logos*.

Logos as (Arithmetic) Proportion

We have been discussing *logos* from the standpoint of spoken speech, which is arguably its most important aspect. However, the ability to "gather" *numerically* is also rooted deeply in our nature. A mathematical proportion is a gathering-separation of two quantities. In the expression "$\frac{1}{2}$" for example, the 1 is "taken as," or in terms of, the 2; it is taken as a kind of 2, while the 2 is treated as—becomes, we might say—a kind of 1. The full oneness of the 1 is restricted so it can take on a new power. It becomes like someone married, both less and more than itself. The two quantities of a ratio are bound together yet held apart.

Clearly *logos* as binding-release operates in our conscious mathematical reasoning. I would now like to suggest that a quantifying *logos* may be glimpsed in our daily perception and life, in addition to the *qualifying logos* mentioned above. My suggestion may seem to be much ado about nothing, since my evidence boils down to mathematical metaphors in ordinary speech. However, along with other researchers in the area of psycho-linguistics, I believe that our metaphors are powerful indications of the psychology "beneath" them.[28] We "size up" a situation, "rate" our experiences, and give a good "account" of ourselves when reporting to parents after Spring Break (an investment metaphor). I want to hang out with people who "count," that is, who are numbered among the successful, and I want to "amount to something." People may be "all accounted for," and when an absence is explained, we say it is "discounted."

Because our structured world is flexible and shaped by our will to some extent, we are always "double-checking" it, that is, "checking-off" or verifying the presence of each piece. Think about getting into a car: quickly and almost unconsciously you run down a checklist of requirements for driving. Seat belt – check. Mirrors – check. Music – check. Coffee – check. Kids' belts – check. Directions to destination – check. Look behind before backing up – check. The countdown to drive-off is a necessary, precise, and regulated formality, like showing one's work in an arithmetic problem. Or it is like checking a manifest for a delivery insofar as you are only interested in the bare existence of each item. You are skimming over the surface of these things—counting them off—in preparation for something else.

We see in these examples, I think, evidence for *logos* as quantitative gathering-separation.

---

[28] See, for example, George Lakoff and Mark Johnson, Metaphors We Live By, 2nd ed. (Chicago: University of Chicago Press, 2004).

Logos as Personal Relation

At this point it might seem like we could assemble the qualitative and quantitative aspects of *logos* for a complete picture of human nature. However, that would be to neglect a third aspect—one that includes, transcends, and completes the first two. In the mode of *personal relation*, *logos* "gathers" human beings into communion.

It is well known that human babies fail to flourish without the bodily presence of a caregiver, but any adult's experience testifies to the same need. It's hard to be productive in a busy coffee shop even when I don't expect any acquaintance to drop in, since I feel an *obligation* to look up and acknowledge passersby. Perhaps we feel an interior call to give a fellow human being, whoever it is, some modicum of respect. Like you would feel a duty to glance at a world-famous monument when driving by even if you weren't particularly interested. If you were hiking alone in a wilderness and had been for some time, your eyes would certainly still be drawn to an eagle or bear; but *much more* would they be attracted by another hiker. Say you "escape" to a secluded corner of the library to be "productive;" yet, if footsteps tap nearby, you would be more likely to look up than if you were in a busy lobby. The greater our isolation, whether spatial or relational, the greater the compulsion to reach out to another person. We want to see and be seen, to love and be loved. Two questions, "is someone there?" and "who is there?," lie at the core of our existence.

Logos as speech is the clearest means whereby we bind to each other, penetrating more deeply but allowing other persons the free space wherein to reveal themselves. But all relationships are created and sustained verbally. For children and parents they begin symbolically with the naming of the child. Until recently, in much of the Christian West children were named after saints or ancestors. With its name the child bore the weight of tradition, family character, and communal expectation. When children begin to talk, their first words are the names of their parents—their most important relationship. Then they learn to name the objects in their environment, the ones they are chewing on and staring at. Their first lesson is to sort out categories from what William James called the blooming, buzzing confusion of particulars. Not all bugs are ants. Studies show both that relational insecurity inhibits language acquisition and that silence stunts the development of relationships.

A conversation may be provoked by the welcoming nod, but more significant is the personal address: when you name me by my proper name, you knock on a door to the vast region of memories, traits, and experiences— all the various relations that constitute me. When I hear my name I instinctually believe you want to explore this frontier, to discover, for instance, that I once trapped gophers for twenty-five cents a head in an orange orchard in Santa Paula, CA. The importance of name-days and first-name bases implies a covenantal function because they open a future of mutual obligations. I will pray/hope/live for my daughter and she must "live up" to her name. Similarly, the personal address means you want to share my personality, dreams, and life but that you will not betray, must even steward well, the treasures I give to you and must not take without sharing in turn. In conversational *logos*, I give over my private sphere to the "common ground" that binds myself and you more intimately. I become better known/bound to the degree I give up my freedom to "start over" and "be whatever I want to be."

As Colin Gunton has put it, "Freedom is found in the space in which persons can be themselves in relation with other persons."[29] This shared space of conversation can be barred by shy silence or arrogant verbosity. That is because human beings have a necessarily guarded interior transcendence, an interior "self." Those who fail to maintain this transcendence are regarded as shallow, thoughtless chit-chats; which is to say they lack transcendence of thought over expression. We need to be in relation (*logos*) to others in such a way that they are received and challenged, respected and rebuked. But that honesty only obtains if we are free from posing, free to weep, free to get

---

[29] Colin Gunton, *The Promise of Trinitarian Theology*, 2nd ed. (Edinburgh: T & T Clark, 1997), 128.

weakness and doubt in the open. Free to hear any rebuke of folly and pettiness. Free to be bound.

All these attributes of our informed covenants are intensified, even archetypified, in the formal covenants out of which the fabric of human community is woven. The most important of these is the vertical covenant of a person or people with an ultimate project (nationalism), thing (materialism), idea (ideologism), or person ("religion" in the narrow sense). But, the most important horizontal covenant, which reflects its vertical counterpart to some extent (Eph. 5), is marriage. Marriage is the most important *logos* aside from our communion with God; it is the richest and most ramifying "taking as." The words that effect a marriage are the most powerfully subcreative of all "speech acts." They are in fact the most divine of all human speech acts, since they bring a new reality into being instead of merely signifying like other *logoi*. "I take you." The "take" here is in effect the "/" of a proportion; it is the energy catalyzing a new subject-predicate compound in any sentence-*logos*. But deeper than any other *logos*, the counterforce of the marriage bond pervades the heart, soul, mind and strength of a man and woman. Our culture today, eaten by the acid of individualism, longs for this binding-freedom. It is a freedom *from* the chaos of selfishness and self-delusion; it is a freedom *for* genuine subcreation through orientation to others.

Tim Keller eloquently states the paradox at the core of marriage. "A covenant relationship is a stunning blend of law and love… Love needs a framework of binding obligation to make it fully what it should be."[30] He continues: "The legal bond of marriage creates a space of security where we can open up and reveal our true selves" (89). "In promising, you limit options now, … so that you can be free to be there in the future for people who trust you" (98). A promise, like the marriage vow, is a speech-*logos* that creates a relation-*logos*, which in turn, by blocking demotivation or shifts in desire,

---

[30] Timothy Keller, with Kathy Keller, *The Meaning of Marriage* (New York: Riverhead Books, 2011), 88. Other quotations in the paragraph are from this book.

releases a wider realm of creative energy—the energy of culture-building. Because others, especially your spouse, can count on you, they are free to use their gifts, to risk, to fail, to try again. According to Keller, such covenantal obligations function by securing our commitments against shifts in feeling:

> The only way for you to be truly free is to link your feeling to an obligation. Only if you commit yourself to loving in action, day in and day out, even when feelings and circumstances are in flux, can you truly be a free individual and not a pawn of outside forces. Also, only if you maintain your love for someone when it is not thrilling can you be said to be actually loving a person.[31]

Freedom within any covenantal *logos*, but especially in marriage, occurs *through* bondage.

By widening our perspective to other social areas, we can elaborate on the claim that marriage frees *for* subcreation and other *logoi*. Sociologists talk about three spheres of relationships. First is the smallest sphere constituted by our vertical *logos*, then marriage, then our extended family and closest friends. The next sphere is our fixed social *logoi*, "institutional" connections such as church, business, and social clubs. Then there is the outer sphere of occasional acquaintances. Now *here* is what these spheres have to do with freedom. In marriage I am most free to be myself but most bound to another, most free to speak but most compelled to listen, most free to receive but most bound to give. What this means is that as it goes in marriage, so it goes in society. A man who relates to his wife poorly—who hides his vocational trials and triumphs and goals, who always merely listens and nods, who speaks without acting or vice versa—this man cannot compensate with an intimate male-friend *logos*. He can appear to be honest and self-revealing, but in fact wanders into ignorance of self at best and disingenuousness at worst. He can appear creative and spirited, but in fact many energies are blocked by

---

[31] Ibid., 103.

silence, miscommunication, and lack of support from his wife. (It is well-known that married men and women are more economically productive than singles.) For many middle-class urban couples, "social activities"—activism, entertainment, fitness, parties—are an elaborate diversion from the real work of being married.

By tracing *logos* to its deepest horizontal levels, I have gone as far as space allows to say, in answer to the first question, *why* human beings are religious. It remains to argue that Christianity is *the* religion. That is to say, is Christianity, more than other religions—in its stories, practices, and doctrines—a "liberating constant-binding"? The answer has already been hinted at. It is "yes," for in orthodox Christian belief, more than in any other religion, the ultimate binding force is *in itself* a *logos*, one substance entailing three persons. Their co-allegiance is not compulsory; rather they freely submit and give themselves to one another. Moreover, the Triune God created the angels and physical reality as traces of themselves (*similitudines dei*), while creating a special class of beings to imitate them specially (*imagines dei*).[32] With these beings God establishes a covenantal link of love, not "free" or uncommitted love, but love that includes mutual obligations.[33] By contrast, because Islam's Allah lacks plurality ("the space in which persons can be themselves"), Islamic culture can only be oppressive (when consistent). On the other hand, polytheistic religions lack unity, and so the weight their many obligations is also oppressive. In Christianity, the most important horizontal bond, when functioning properly, imitates the vertical bond and extends

---

[32] Keller, *The Meaning of Marriage*, 120: "Being created in God's image means that we were designed for relationships."

[33] The literature on the trinity and the Trinitarian *imago dei* is immense and has especially proliferated since Karl Rahner's *The Trinity*, trans. Joseph Donceel (New York: Crossroads, 2004 [1967]) and John D. Zizioulas's *Being as Communion: Studies in Personhood and the Church* (Yonkers: St. Vladimir's Seminary Press, 1997). Much Trinitarian theology is too reliant on philosophical categories; but recent exceptions are R. A. Smith, *Eternal Covenant: How the Trinity Reshapes Covenant Theology* (Moscow, ID: Canon Press, 2003) and *Trinity and Reality* (Moscow, ID: Canon Press, 2004), both of which are deeply rooted in biblical and covenantal theology.

productive freedom to all of life. It was Jesus Christ who pointed out the interrelation of the two bonds most clearly: love God with all your heart and your neighbor—whoever is closest to you in the first circle, wife or sibling or friend (Matt. 22:37-9). But it was Martin Luther who called attention to the freedom-bondage implied by the *command* to love:

> A Christian is a perfectly free lord of all, subject to none.
> A Christian is a perfectly dutiful servant of all, subject to all.[34]

Conclusion

Thinkers such as Herman Dooyeweerd and R. J. Rushdoony have shown that, to the extent Western culture departs from a Trinitarian-theological worldview, to that extent it falls into a series of dualisms. Freedom or determinism, organism or machine, culture or pure nature, individual or collective, reason or feeling—when tormented by these opposite options, culture has to choose, and the history of modern thought is a series of oscillations.[35] Right now the dominant set of binaries is as follows:

Freedom	Commitment
Private	Public
Feeling	Duty
Absolute Self-Determination	Deep Accountability

In sorting out their options this way, popular culture constructs false dichotomies and misses the deep unity of freedom and bondage. Tragically, this dualism presupposes *debased versions of both freedom and religion*. On the one hand, freedom is primarily external; it means not only "the absence of restraint from" but even "support for being or doing whatever the hell I want

---

[34] "Treatise on Christian Liberty," in *Three Treatises*, trans. W. A. Lambert, rev. Harold J. Grimm (Fortress Press, 1970), 277.

[35] See Rushdoony, *The One and the Many* (Fairfax, VA: Thoburn Press, 1971).

to do or be." It is freedom *from* every judgment, tradition, and standard, except perhaps the standard of absolute tolerance. No tradition, expectation, duty, or vocation binds me, except perhaps the duty to tolerate the whims of others. I am not even bound by nature in the form of gender, since (my) nature is only a certain state of matter, ever evolving in itself and so reconfigurable according to whim. On the other hand, "religion" as an intellectual or social hobby is just one of those many things I may or may not choose to do. Whereas the premodern understanding of persons saw freedom *through* religion, moderns sever it from its internal anchorage in virtue and the human good (now we are not free *for* anything in particular). And also they sever religion from our nature as *logos*. Thus, freedom is debased into free time and religion into pastime.

So it is little wonder that *logos* in all its forms is undervalued and undermined. As our discourse and media interactions become increasingly visual, virtual, and digital, ordinary spoken speech loses the respect it once enjoyed as the principle mark of human dignity. On the one hand, ordinary language has been degraded by the proliferation of texts, the perpetual chatter of digital mass communication, and the emotionalistic banalities of pop music. On the other hand, while dismissing ordinary human language as subjective and untrustworthy, our culture seeks practical wisdom in the quantitative discourse of the hard sciences (notice, for example, the bar-graph statistics that populate Newsweek). We seek to address our most pressing concerns—whether political, medical or economic—with "unbiased," quantitative answers. Everywhere language and its arts are neglected and trivialized.

The decline of speech *logos* inevitably leads to the decline of *logos* as personal relation. This happens on multiple fronts at once. Increasingly a person reads information in digital and converses in the snippets of texts and tweets. Then he has less patience, memory, and vocabulary for reading longer articles and books. He becomes less able and willing to read and understand long, technical documents such as contracts, much less philosophy. At the same time, he is less able to reason prudentially about choices, about cause and effect, about proportions and consequences—less able to reason analogically. He is less able to imagine alternatives, less able to detach from the immediacy of feelings and short-term gratification. These subtle weaknesses produce series of bad decision—such as financial or health decisions—that damage relationships and quality of life in the long-term. Occasionally there is momentous folly, such as taking on massive debt for a house with insufficient collateral, income, or down payment. Such financial struggles are the leading cause of divorce.

Then there is the relational shallowness reinforced by technologies of distraction. You have probably walked into a restaurant and been cheered by the scene of a family at table with every head bowed. Then a closer look shows all eyes glued to the screens of iPhones. This shallowness means that instead of relating to others, we consume them—their status updates, pictures, "shares," and what Facebook now calls "Reactions."[36] Sustained conversation and argument are as rare in the world of social media as they are in contemporary politics.

We certainly appear free to choose what and whom to consume from an infinite array. But we are less and less free *not to consume*, not to bite off merely the surface of an idea, argument, system, or person and then project our own will on it, rather then perhaps submitting to its counter-pressure and consequent expansion of our being. Indeed, consumption just is the religious thread that ties together the life of the Facebook addict and the user who feels naked without her phone in her pocket. Similarly, by denying any constant binding to God, spouse, church, friends, civic responsibility—we simply allow the impersonal pressure of nation-state bureaucracy to fill those spaces. It is not whether we will be bound but how. Will it be from the inside in a way that humanizes or from the outside in a way that makes us beastly or mechanical?

In the last analysis, our being as *logos* will collapse unless it is based upon the logos of personal relation, the gathering of love. This Trinitarian

---

[36] At least one now has several ways to "react" instead of just "Like"!

"gathering" is currently in danger of being erased altogether from a culture that enjoys much freetime but little freedom, much communication but little community.

3

Enrichment versus Job-Training: An Answer to the Forces of Educational Disruption

Hunter Baker

In the process of trying to follow the conversation about higher education and its potential transformation, I came across a discussion between Walt Mossberg (then of the *Wall Street Journal*, Sal Khan of Khan Academy), and John Hennessy, the president of Stanford University. One of the interesting moments was when Khan (if memory serves) said something about students coming to college to learn a skill or to prepare for a job. John Hennessy immediately jumped in and said that what the universities offer is "an enriching experience" that is greater than just professional training. Khan quickly countered that parents and students should understand what is really being offered. He felt that the economic aspect was the most compelling one. Mossberg noted the disconnect in expectations.[1]

---

[1] See Kara Swisher, "Sal Khan and John Hennessy on Online Education: The Full D10 Interview." *All Things.* (June 28, 2012).

Khan has been on the vanguard of the effort to disrupt and transform the nature of education with his hugely popular short videos that tackle a wide variety of academic subjects. There are others who tilt in the direction of giving up on higher education entirely. I recently listened to an interview between Peter Robinson and two highly successful venture capitalists in the technology sector: Peter Thiel and Andy Kessler.[2] Thiel is especially notable. Along with Elon Musk, he is a founder of Paypal and one of the original investors in Facebook. He gained additional notoriety a few years ago when he announced the Thiel Fellows program which actually pays talented college-aged students $100,000 *not* to go to school. The purpose of the interview was to pit Thiel's growing pessimism about American innovation and our future against Kessler's optimism, but a question about higher education brought the two together as critics. Both men essentially endorsed the notion that the only value of universities is as a sorting mechanism for intelligence. In other words, what is significant about a student having attended Harvard or Yale is simply the fact that they had the ability to get into Harvard or Yale. That view implies perforce that the actual education received at either of those institutions is of no value. Better yet, the two men agreed, would be to spend a few dollars on a good test of intelligence to identify the real talents among the young student population. Having those results in hand, employers could simply choose among the brightest test takers.

Is the Thiel/Kessler view an accurate appraisal of the good that comes to us from higher education? Is it just an overly expensive way to separate wheat from chaff? What's a college for?

I have to say, though, that I did find myself wondering whether Thiel attaches too little significance to the education he received at Stanford. His undergraduate studies in philosophy and graduate studies in law appear to

---

[2] *Uncommon Knowledge* podcast, Peter Robinson interview of Peter Thiel and Andy Kessler on September 13, 2013.

serve him quite well both as a venture capitalist and as a public intellectual. Better I think than just some sorting mechanism for talent would have.

What is being offered when we speak of higher education? There is a second question, as well, that goes beyond the individual expectation. *What are the cultural stakes* involved? Does higher education bear some relationship to things like political freedom and a good life?

What's a College For?

In his highly stimulating 1957 book, *Landmarks of Tomorrow*, Peter Drucker examined higher education and several other critical social levers. Drucker, one of several Austrians who exerted a significant impact on thinking in the U.S. during the previous century, identified key questions faced by colleges and universities. Will the employee be a technician, a simple master of technique, "a barbarian in thrall to his tools," or will he be something more? Will he be interested in the common good? Or rather will he be little more than a self-interested individual looking to extract the maximum reward from the broader society with the least personal investment possible?[3]

What about the institutions themselves? Are the universities grounded in such a way as to be able to prepare students for a more responsible existence? *Landmarks of Tomorrow* includes a disheartening story about a German university during the early period of Nazi rule. When a new Nazi commissar was appointed to head the institution, the professors became obsequious. Would the biology department get more money? Would the law library be able to expand its holdings? The answer was that there would be plenty of funds for those willing to cooperate. The man who shared the account with Drucker said that he feared the same would be true of his own school where the focus was increasingly on narrow interests and pet projects.[4] Without a

---

[3] Peter F. Drucker, *Landmarks of Tomorrow* (New York: Harper, 1959), 105.

[4] Ibid, 105-106.

strong foundation, the university becomes a collection of budget-maximizing centers in which the various players are primarily concerned about what share of the university resources they can command for their own initiatives. Students are just as capable of drawing a lesson from such a structure of incentives as they are from eloquent lectures.

In a less sinister, but still concerning vein, a half century later Yale University's Anthony Kronman would write *Education's End: Why Our Colleges and Universities Have Given Up on the Meaning of Life*. In the book, he bemoaned the modern student's loss of interest in the liberal arts and the big questions that go along with them.[5] Around the same time the historian C. John Sommerville from the University of Florida would describe *The Decline of the Secular University*. In that book he detailed the disappointment of enlightenment liberals who had dreamed of dispensing with Christianity's influence in the academy so as to replace it with their own only to find that professors and students became increasingly oriented around careerist objectives.[6] Instead of goodbye Jerusalem and hello, Athens (or maybe Paris), the result has been more like goodbye to Jerusalem *and* Athens and hello, Wall Street and Silicon Valley. Technology and finance seem to shape the lives of Americans far more than philosophy and religion.

The discussion goes to the core of the crisis we are in. The price of education is high. As it has grown, the customers are getting cagier about asking, "Just what exactly am I getting here?" In the process, the people who work in admissions emphasize the great jobs students will get and the salaries they will be paid. The overall impression tilts more to the side of professional training and less in the direction of the enriching experience I mentioned earlier. This situation helps explain why we are having trouble maintaining strong core curricula. Every professional training program wants to claim

---

[5] Anthony Kronman, *Education's End: Why Our Colleges and Universities Have Given Up on the Meaning of Life* (New Haven: Yale University Press, 2007), 32-33.

[6] C. John Sommerville, *The Decline of the Secular University* (New York: Oxford University Press, 2006), 8.

more hours. And their students expect mostly to train in their professional majors. The broader sense of the educated person is being lost.

It seems like an uneven match. Can we interest our fellow citizens in the idea of college as life enrichment over against a predominant vision of job training? I would like to try it anyway. I'll begin with a discussion of the value of the liberal arts (even if that means thinking about careers) and then move into areas of citizenship and then the soul.

Defending the Liberal Arts

If you really think about learning, there are some master disciplines which unlock all the others. They are philosophy, history, mathematics, language (reading/writing), and science (mainly mastery of the scientific method). My friend John Mark Reynolds puts it this way: "Students need to read well, write well, think well, and figure." These disciplines form the core of learning and comprise the engine of its expression. The student who gains proficiency in these areas will maintain, for virtually the rest of his/her life, the capacity to learn new things and to organize those new things within the context of the older things. The learning that takes place in these traditional subjects does not really expire. It does not become dated. It is a fund that maintains its value. The same is not necessarily true of knowledge gained in programs more directly focused on job training.

Peter Drucker addressed the matter insightfully in *Landmarks of Tomorrow*:

Whatever does not add to the capacity for sustained growth of personality or contribution is impractical – and may indeed be deleterious. That this or that subject adds to a man's ability to get a job, or to do well on his first job, is not irrelevant. But as a measure of the effectiveness of a long-term advanced investment it may be the most impractical yardstick, may indeed cost heavily in terms of the really practical results. The practical test of education in educated society is whether it prepares for the demands of the world fifteen years after graduation. Since we live in an age of innovation, a practical education must prepare a man for work that does not yet exist and cannot yet be clearly defined. To be able to do this a man must have learned to learn.[7]

The person who has mastered a particular market-driven skill of today is in a good position to profit in the short term, but given that we live in a highly dynamic society, the better long term investment is an education that equips the person to learn for the rest of his life. The liberal arts, if taught well and approached with desire by the student, have the ability to unlock almost any subject the student wishes to learn for years to come. If you understand how to think, how to draw lessons from past experience, how to write and speak, how to calculate, and how to put information through the kinds of tests which yield deeper knowledge, then you have the tools you need.

Drucker was right about the kind of education people require in order to thrive. But if we are to put the liberal arts to work and get the most out of them that we can, we have to address our cultural expectations. All the players in the higher education world—students, parents, colleges, governments— need to give proper priority to the traditional arts and sciences as the keys to further learning. In other words, we have to throw out the self-defeating view that those courses are just hurdles students must jump because they have in the past. They are not hurdles. The traditional fields are fulcrums, levers, and pulleys that magnify the strength of subsequent learning.

Institutions should stop throwing together core curricula on the basis of turf battles, faculty preference, and expedience and instead should come up with principled plans for liberal arts cores that will make them what they should be. Various professional majors should stop demanding more and more hours at the expense of liberal arts core curricula. Without a solid foundation at the bottom, the education at the top will be poured into a sieve. At a minimum, it will not be as effective as it otherwise would have been.

There is one more point I need to make in this connection. We often hear that employers want people on their staff who can "think critically" or

---

[7] Drucker, *Landmarks*, 128-129.

"think outside the box." These descriptors have become clichés, but the intent is simply to refer to a person who is not captured by the conventional wisdom. The liberal arts speak to this point, too.

Students at an institution like John Witherspoon College are less likely to be trapped in the materials of modernity having little or no knowledge of what was said, thought, and believed before their century or why those things are important. They will not simply run after the latest social media meme or be easily changed by the endless popularity contests of the contemporary scene. In his essay "Learning in Wartime," C.S. Lewis makes a case for a life of the mind of the type pursued here in your college:

> Most of all, perhaps, we need intimate knowledge of the past. Not that the past has any magic about it, but because we cannot study the future, and yet need something to set against the present, to remind us that the basic assumptions have been quite different in different periods and that much which seems certain to the educated is merely temporary fashion. A man who has lived in many places is not likely to be deceived by the local errors of his native village; the scholar has lived in many times and is therefore in some degree immune from the great cataract of nonsense that pours from the press and microphone of his own age.[8]

The kind of person described here by Lewis is a truly free man or woman with the capacity to exercise shrewd judgment. He or she knows the wisdom and the errors of many times and places. A person of this type is far better equipped to truly see and reflect in a meaningful fashion on their own period.

---

[8] C.S. Lewis, "Learning in Wartime," in *The Weight of Glory* (New York: HarperOne, 2001), 58-59.

Higher Education and Citizenship

We have begun with an argument about the relevance of the liberal arts to learning and functioning in the world. In essence, what I have done is to try and establish that the traditional fields retain their relevance despite the dominance of the professional fields in the modern mind. I would like to proceed to make a case for the importance of a certain type of higher education when it comes to citizenship.

I teach in the area of politics. One of the goals of modern political science is to develop theories of human action. For example, can we achieve a level of confidence that the chance of democratic nations engaging in war against one another is significantly lower than some of the alternatives (democracy v. authoritarian nation, authoritarian nation v. authoritarian nation, etc.)? There are many other interesting questions. Can the behavior of legislators be predicted under certain circumstances? Does a standing assembly act significantly differently from one that meets only every other year? In what ways will the presence of a professional army change the tenor of politics in a society as compared to one that relies upon emergency conscription? These are some of the questions that pre-occupy us.

There are some iron laws of politics which are more fundamental and important than any that might be developed by answering these questions and which almost inexplicably fail to take root in our thinking despite their simplicity. One of those was considered to be of primary importance by the founding generation in the United States. It is this: *Freedom requires the exercise of virtue. If a people cannot govern themselves through the exercise of virtue, then they will not be free.*

The United States of America, as an ongoing project, is a dramatic and dynamic act of balancing law and virtue. The more virtuous the people, the less will we require the coercive and paternal action of the state. Indeed, the more we strive to be virtuous people, the more we will be "men with chests," as C. S. Lewis would have us, rather than mass men under the sway of elite "conditioners" who manipulate the public like puppets.[9] We will participate in bringing about the good society rather than simply drifting along with whatever state of affairs a set of Masters determines to create.

The American Constitution is set up with an eye toward maintaining freedom, and therefore, virtue. One such way is to avoid tempting human beings with too much power. Rather than deal in the old question of "who has the power?" the American founders sought to answer a more insightful inquiry: "How much power?" To that end, the power of the American government is limited, checked, and balanced. The government created by the constitution is inherently a modest one, one that is suited to a free and virtuous people. But how could the founders ensure that the people would be virtuous and therefore capable of being free? One important answer to that question was religion. The American founders were clearly somewhat heterogeneous when it came to the matter of religious orthodoxy (though not nearly so much so as we are today). We can find a motley collection of Christians, deists, and so-called "freethinkers" (a self-flattering designation) in the founding generation. But they were more united on the positive value of faith for building republican virtue. Washington's statement in his farewell address captures the sense of the founders well:

> *Of all the dispositions and habits which lead to political prosperity, religion and morality are indispensable supports.* In vain would that man claim the tribute of patriotism, who should labor to subvert these great pillars of human happiness, these firmest props of the duties of men and citizens. The mere politician, equally with the pious man, ought to respect and to cherish them. A volume could not trace all their connections with private and public felicity. Let it simply be asked: Where is the security for property, for reputation, for life, if the sense of religious obligation desert the oaths which are the instruments of investigation in courts of justice? And let us with caution indulge the supposition that morality can be maintained without

---

[9] C.S. Lewis, *The Abolition of Man* (New York: HarperOne, 2015), following his argument across the three parts of the book.

religion. Whatever may be conceded to the influence of refined education on minds of peculiar structure, *reason and experience both forbid us to expect that national morality can prevail in exclusion of religious principle.*

It is substantially true that virtue or morality is a necessary spring of popular government. The rule, indeed, extends with more or less force to every species of free government. Who that is a sincere friend to it can look with indifference upon attempts to shake the foundation of the fabric?[10] (italics mine)

In addition to religion, he pointed to the value of education:

Promote then, as an object of primary importance, institutions for the general diffusion of knowledge. In proportion as the structure of a government gives force to public opinion, it is essential that public opinion should be enlightened.[11]

When we consider the two quotes from the same source, we see Washington proclaiming that the nation should look to both religion and education for sustenance. It is especially interesting that he rejects the idea that "refined education" is adequate in itself to sustain virtue in the people. The United States of America would need a religious morality (based on Christianity) and educational institutions working together for the health of the republic. It was in this way that the citizens would be instilled with the virtue necessary to the cultivation and preservation of freedom.

Citizenship and Christian Civilization

This thing that Washington held up as the realistic ideal is what we might call the Christian civilization project. Christian civilization helped foster the

---

[10] Washington's 1796 Farewell Address has been reproduced and reprinted in more editions and forms than anyone likely knows. It may be easily found and examined online at a wide variety of archive sites.

[11] Ibid.

emergence of a broad-based citizenship in America that was applauded by Alexis de Tocqueville when he visited the country in the 19th century.[12]

America's schools and churches worked in concert to train Americans for a largely new kind of life in the polis for many. Gone was the old passivity and deference to rulers exhibited by mere subjects. In its place came the engaged role of the citizen. It is true that the Bible counsels Christians to obey their sovereigns, but one of the great differences of the new American life was that the people possessed a real share of the sovereignty. Sovereignty did not exist outside of them, but within them and had to be used morally. While subjects need only obey, citizens have the weighty task of making a right use of freedom and the even more awesome challenge of deciding when to curtail wrong uses of freedom, which might be called license.

Lest we give in to the temptation to follow some commentators who attribute this free citizenship primarily to secular impulses, it is good to remember, as Patricia Bonomi wrote in *Under the Cope of Heaven,* that the revolution occurred in between the First and Second Great Awakenings in the United States.[13] It would be odd to think that the middle portion of that period was especially godless as some have suggested.

In this analysis, I have made much of the importance of liberty and the vitality freedom mixed with virtue can give to a society. Benjamin Constant's famed 1819 essay, *The Liberty of the Ancients Compared with that of the Moderns,* is instructive in that regard. In the essay, Constant's goal was to argue for a different kind of liberty than the one Jean Jacques Rousseau (a darling of the French Revolution) had promoted in his work.[14] Rousseau's ideal of liberty (ancient liberty, per Constant) amounted to something like true direct democracy in which citizens attempted to cast their vote in favor of the general will. Citizens were not urged to exercise their judgment with regard

---

[12] See Alexis de Tocqueville, *Democracy in America*, Vol. I, Part I, Ch. V. Tocqueville's book (1835, 1840) has been reprinted many times and in many editions.

[13] Patricia U. Bonomi, *Under the Cope of Heaven* (New York: Oxford, 1986).

[14] Constant's essay can be readily found online. One such place is:

http://www.uark.edu/depts/comminfo/cambridge/ancients.html/

to the good so much as they were instructed to guess properly about the will of the group and then add their consent to it. Such a government would have tremendous power to regulate much of life. Constant argued for what he called modern liberty (which in a sense is American liberty). He hoped to limit the business of government to a circumscribed space in life and then to rely on citizens to largely govern themselves. Rather than accept the command to "obey and pay" in exchange for a government that promises to deliver happiness, Constant insisted that citizens should keep the work of gaining a happy life in their own hands. The following passage sums up his view nicely:

> Political liberty, by submitting to all the citizens, without exception, the care and assessment of their most sacred interests, enlarges their spirit, ennobles their thoughts, and establishes among them a kind of intellectual equality which forms the glory and power of a people.[15]

Constant dreamed of a humane, reinforcing cycle between liberty and virtue. He hoped that the responsibility of freedom would bring maturity and wisdom along with it. That cycle is possible, but it is far from guaranteed. There must be some legitimate source of virtue within the culture. Something must make morality more than a social construct to be embraced or disregarded on the basis of cynical, calculating interest.

We are in danger of giving up on the founding vision. More and more we seem to look to the government both to define our virtue and to set the conditions of our lives. Rousseau, rather than Locke or Constant, seems to be coming back to the fore. We can only jump out of this track by becoming aware of our need for renewal. This is not some general feeling that will fall unbidden upon us. Rather, such a movement would come, as Os Guinness has noted, in the way the Renaissance and the Reformation did, through a

---

[15] Ibid.

group of individuals pointing back to original sources.[16] *Ad fontes*. Renewal emerges through rediscovery of those things that spurred us on in the first place. This is good work for our colleges and universities. Higher education should be as focused on helping us to remain free in our capitals and courts as it is on helping us to function in the marketplaces of the world.

Higher Education and the Platonic Soul

Education is needed for work. And it is an important part of sustaining informed citizenship. Is there a unifying thread to tie the two together and to help us have some idea of the shape our efforts in colleges and universities should take?

I tipped my hand in this direction earlier by mentioning C.S. Lewis and his men without chests. Let's work backward from that reference. Lewis's built his image upon Plato's tripartite division of the human soul.

In the course of his discussion of justice in *The Republic*, Plato divides the soul into the reason (the head), the will (the chest or heart), and the appetite (the stomach). His definition of justice is that everyone in the republic and every part of the soul do the thing for which they are born or made. The just man is governed by his reason, which joins forces with the will to keep the appetite in its place. A man ruled by his appetites is disordered. So, too, is the man who allows his love of honor (through its appeal to the will) to overwhelm his reason. There must be a proper balance in the soul. We must tutor the will so that it will aid our reason.

C. S. Lewis applied Plato's framework to the problem he observed in the two young schoolMasters who wrote what he called The Green Book. Lewis dwelt at length upon an example in that book. The authors claimed that when a person looks at a waterfall and declares it to be sublime, he would merely be expressing an opinion with no basis in reality. These schoolMasters went

---

[16] Os Guinness, *A Free People's Suicide: Sustainable Freedom and the American Future* (Downers Grove: InterVarsity Press, 2012), 197.

on to express a view of the world that is cynical and reductive. Their philosophy exalted the reason by demeaning the heart. The schoolboy who reads the textbook will conclude, as Lewis says, that "all sentences containing a predicate of value are statements about the emotional state of the speaker" and "that all such statements are unimportant."

What is especially insidious about this teaching is that the pupil is likely to simply see this shallow philosophy as the default view. He will not realize "that ethics, theology, and politics" are at stake. He is being conditioned into taking a side in a controversy without even realizing it.[17]

Things such as patriotism, honor, bravery, self-sacrifice, respect for elders, reverence, and other virtues dissolve under the implicit accusation that they are merely romantic fantasies designed to manipulate suckers. The scholars who undertake this as their philosophy become professional debunkers.

Abraham Kuyper addressed this matter well in one of his convocation addresses to the Free University of Amsterdam, which he helped found. Kuyper begins with a beautifully descriptive meditation on the joy involved in seeking. He talks about hunters and fishers—men of means who could easily afford to purchase richly prepared fish and game for their dining pleasure. But they want something more. They want the thrilling experience of seeking.

Kuyper, though, enjoins his young charges not to settle for mere seeking. An over-dedication to the search can spoil the appetite for something better, *which is the finding*. He critiques scholars who, in refusing to accept any answers as sufficiently revealing of the truth, are committed to a never-ending project of deconstruction. Clearly, Kuyper's concern has been vindicated by the subsequent movements of the academy. He calls these permanent seekers the "real children of Pilate" who are "left with not one fixed starting point for

---

[17] Lewis, *The Abolition of Man*, 20.

their thinking, not a single pillar in their temple of justice, not one firm rule for their moral code."[18]

Lewis, I think, would point us to the Tao or the natural law or the virtues as things that we have found and that offer us answers about how we should live. Rather than trying to debunk these sensibilities, we should be trying to reinforce them and to help students grow strong in love and wisdom. He offers the best case for the two young schoolmasters when he suggests that they may merely have believed that "the world around them" is "swayed by emotional propaganda" against which they must fortify students. Regardless, Lewis believes they are wrong. He writes:

> My own experience as a teacher tells an opposite tale. For every one pupil who needs to be guarded from a weak excess of sensibility there are three who need to be awakened from the slumber of cold vulgarity. The task of the modern educator is not to cut down jungles *but to irrigate deserts*. The right defense against false sentiments is to inculcate just sentiments. By starving the sensibility of our pupils we only make them easier prey to the propagandist when he comes.[19]

Higher education, at its best, is much more than an enterprise centered around mere rationality. We should recognize that we are more than calculating creatures. Education is primarily about the head, but it should also address the chest. So many professors see themselves as great intellects who relieve students of their credulousness and innocence, but it would be better to offer them a grounded belief in truth. Lewis calls it "the doctrine of objective value," which means "that certain attitudes are really true, and others really false, *to the kind of thing the universe is and the kind of thing we are.*"[20]

---

[18] Abraham Kuyper, *Scholarship: Two Convocations on University Life* (Grand Rapids: Christian's Library Press, 2014).

[19] Ibid, 13-14.

[20] Ibid, 18.

Plato had a sense of education as a kind of tuning of the soul. He specifically imagined a mixture of gymnastic and music (which included things like poetry). Within the world of Christian higher education, we envision a different program. But the intent is the same. We want to offer education that helps to achieve a right balance between what the reason knows and can determine and what the will chooses.

I made some remarks in a faculty meeting years ago that continue to follow me. We were talking about technology and education. I argued that the critical issue was not the tools we use, but rather what we bring to the table as professors. There is a scene in the film *Good Will Hunting* in which the young prodigy taunts a Harvard bully by holding up his library card and declaring that the student is a sucker for paying a great deal of money for an education that could be had for the cost of the card. It seems to me that every instructor should take that scene as a challenge. Part of what we do is to choose the books that students will read, but they also depend upon us to guide them, to translate, to ask good questions, to help them to join the centuries long conversation.

What got me in trouble was that I encouraged my colleagues to ask themselves "What is your value added?" I think that to them it seemed like a silly example of the corporate speak to which I was exposed in my early career. But I don't shy away from that expression. Instead, I think it is more apt than I realized. My original intent was to inspire colleagues to take the challenge posed by technology to make the instructor's role *more compelling* and useful and helpful than ever before. Now, I would simply expand my definition of value. The instructor should prove valuable in teaching the course, but should also add value in the moral and spiritual sense.

We talk a lot about the integration of faith and learning in the world of Christian higher education. That mystifies a lot of people. In reality, it's pretty simple. Integration simply refers to integrity. Do your beliefs translate into the words that you speak and the actions you perform? There is tremendous power in the witness of an integrated life. That's part of what we are trying to accomplish in schools like mine in Tennessee and this one here in South

Dakota. We are cultivating the Platonic chest right along with the head in service of the sanctified soul.

Conclusion

It sometimes seems that the world has grown frustrated with the grand tradition and ideas of higher education. Increasingly, we are urged to forget the large, overarching purposes and lofty visions. Go all-in on a strategy rooted in technique and vocation. Make education instrumental. Stop selling ends and major in means.

But the problem is that despair about what education can do in the civilization project doesn't solve our problems. How will we prepare citizens for life in a democratic republic? How will we maintain true political ends worth pursuing? How will we preserve liberty if we fail in educating for virtue? What will happen if our stock of cultural capital is depleted? What kind of judgments will human beings make when they are poorly equipped with overconfident heads and shrunken chests?

The great Quaker philosopher D. Elton Trueblood is justly remembered for his metaphor of the cut flower civilization. His argument was simple. We have cut our civilization at the stem. Down in the soil is a rich mixture heavily seeded with the Judeo-Christian influence. It has made us more free, wise, and humane than we otherwise would have been. When you cut the flower (and maybe we did that decisively in the West sometime in the 20th century) it continues to look beautiful and healthy. You can place it in water and continue to enjoy it. But in time, it will wilt and eventually rot.[21]

The metaphor is not a hopeful one. But maybe there is hope. Maybe there can be new seedlings, a new work of planting and cultivation, a new time of growth. In any case, Christians are not free to live without hope. We have the task of preserving our inheritance until such time as it can once again enjoy greater cultural expression.

---

[21] D. Elton Trueblood, *The Predicament of Modern Man* (New York: Harper & Row, 1944), 59.

During the introduction to this talk I mentioned Anthony Kronman of Yale and his concern for preserving the liberal arts. In his book, there is an intriguing note in which he observes that while elite institutions such as his own have given up on discovering the meaning of life, the quest moves forward at Christian colleges and universities.[22] We are the ones undertaking the projects aimed at the reading of old books. We are the ones designing honors programs around primary texts and Socratic instruction. Kronman, a secular man, despaired a little to see the Christians gaining in the work he wanted for his own people, but perhaps he will end up proud of what we do with it and how we strive to revitalize the culture. Amidst ruins there will be new birth and shoots of green. While others watch the old flower wilt, let us continue our work of gardening.

---

[22] Kronman, *Education's End*, 200.

4

Nullification: The Rightful Remedy

Michael Maharrey

In Federalist No. 45, James Madison encapsulated the intended structure of America's system of government under the Constitution. The federal government was to operate within a limited scope of power, most authority remaining with the state government and the people themselves:

> The powers delegated by the proposed Constitution to the federal government are few and defined. Those which are to remain in the State governments are numerous and indefinite. The former will be exercised principally on external objects, as war, peace, negotiation and foreign commerce; with which the last the power of taxation will for the most part be connected. The powers reserved to the several States will extend to all objects which, in the ordinary course of affairs, concern the lives, liberties and properties of the people, and the internal order, improvement and prosperity of the State.[1]

---

[1] James Madison. "The Federalist No. 45: Alleged Dangers From the Powers of the Union to the State Governments Considered." (1788). The Constitution Society. http://www.constitution.org/fed/federa45.htm

The central debate during the ratification process wasn't whether or not the federal government would exercise expansive powers or limited authority; all parties broadly agreed that it was intended to remain limited. Debate centered on whether or not the provisions in the Constitution would adequately restrain federal power. Anti-federalists like Patrick Henry argued that it would not: "My great objection to this government is, that it does not leave us the means of defending our rights, or of waging war against tyrants."[2]

But the Federalists won the day, promising that the general government would exercise only its enumerated powers and the states would retain their sovereignty in all spheres where powers were not delegated. Several of the state ratifying instruments reflect this understanding. For instance, the New York ratifying document specifically asserts the states authority to withdraw delegated powers.

> We, the delegates of the people of the state of New York, duly elected and met in Convention…Do declare and make known…That the powers of government may be reassumed by the people whensoever it shall become necessary to their happiness; that every power, jurisdiction, and right, which is not by the said Constitution clearly delegated to the Congress of the United States, or the departments of the government thereof, remains to the people of the several states, or to their respective state governments, to whom they may have granted the same; and that those clauses in the said Constitution, which declare that Congress shall not have or exercise certain powers, do not imply that Congress is entitled to any powers not given by the said Constitution; but such clauses are to be construed either as exceptions to certain specified powers, or as inserted merely for greater caution.[3]

---

[2] Patrick Henry, "Against Ratification of the Constitution" (Virginia Ratifying Convention, 1788), in Neil Cogan, ed., *The Complete Bill of Rights: The Drafts, Debates, Sources, and Origins* (New York: Oxford University Press, 2015), 641.

[3] "Ratification of the Constitution by the State of New York" (July 26, 1788). Yale Law School: Lillian Goldman Law Library. http://avalon.law.yale.edu/18th_century/ratny.asp

But merely asserting that the federal government must operate with limited powers means nothing without some means to ensure that it remains within its proper bounds. How do the states and the people check federal power?

The Alien and Sedition Acts

It wasn't long until this concern became more than just a theoretical question. During the summer of 1798, Congress passed—and President John Adams signed into law—four acts together known as the Alien and Sedition Acts. With winds of war blowing in Europe, the Federalist Party majority wrote the laws to prevent "seditious" acts from weakening the U.S. government. Federalists utilized fear of the French to stir up support for these draconian laws, expanding federal power, concentrating authority in the executive branch and severely restricting freedom of speech.

The *Naturalization Act* passed on June 18 and extended the amount of time immigrants had to live in the United States before becoming eligible for citizenship from five to 14 years. Like most things political, the stated and the underlying purposes of tightening naturalization requirements were two different things. The law was advanced as a national security measure. But it provided a great benefit to the Federalist Party in power because most recent French and Irish immigrants supported the Democrat-Republican Party.

The *Alien Friends Act* passed a week later and gave the president sweeping power to deport "dangerous" aliens, in effect elevating the president to the role of judge, jury and "executioner."

> It shall be lawful for the President of the United States at any time during the continuance of this act, to order all such aliens as he shall judge dangerous to the peace and safety of the United States, or shall have reasonable grounds to suspect are concerned in any treasonable or secret

machinations against the government thereof, to depart out of the territory of the United States, within such time as shall be expressed in such order.[4]

Note the wide latitude afforded the president by undefined terms in the act. What constituted "dangerous" and what exactly is a "secret machination?"

On July 6, Congress passed *The Alien Enemies Act*, allowing for the arrest, imprisonment and deportation of any male citizen of a nation at war with the U.S., even without any evidence that he was an actual threat.

> All natives, citizens, denizens, or subjects of the hostile nation or government, being males of the age of fourteen years and upwards, who shall be within the United States, and not actually naturalized, shall be liable to be apprehended, restrained, secured and removed, as alien enemies.[5]

The *Sedition Act* was arguably the most draconian of the four laws. Enacted on July 14, it declared any "treasonable activity" a high misdemeanor punishable by fine and imprisonment. Treasonable activity included "any false, scandalous and malicious writing" against the government or its officials.

> If any person shall write, print, utter or publish, or shall cause or procure to be written, printed, uttered or published, or shall knowingly and willingly assist or aid in writing, printing, uttering or publishing any false, scandalous and malicious writing or writings against the government of the United States, or either house of the Congress of the United States, or the President of the United States, with intent to defame the said government, or either house of the said Congress, or the said President, or to bring them, or either of them, into contempt or disrepute; or to excite against them, or either or any of them, the hatred of the good people of the United States, or to stir up sedition within the United States, or to excite any unlawful combinations therein, for opposing or resisting any law of the United States, or any act of

---

[4] Ibid.
[5] Ibid.

the President of the United States, done in pursuance of any such law, or of the powers in him vested by the constitution of the United States, or to resist, oppose, or defeat any such law or act, or to aid, encourage or abet any hostile designs of any foreign nation against the United States, their people or government, then such person, being thereof convicted before any court of the United States having jurisdiction thereof, shall be punished by a fine not exceeding two thousand dollars, and by imprisonment not exceeding two years.[6]

Based on the *Sedition Act*, federal officials arrested some 25 men, mostly editors of Republican newspapers. There were at least 17 verifiable indictments, 14 under the *Sedition Act* and three under common law.[7] The Act also effectively shut down many dissenting party presses.

Benjamin Franklin's grandson was among those prosecuted. Federalists sent "committees of surveillance" to spy on Benjamin Franklin Bache, editor of the *Philadelphia Democrat-Republican Aurora*.[8] Bache called the Alien and Sedition Acts an "unconstitutional exercise of power."[9] He was ultimately charged with libeling President John Adams and sedition for his French sympathies. Bache died of yellow fever before he was brought to trial.

Recognizing the grave danger these acts posed to the basic constitutional structure, Thomas Jefferson and James Madison drafted resolutions that were passed by the Kentucky and Virginia legislatures on November 10 and December 21, 1798, respectively. The "Principles of '98" formalized the

---

[6] Ibid.

[7] Gordon T. Belt, "Sedition Act of 1798: A Brief History of Arrests, Indictments, Mistreatment & Abuse First Amendment Center Library." First Amendment Center. http://www.firstamendmentcenter.org/madison/wp-content/uploads/2011/03/Sedition_Act_cases.pdf

[8] Richard N. Rosenfeld, *American Aurora: A Democratic-Republican Returns* (New York: St. Martin's Griffin, 1997), 80.

[9] Carol Sue Humphrey, *The Revolutionary Era: Primary Documents on Events from 1776 to 1800* (Westport: Greenwood Press, 2003), 325.

principles of nullification as the "rightful remedy" when the federal government oversteps its authority.

Jefferson's Dissent

The Alien and Sedition Acts outraged many in Kentucky. Several counties in the Commonwealth adopted resolutions condemning the acts, including Fayette, Clark, Bourbon, Madison and Woodford. A Madison County Kentucky militia regiment issued an ominous resolution of its own, stating, "The Alien and Sedition Bills are an infringement of the Constitution and of natural rights, and that we cannot approve or submit to them."[10] Several thousand people gathered at an outdoor meeting protesting the acts in Lexington on August13.

The push to nullify the Alien and Sedition Acts was not simply the act of opportunistic politicians. It rose out of the passionate demands of the citizenry in Kentucky, as well as Virginia.

Jefferson penned the original draft of the Kentucky Resolutions within a month of Congress passing the *Sedition Act*.

> That the several States composing, the United States of America, are not united on the principle of unlimited submission to their general government; but that, by a compact under the style and title of a Constitution for the United States, and of amendments thereto, they constituted a general government for special purposes — delegated to that government certain definite powers, reserving, each State to itself, the residuary mass of right to their own self-government; and that whensoever

---

[10] Robert H. Churchill, "Manly Firmness, the Duty of Resistance, and the Search for a Middle Way: Democratic Republicans Confront the Alien and Sedition Acts" (1999 Annual Meeting of the Society for Historians of the Early American Republic, Lexington, Ky., July 17, 1999) (http://uhaweb.hartford.edu/CHURCHILL/SHEAR_Paper.pdf)

the general government assumes undelegated powers, its acts are unauthoritative, void, & of no force.[11]

After outlining each constitutional violation and overreach of federal power, Jefferson called for action:

> Therefore this commonwealth is determined, as it doubts not its co-States are, to submit to undelegated, and consequently unlimited powers in no man, or body of men on earth: that in cases of an abuse of the delegated powers, the members of the general government, being chosen by the people, a change by the people would be the constitutional remedy; but, *where powers are assumed which have not been delegated, a nullification of the act is the rightful remedy*: that every State has a natural right in cases not within the compact, (casus non fœderis) to nullify of their own authority all assumptions of power by others within their limits: that without this right, they would be under the dominion, absolute and unlimited, of whosoever might exercise this right of judgment for them.[12]

Jefferson sent former Virginia ratifying convention delegate Wilson Cary Nicholas a draft of the resolution, likely hoping the state legislator could get them introduced in Virginia. In October, 1798, Wilson indicated that state representative John Breckinridge was willing to introduce the resolutions in Kentucky. Breckinridge suffered from tuberculosis and made a recuperative trip to Sweet Springs, VA late in August of that year. Nicholas likely gave the Kentucky lawmaker a copy of Jefferson's draft during that trip.

On November 7, 1798, Gov. James Garrard addressed the Kentucky state legislature, noting the vehement opposition to the Alien and Sedition Acts. He said Kentucky was, "if not in a state of insurrection, yet utterly disaffected to the federal government," and noted that the state "being deeply

---

[11] Thomas Jefferson, *The Papers of Thomas Jefferson*, Vol. 30: 1, January 1798 to 31 January 1799 (Princeton: Princeton University Press, 2003), 536-43.

[12] Ibid. Emphasis mine.

interested in the conduct of the national government, must have a right to applaud or to censure that government, when applause or censure becomes its due," urging the legislature to reaffirm its support of the U.S. Constitution while, "entering your protest against all unconstitutional laws and impolitic proceedings."[13]

That same day, Breckinridge announced to the House he intended to submit resolutions addressing Garrard's message. The following day, the Fayette County lawmaker followed through, introducing an amended version of Jefferson's draft. Most notably, Breckinridge omitted the word "nullification" from the actual version considered by the Kentucky legislature, seeking to moderate the tone of the resolution. Removal of the nullification reference apparently didn't bother Jefferson, and in fact, did little to change the fundamental thrust of the resolution. By declaring the Alien and Sedition Acts unconstitutional, null and void, the Kentucky legislature voted on a nullification bill, even with the actual word omitted.

The resolution passed the House on November 10 with only three dissenting votes. The Senate unanimously concurred three days later, and Gov. Garrard signed the resolution on November 16.

A week after the resolutions passed in Kentucky, Jefferson sent Madison a copy, along with a letter urging him to press forward:

> I enclose you a copy of the draught of the Kentucky resolves. I think we should distinctly affirm all the important principles they contain, so as to hold to that ground in future, and leave the matter in such a train as that we may not be committed absolutely to push the matter to extremities, & yet may be free to push as far as events will render prudent.[14]

---

[13] James Gerrard, *Kentucky Gazette* (November 14, 1798).

[14] Thomas Jefferson. "Letter from Thomas Jefferson to James Madison, 17 November." (1798). U. S. National Archives. http://founders.archives.gov/documents/Jefferson/01-30-02-0392

Madison did just that, drafting resolutions for introduction in the Virginia legislature. The *Virginia Resolutions of 1798* declared the Alien and Sedition Acts "unconstitutional." Madison also asserted that the states had an obligation to act against egregious federal exercises of undelegated power.

> That this Assembly doth explicitly and peremptorily declare, that it views the powers of the federal government, as resulting from the compact, to which the states are parties; as limited by the plain sense and intention of the instrument constituting the compact; as no further valid that they are authorized by the grants enumerated in that compact; and that in case of a deliberate, palpable, and dangerous exercise of other powers, not granted by the said compact, the states who are parties thereto, have the right, and are in duty bound, to interpose for arresting the progress of the evil, and for maintaining within their respective limits, the authorities, rights and liberties appertaining to them.[15]

Madison gave his draft of the Virginia Resolutions to Wilson Cary Nicholas, who showed them to Jefferson. In a letter dated November 29, 1798, Jefferson recommended adding more emphatic language in declaring the Alien and Sedition Acts unconstitutional:

> The more I have reflected on the phrase in the paper you shewed me, the more strongly I think it should be altered. suppose you were to instead of the invitation to cooperate in the annulment of the acts, to make it an invitation: 'to concur with this commonwealth in declaring, as it does hereby declare, that the said acts are, and were ab initio—null, void and of no force, or effect' I should like it better. health happiness & Adieu.[16]

---

[15] "Virginia Resolution of 1798." The Constitution Society. http://www.constitution.org/cons/virg1798.htm

[16] Thomas Jefferson. "Thomas Jefferson to Wilson Cary Nicholas, 29 November." (1798.) U. S. National Archives. http://founders.archives.gov/documents/Jefferson/01-30-02-0399

Nicholas added words declaring that the Alien and Sedition Acts we unconstitutional "not law, but utterly null, void and of no force or effect."

John Taylor of Caroline introduced Madison's resolutions with Nicholas' addition on December 10, 1798. He described the resolutions, "as a rejection of the false choice between timidity and civil war." Taylor argued that state nullification provided an alternative to popular nullification – in other words outright armed rebellion. In legislative debates, he argued that "the will of the people was better expressed through organized bodies dependent on that will, than by tumultuous meetings; that thus the preservation of peace and good order would be more secure."[17]

In the course of the debate, Jefferson's suggested wording was removed. During the period following passage of the Alien and Sedition Acts, there was talk of outright revolution. Both the Kentucky and Virginia legislatures went to great pains to ensure they were striking a balance between a hard line and moderation. They wanted to make their point, but they did not want to spark violence.

Removing Jefferson's wording did not change the substance of the resolutions. In fact, declaring a law "unconstitutional" was essentially the same as calling it "null, void and of no effect." Alexander Hamilton inferred this distinction during the New York ratification debate.

> The acts of the United States, therefore, will be absolutely obligatory as to all the proper objects and powers of the general government…but the laws of Congress are restricted to a certain sphere, and when they depart from this sphere, they are no longer supreme or binding.[18]

---

[17] *Resolutions of Virginia and Kentucky: Penned by Madison and Jefferson in Relation to the Alien and Sedition Laws; and the Debates and Proceedings of the House of Delegates of Virginia on the Same, in December 1798.* (Richmond: Robert Smith, 1835), 175.

[18] Jonathan Elliot, ed., *Debates in the Several Conventions, on the Adoption of the Federal Constitution, as Recommended by the General Convention at Philadelphia in 1787,* 2nd ed. (Washington, D.C.: Jonathan Elliot, 1836), 2:362-63.

The Virginia House of Delegates passed the resolutions on Dec. 21, 1798, by a vote of 100 to 63. The Senate followed suit on Dec. 24, by a 14 to 3 margin.

Kentucky followed up with a second resolution affirming its position in 1799, notably including the word "nullification," omitted in the final version of the Kentucky Resolutions of 1798 passed by the state legislature.

> That this commonwealth considers the federal Union, upon the terms and for the purposes specified in the late compact, conducive to the liberty and happiness of the several states: That it does now unequivocally declare its attachment to the Union, and to that compact, agreeably to its obvious and real intention, and will be among the last to seek its dissolution: That, if those who administer the general government be permitted to transgress the limits fixed by that compact, by a total disregard to the special delegations of power therein contained, an annihilation of the state governments, and the creation, upon their ruins, of a general consolidated government, will be the inevitable consequence: That the principle and construction, contended for by sundry of the state legislatures, that the general government is the exclusive judge of the extent of the powers delegated to it, stop nothing short of despotism—since the discretion of those who administer the government, and not the Constitution, would be the measure of their powers: That the several states who formed that instrument, being sovereign and independent, have the unquestionable right to judge of its infraction; and, That a nullification, by those sovereignties, of all unauthorized acts done under color of that instrument, is the rightful remedy.[19]

Taken together, the *Kentucky and Virginia Resolutions* lay out the principles of nullification. But they did not actually nullify the Alien and Sedition Acts.

---

[19] "Kentucky Resolution—Alien and Sedition Acts: Resolutions in General Assembly." Yale Law School: Lillian Goldman Law Library. The Avalon Project.
http://avalon.law.yale.edu/18th_century/kenres.asp

These non-binding resolutions merely made the case and set the stage for further action.

Correspondence between Jefferson and Madison indicate they didn't plan to stop with the resolutions. They hoped to use them as a springboard for state action against the unconstitutional Alien and Sedition Acts.

The *Kentucky and Virginia Resolutions* weren't all that well received, particularly by states in the northeast. This is unsurprising because these states were controlled by the Federalist Party. Several, including Massachusetts, passed resolutions of their own condemning the rhetoric of Kentucky and Virginia.

Jefferson asserted in a letter to Madison dated August 23, 1799, that the opposition should not remain unanswered.

> I will in the mean time give you my ideas to reflect on. that the principles already advanced by Virginia & Kentucky are not to be yielded in silence, I presume we all agree.[20]

He then went on to specify three steps.

> ...answer the reasonings of such of the states as have ventured into the field of reason, & that of the Commee of Congress. here they have given us all the advantage we could wish. take some notice of those states who have either not answered at all, or answered without reasoning. [2] make a firm protestation against the principle & the precedent; and a reservation of the rights resulting to us from these palpable violations of the constitutional compact by the Federal government, and the approbation or acquiescence of the several co-states; so that we may hereafter do, what we might now rightfully do, whenever repetitions of these and other violations shall make it evident that the Federal government, disregarding the limitations of the federal compact, mean to exercise powers over us to

---

[20] Thomas Jefferson. "Letter from Thomas Jefferson to James Madison, 23 August 1799." U. S. National Archives. http://founders.archives.gov/documents/Jefferson/01-31-02-0145

which we have never assented. [3] express in affectionate & conciliatory language our warm attachment to union with our sister-states, and to the instrument & principles by which we are united; that we are willing to sacrifice to this every thing except those rights of self government the securing of which was the object of that compact; that not at all disposed to make every measure of error or wrong a cause of scission, we are willing to view with indulgence to wait with patience till those passions & delusions shall have passed over which the federal government have artfully & successfully excited to cover it's own abuses & to conceal it's designs; fully confident that the good sense of the American people and their attachment to those very rights which we are now vindicating will, before it shall be too late, rally with us round the true principles of our federal compact…[21]

Madison took Jefferson's advice and penned a lengthy defense of the Virginia Resolutions known as the Virginia Report of 1800 (sometimes called the Virginia Report of 1799). Madison fleshed out the Virginia Resolutions at length and answered the opposition's arguments point by point. Most notably, he asserted the people of the states have the final authority to determine the constitutionality of an act.

The States then being the parties to the constitutional compact, and in their sovereign capacity, it follows of necessity, that there can be no tribunal above their authority, to decide in the last resort, whether the compact made by them be violated; and consequently that as the parties to it, they must themselves decide in the last resort, such questions as may be of sufficient magnitude to require their interposition.[22]

---

[21] Ibid., numbering added.
[22] Elliot, 4:546–50, 579.

The Logic of Nullification

While the Kentucky and Virginia Resolutions did not actually nullify the Alien and Sedition Acts, they form the philosophical foundation nullification actions rest upon. Ultimately, it remains up to states to take action in the ways they see fit to stop the exercise of unconstitutional federal power—or as Madison eloquently put it, to "interpose for arresting the progress of the evil."

We cannot judge the validity of the Principles of '98 based on short-term political outcomes. A Democrat–Republican assent to power, driven by popular opposition to the Alien and Sedition Acts and capped by Jefferson's presidential victory in the 1800 election, rendered the nullification issue moot, at least for the time being. But the staying power of the principles became evident just a few years later when the same northeastern lawmakers who condemned the Kentucky and Virginia resolutions invoked those very principles to fight Jefferson's embargo of 1807.

With both the British and French seizing American shipping bound for each other's ports, Jefferson chose to wage economic warfare, forbidding any U.S. merchant vessel to sail for any foreign port anywhere in the world. Finding the usurpation shoe on the other foot, Massachusetts suddenly became an ardent supporter of a state's right to judge the constitutionality of an act, declaring the embargo, "in many respects unjust, oppressive and unconstitutional, and not legally binding on the citizens of this state."

And Connecticut Governor Jonathan Trumbull channeled James Madison.

> Whenever our national legislature is led to overleap the prescribed bounds of their constitutional powers, on the State Legislatures, in great emergencies, devolves the arduous task – it is their right – it becomes their

duty, to interpose their protecting shield between the right and liberty of the people, and the assumed power of the General Government.[23]

Over the next 50 years, states advanced the Principles of '98, fighting against federal overreach on a wide range of issues, including federal conscription during the War of 1812. Daniel Webster of New Hampshire wrote:

> The operation of measures thus unconstitutional and illegal ought to be prevented by a resort to other measures which are both constitutional and legal. It will be the solemn duty of the State governments to protect their own authority over their own militia, and to interpose between their citizens and arbitrary power. These are among the objects for which the State governments exist.[24]

Nullification was also invoked during the battle against the Second National Bank, against tariffs in the 1830s and to fight fugitive slave laws in the 1840s and 50s. In an argument against the bank, Ohio "recognized and approved" the Kentucky and *Virginia Resolutions of 1798*.

Members of every political party appealed to the nullification principles at various times, proving that they stand the test of time as more than partisan tools used to advance specific agendas, or the property of one political wing.

---

[23] Carol Sue Humphrey, *The Revolutionary Era: Primary Documents on Events from 1776 to 1800* (Westport, Connecticut: Greenwood Press, 2003), 325.

[24] Edward Everett, *The Writings and Speeches of Daniel Webster: Writings and speeches hitherto uncollected, v. 2. Speeches in Congress and diplomatic papers* (Boston: Little, Brown, & Company, 1903), 14:68.

Nullification Today

Still, the question remains: how can states effectively put nullification into practice? Without some mechanism to actually confront and stop federal overreach, we have nothing more than an intellectual exercise.

Some have advocated arresting federal agents acting in ways that violate the Constitution. For instance, a state could pass a law criminalizing enforcement of acts violating the Second Amendment. Under such a law, a county sheriff could arrest and charge an ATF (Alcohol, Tobacco, Firearms) agent. But this would likely accomplish nothing. The agent's attorney would have the case remanded to federal court and a federal judge would quickly dismiss it.

Under federal law, impeding a federal official with force or threats constitutes a federal crime.[25] So attempting to physically impede or arrest a federal officer won't work in practice.

In today's system, everyone generally assumes that any action taken by the federal government automatically qualifies as legal and legitimate. In the minds of most Americans, every act of Congress, every presidential edict and every federal judicial opinion stands supreme simply by virtue of its existence. Thousands of academics, lawyers and legal scholars will quickly line up to prop up the system, endlessly quoting the "supremacy clause."

But every law enacted by Congress doesn't become supreme just by virtue of its passage and a presidential signature. Every presidential utterance doesn't automatically become the law of the land. And every opinion issued by politically connected lawyers serving on the federal bench doesn't qualify as "constitutional." The Constitution's supremacy clause contains a condition. Legitimate federal laws must be "in pursuance" of the Constitution. Any federal act not in pursuance of the constitution is, as Thomas Jefferson put it, "unauthoritative, void, and of no force."

---

[25] *U.S. Criminal Procedure Law 2015 (Annotated)*: *U.S.C. Title 18.* § 372. "Conspiracy to impede or injure officer."

Alexander Hamilton summed up this principle succinctly and clearly in *Federalist #78*:

> There is no position which depends on clearer principles, than that every act of a delegated authority contrary to the tenor of the commission under which it is exercised, is void. No legislative act, therefore, contrary to the constitution, can be valid.[26]

But no matter how true all of this may be in theory, it really makes no difference in a system run by federal judges. The federal government will meet any efforts to constrain its power by force with superior force, using the weight of a legal system most Americans consider legitimate. As Saul Alinsky wrote in *Rules for Radicals*, "'Power comes out of the barrel of a gun!' is an absurd rallying cry when the other side has all the guns."[27]

It seems we have only two options: violent revolution (which will fail), or complete submission.

However, a third way exists, a moderate middle road between violence and submission: *nullification through noncooperation*.

Americans can impede federal actions without using threats or intimidation. They can simply refuse to cooperate with the federal government. This was the blueprint James Madison gave us in *Federalist #46*.

During the ratification debates, many Americans remained skeptical of the Constitution because they did not believe the federal government would remain limited—as all of the supporters of the Constitution promised it would. They asked a very good question: how will we keep this "limited" federal government in check? This was Madison's answer:

> Should an unwarrantable measure of the federal government be unpopular in particular States, which would seldom fail to be the case, or even a

---

[26] Alexander Hamilton. "The Federalist No. 78." (1788). The Constitution Society. http://www.constitution.org/fed/federa78.htm

[27] Saul Alinksy, *Rules for Radicals* (New York: Vintage Books, 1989), xx-xxi.

warrantable measure be so, which may sometimes be the case, the means of opposition to it are powerful and at hand. The disquietude of the people; their repugnance and, perhaps *refusal to cooperate with officers of the Union,* the frowns of the executive magistracy of the State; the embarrassment created by legislative devices, which would often be added on such occasions, would oppose, in any State, very serious *impediments;* and were the sentiments of several adjoining States happen to be in Union, would *present obstructions* which the federal government would hardly be willing to encounter.[28]

Madison had no problem with the concept of impeding or obstructing the federal government when it imposes "unwarrantable measures" or even simply unpopular measures. In fact, he encouraged it. He intended for the states to serve as a check on federal power.

But not through violence, nor by intimidation. Madison said simply refusing to cooperate would be enough to impede or obstruct federal actions.

The federal government depends on state and local cooperation for virtually every action it undertakes. It needs state and local police to enforce federal gun and drug laws. It needs state and local assistance to implement programs such as Obamacare. It needs state and local cooperation to "manage" lands. It lacks the resources to implement all of its laws, rules, regulations and programs alone. Pull the rug of state cooperation out from under their feet and the feds will find themselves impotent. We've seen this vividly play out as states have legalized marijuana, effectively nullifying federal prohibition in practice within those states.

During the partial federal government shutdown in 2013, the National Governor's Association sent out a letter noting "states are partners with the

---

[28] James Madison. "The Federalist No. 46." (1788). The Constitution Society. http://www.constitution.org/fed/federa46.htm. Emphasis added.

federal government on *most federal programs.*"[29] That means by refusing state cooperation, we have within our power the ability to thwart "most federal programs."

The beauty of this approach lies in the fact that it uses the federal system against itself. The Supreme Court has consistently held since 1842 that the federal government cannot force states to help implement or enforce any federal act or program. The anti-commandeering doctrine rests primarily on four Supreme Court cases. *Printz v. US* serves as the cornerstone. Justice Antonin Scalia wrote the majority opinion:

> We held in New York that Congress cannot compel the States to enact or enforce a federal regulatory program. Today we hold that Congress cannot circumvent that prohibition by conscripting the States' officers directly. The Federal Government may neither issue directives requiring the States to address particular problems, nor command the States' officers, or those of their political subdivisions, to administer or enforce a federal regulatory program. It matters not whether policy making is involved, and no case by case weighing of the burdens or benefits is necessary; such commands are fundamentally incompatible with our constitutional system of dual sovereignty.[30]

For Americans today, non-cooperation provides a moderate middle-road we can follow to impede and obstruct federal actions and nullify them in effect.

While many academics and legal scholars will take issue with Thomas Jefferson and James Madison's conception of the Union, and the role of states as the final arbiters in settling disputes concerning the limits of federal

---

[29] "Federal Government Shutdown." National Governors Association. (September 20, 2013). http://www.nga.org/cms/home/federal-relations/nga-letters/executive-committee-letters/col2-content/main-content-list/federal-government-shutdown.html. Emphasis mine.
[30] *Printz v. United States.* 521 U.S. 898, 117 S. Ct. 2365 (1997). Cited in Donald Kommers, John Finn, and Gary Jacobsohn, eds., *American Constitutional Law* (New York: Rowman & Littlefield, 2010), 1:293.

power, *there is no question that the states have the legal right to simply refuse to cooperate.* State governments cannot effectively block federal actions, but they can simply withdraw state personnel and resources. While a given federal law will remain on the books, enough states refusing to help enforce or implement it can nullify it in practice. It becomes unenforceable and practically speaking— void.

We've seen this strategy play out in the realm of marijuana policy. Beginning in California with legalization of cannabis for medical use in 1996, states have advanced the issue each year, in spite of a 2005 Supreme Court opinion against the efforts, and a relentless year-to-year increase in spending and enforcement efforts by the federal government.

Today, 17 states have decriminalized marijuana possession, 19 states have legalized it for medical use, and Colorado, Washington state, Oregon and Alaska have legalized it for recreational use. Each year, new state laws and regulations continue to expand the industry, and each expansion further nullifies in practice the unconstitutional federal ban. The feds need state cooperation to fight the "drug war," and that has rapidly evaporated in the last few years with state legalization and decriminalization.

While state legalization does not alter federal law, it takes a step toward nullifying in effect the federal ban.

Conclusion

Nullification rests on a solid moral, philosophical and historical foundation. If government is to remain limited, some mechanism must exist to hold it within its prescribed bounds. Relying on a branch of the federal government to limit the federal government is not only a logical absurdity, it has proven completely ineffective.

On the other hand, nullification through non-cooperation has proven an effective tool. It was the remedy for federal overreach offered by the "Father of the Constitution." It stands on solid legal ground affirmed by the Supreme Court. And most importantly, it works.

The federal government bears no resemblance to the vision Madison cast in *Federalist #45*. In fact, it has been flipped on its head. The federal government exercises powers "numerous and indefinite," while those remaining with the states and the people have become "few and defined." If the American people ever want to reclaim the founding generation's vision, it will take a revolution. But not a revolution fought with guns and bombs, not an uprising characterized by a physical upheaval against the established order. Instead America needs a deeper, more philosophical revolution.

A revolution in thought.

John Adams described the American Revolution in much the same way. In his 1818 letter to Hezekiah Niles, he wrote:

> But what do we mean by the American Revolution? Do we mean the American war? The Revolution was effected before the war commenced. The Revolution was in the minds and hearts of the people; a change in their religious sentiments of their duties and obligations. … This radical change in the principles, opinions, sentiments, and affections of the people, was the real American Revolution.[31]

Today's nullification movement counts as revolutionary because it offers the hope of smashing the established political order; an alternative to "voting the bums out" only to see them replaced by new "bums" who violate the Constitution in more costly and dangerous ways each year, or relying on the federal government to limit its own power.

This revolution of thought may still seem small at this time, but it grows a little bit every day. In the words of American revolutionary John Dickinson, "*Concordia res parvae crescunt.*" (Small things grow great by concord).[32]

---

[31] John Adams. "Letter from John Adams to H. Niles February 13." (1818). The Constitution Society http://www.constitution.org/primarysources/adamsniles.html?PageSpeed=noscript

[32] John Dickinson. "Letters from a Farmer" (1767), in *The Writings of John Dickinson: Political Writings, 1764-1774* (Philadelphia: The Historical Society of Pennsylvania, 1895), 1:312.

5

Fake Money and Fraudulent Banking: The Greatest Threats to American Liberty

Jamin Hübner

When people talk about "threats to American liberty," we think of many things. We might think of bad policies proposed in U. S. Congress. Or we might think of foreign enemies, like the Islamic State. Or we might even think of the next President as a threat to American liberty.

One of the last things we consider threatening is *money and banking*.

Money, we believe, is just a politically-neutral medium of exchange. Banks, likewise, are just those institutions that hold on to money, protecting it for our good and for our convenience.

Nothing could be further from the truth. Dollars are not neutral and banking today has nothing to do with protecting anyone's money. America's founders knew this very well.

This corner of U.S. history is commonly forgotten. We've all heard the cold, treacherous story of the soldiers at Valley Forge, but we forget that it was the fake money and fraudulent banking that left the soldiers starving without food and necessary provisions (the paycheck they received from the government was virtually worthless). And what about "Shay's Rebellion," which threatened to divide the new nation in the 1780s? We were taught that it occurred because of a five-fold increase in taxes, which is largely true—but why did the government raise taxes to begin with? Because the government was going bankrupt by having to pay back all the money it had borrowed from the war. The government refused to pay with real money and instead issued yet another IOU certificate. But when it came time for everyone *else* to pay higher taxes to the government, they were the ones who had to pay with *real* money. Thus it was an unavoidable, double-standard of monetary policy that caused the frustration, not merely another tax increase.

These are just two of countless examples of how problems with money and banking undergird the very fabric of America's founding *and* how they come into direct conflict with personal freedoms. My plan for this two-part essay is to look at just how destructive it is when large authoritarian groups—like governments or central banks—use counterfeiting and legalized fraud to harvest profits from the masses.

Now, you might say, "Of course bad things are going to happen when people counterfeit and commit fraud. I don't need someone to tell me that." Perhaps not. The problem is that almost no one sees the counterfeit and fraud anymore. In fact, if we were to believe most of our Senators and Representatives, it would be unAmerican to *object* to it. And of course, it is never actually called "counterfeit" and "fraud" (that would hardly fly). Instead it's "fractional reserve banking," "monetary policy," "inflation," "expansionary program," and other big, intimidating terms that usually confuse people.

So I want to examine some basic ideas about money and banking and then talk about these issues in the context of America's history. I know this sounds boring. So I figure the only way I'm going to keep your attention is by telling a good story with lots of pictures…

A Simple Story of (Easy) Money

Please meet Mr. and Mrs. Gold.

The Golds have been alive since the dawn of creation. In the ancient account of Genesis, the Golds get immediate attention by the second chapter: "A river flows out of Eden to water the garden, and from there it divides and becomes four branches. The name of the first is Pishon; it is the one that flows around the whole land of Havilah, *where there is gold. and the gold of that land is good*" (Gen 2:11-12, emphasis mine). As you can tell, the Golds were a special family, for they generally functioned as the world's medium of exchange. Gone were the days of inconvenient, Craigslist-style bartering. If you wanted to purchase something, you bought it using a physical object that required serious work to produce. This labor limited how much there could be. Furthermore, nature itself exhibited a limited quantity ("scarcity") that couldn't be easily overcome. These limitations provided stability.[1]

The Golds, however, weren't alone. There were also the Silvers, Coppers, and other commodities like olive oil. In the case of early America, rice and tobacco functioned as currencies. But all of these currencies shared some common features: they were (1) physical, (2) easily quantifiable, and importantly, (3) they were measured in terms of physical *weight*. These features wouldn't prevent all fraud, of course. But they certainly made it difficult; gold in particular is really dense; when someone has a certain *size* of coin, it's very difficult to fake the weight.

---

[1] Cf. Lew Lehrman, "Reflections on the Case for a True Gold Standard," in *Roads to Sound Money*, ed. Alex Chafuen and Judy Shelton (Washington D.C.: Atlas Economic Research Foundation, 2012). I mean "stability" in relative, not absolute terms. For a critique of absolute monetary stability as an economic goal, see Ludwig Von Mises, *Human Action: Scholar's Edition* (Auburn: Ludwig Von Mises Institute, 2008), 419.

All of these currencies were popular around the world. While Squanto was cooking up thanksgiving turkey in the colonies (not really, of course),[2] the most common coin in circulation was the Spanish silver dollar. But, the Golds were still generally the most respected and used currency.

But then, something terribly tragic happened: Mr. and Mrs. Gold became slaves.

For thousands of years the Golds served no particular masters. They were servants of all. But then a powerful group came together to monopolize and control the Gold family so that if anyone else even dared to make coins out of the Gold family tree, *violence* could be committed against them. "The government," in one author's words, "nationalized the mint."[3]

Then, yet another tragedy struck: the faces of their children were marred and distorted. The Golds were now stamped with a picture of their despotic Masters. How humiliating!

And then it got even worse: the Golds' own *value* became debased. The Masters *lied* about their weight. The Golds had "5" etched on them when in actuality they weighed 4.5.

What a sudden change of events! Sadly, the people who used the Golds never even took notice of these changes. They just thought, "oh, what a wonderful new picture on this coin! I can trust this person's face…yes indeed." Eventually, the Masters didn't even try to hide their deceit. They shamelessly made it legal for themselves—and *required* everyone else—to give and demand money at the stamped values and not the weighted values. Now the Golds' pure family tree was dispersed in a flurry of all kinds of other materials. (To use but one example, from 1783 to 1857, the penny in the U.S. was made of 100% copper. Today, the penny is 2% copper, and 98% zinc. A copper penny used to be worth a penny; that same copper penny is worth 9 of today's cents.)

---

[2] See the more accurate "Thanksgiving" story in Nathaniel Philbrick, *Mayflower* (New York: Penguin Books, 2007).

[3] Walter Block, *Defending the Undefendable* (Auburn: Ludwig Von Mises Institute, 2013), 105.

US Penny: 1783-1857, and Today

= 1 cent (13.5g)
= 9 (today's) cents

= 1 "cent" (2.5g)
=.11 (real) cents

At this point, *money* was no longer in circulation, but tokens that *represented* money. This was a clever swap, and the Masters had a ready-made answer for anyone who might cause a kerfuffle: "Look, friends, we go way back. These tokens are as *good as gold*—the real thing. But if for some reason you want to haul around that…old, clunky gold, just come to the bank and we'll exchange it for its stamped value." And so that's what happened.

This sounded good and dandy, but this didn't address the obvious question: where's the *real* money? Where is the Gold family if they've been quietly replaced?

In the vaults of the Masters, of course. There, the Golds recalled the good old days of hussling bussling markets and quickly running from hand to hand in the sun. But now, they weren't even allowed outside. Instead, they were stuck in a cold, locked chamber.

It wasn't long and the Masters contrived their greatest plan yet. They began to realize something very interesting: *almost no one came back to redeem their tokens for real gold.* Not only were people generally unaware of what had happened, but even when some discovered the truth, they didn't seem to care anyway. As long as whatever "money" they had in their pockets got them groceries at the end of the day, there appeared little reason to complain.

In addition to this, the Masters also took notice that these new fancy tokens were *much* easier to make than obtaining gold and silver. Hard work was no longer a limitation on how much "money" could be produced like in the old days of gold-mining. The sky was now the limit as to how much "money" could be produced.[4] Just think, *unlimited money!* The possibilities!

These two thoughts converged to form the ultimate light-bulb moment in the minds of the Masters: "hmm, yes....*what if we made more tokens than the gold they represent?* Would anyone even notice? This way, we could spend and lend more money than we actually have...just think, *unlimited money!*" It was a stroke of genius that would launch the Masters to the top of the financial food-chain.

Of course, the Masters wouldn't get rid of all the (real) money. They would still reserve a little bit of gold to back the tokens, but only a *fraction*. This way, they could make as many tokens as they want for their own personal use ("Time for a new car, honey!")—but not too many, and not too fast, otherwise people are going to catch on to this (literal) money-making scheme.

Perhaps we should stop for a moment and recap what's happened so far.

At this point in our story, the Masters had achieved both *legalized counterfeit* and *fraudulent banking* in a few simple steps. Regarding legalized counterfeit, the Masters created a money substitute that didn't represent the weighted values of real money, and then forced everyone to play along with the fake money that the Masters controlled. It was "forced" through real, physical armies and police that, in an incredible twist of irony, the people themselves paid for through their taxes. Indeed, the Masters and the state (the government) were partners. (In a way, however, it was an unbalanced relationship. Only the Masters had an unlimited supply of money. The government, on the other hand, could only obtain as much money as could be extracted from its citizens.)

Regarding fraudulent banking, that is simply what fractional-reserve banking is. The Masters made a contractual promise that they *could not fulfill,*

---

[4] "*Fiat money* is a money consisting of mere tokens which can neither be employed for any industrial purposes nor convey a claim against anybody." Von Mises, *Human Action,* 426.

namely, that if people came to redeem their tokens, they would receive the appropriate amount of gold. This used to be possible in the days when the value of a token corresponded to the value of gold. But, since making all of these new tokens, the Masters didn't have enough gold to go around; they only had a *fraction* of what they promised to have.[5] So while the Masters appeared to be gods and goddesses with unlimited wealth, they were actually broke.[6]

What if everyone came to the Masters at once, wanting gold in exchange for tokens? The trick would be found out. Most people would be lined up at the bank from dusk until dawn and still wouldn't get their money back—because it didn't exist. How would the Masters deal with this risk?

Well, for starters, they figured that no one would catch on until they were long dead. But, just in case the day of reckoning came sooner, they would handle any troubles the same way that they enforced the money-making scheme in the first place: putting the law and police on their side. If any riots broke out, riot shields and water canons would come out of the closet and into the streets. Case closed.

As you can see, then, this whole arrangement was a bit of a gamble. The fractional-reserve banking system only works when depositors deposit. It fails when depositors *redeem* their money—at least when they redeem more than the banks have. For that reason, the Masters established various measures to prevent this from happening—such as lag times between

---

[5] "The whole system of 'fractional-reserve banking' involves the issuances of receipts which cannot possibly be redeemed...Instead of preventing inflation by prohibiting fractional-reserve banking as fraudulent, governments have uniformly moved in the opposite direction, and have step-by-step removed these free-market checks to bank credit expansion, at the same time putting themselves in a position to direct inflation." Murray Rothbard, *America's Great Depression* (Auburn: Ludwig Von Mises Institute, 2005), 25.

[6] "The problem assumed much greater importance when governments initiated their policies of long-term irredeemable and perpetual loans. The state, this new deity of the dawning age of statolatry, this eternal and superhuman institution beyond the reach of earthly frailties, offered to the citizen an opportunity to put his wealth in safety and to enjoy a stable income secure against all vicissitudes." Von Mises, *Human Action*, 226.

deposits and redemptions ("you'll get your money in 'two business days'"), daily or monthly withdrawal limits ("no more than $10,000 per month"), and "bank holidays" when everything is froze ("come back next week and maybe we'll have your money!").

The people generally didn't realize this risk of the banks, even when voluntarily exchanging their own money for a money substitute. Banks exist to *protect* our money, not lose it, right?

Not anymore. And, in fact, something really, *really* weird happened on this count.

Instead of being anxious and worried about losing all of their money (as they should have been), the people were, for a time, *incredibly happy* by this new and innovative arrangement. Why? Because the Masters had all this money (from who knows where!) and it had to get spent somewhere. The Masters wanted new houses, for example, so the realtors and home-builders were making big business. The Masters wanted new cars and luxurious clothing, so the retail market was happy. And on it went.

In addition, other *banks* wanted to borrow tokens to lend out so that everyone—not just the Masters—could buy new houses, cars, clothing, and the latest iWidget. This made the banks really happy and the millions of borrowers happy as well.

Money, in a word, became *easy*. Countless tokens burst from the floodgates of the Masters' vaults and eventually made its way into the hands of the people at near zero rates of interest. Now everyone could buy a house, buy a car—become wealthy! It felt like everyone was rich and life was bliss! *Money money money!* The economists were all giving positive numbers— spending and consumption were all at all-time highs. The stock market was driving through the roof, making everyone even more wealthier!

Or so it seemed.

Around the time the "economy" reached its new "high," something really, *really* weird happened: the townspeople woke up one day and realized that everything was really, *really* expensive.

School was now 10,000 tokens when it used to be 5,000. Milk was 4 tokens when it used to be 1. A house that used to cost 40,000 tokens now cost 110,000. People's wages got higher too, *but not as fast.*

Worst of all, people's savings were being destroyed.[7]

The older, wiser people in the community—the people who used to know the *real* Mr. and Mrs. Gold—were very upset about how all the money they saved over the years couldn't even buy them a new house. Younger couples were upset as well because they couldn't afford to have the mother of the family quit her job in order to have kids; it used to be possible to live off of one parent's income, but now that seemed impossible. These younger folk also got irritated when hearing stories from their parents about how a part-time job paid for the College back in the day, and now a part-time job would barely pay for their new textbooks! Some of these parents even got upset at their kids because they assumed that, if they would just work harder, then they could pay for anything they wanted to. This is the land of the free, after all!

---

[7] The image of the inflation monster comes from *Fixing the Economist.* "How to Approach the Problem of Inflation in Economics." (July 31, 2014).
https://fixingtheeconomists.wordpress.com/2014/07/31/how-to-approach-the-problem-of-inflation-in-economics/

What actually happened was that the currency had depreciated, and inflation took its sinister toll—eradication of savings, declining living standards, and disruption of the social order.

But it got worse: this new "money" and artificial growth just couldn't sustain itself. All of sudden prices would come crashing back down, and the boom fell into a bust. A recession!

Now instead of being really happy, everyone was really upset. But they didn't know what happened. They had no idea why everything was getting so darn expensive, or why the mysterious "economy" in the sky fell to the ground and caused them to lose their job. But *somebody* had to be blamed for all of this.[8]

So the people started the blame game:

It was the rich landowners! Yes, they were behind all of this!

Oh no, wait…the wealthy farmers and merchants! Yes, that's it!

No, wait…maybe it was some Wall Street speculators! Yeah, they caused this chaos!

Or, wait…perhaps it was the elected politicians! Yes! They're the ones!

Well, wait, maybe it was…big corporations! Yeah! Overpaid CEOs and…no wait, that's not it.

It's outsourcing jobs to China! Yeah! Foreign competition!…

No…no wait, we got it…it was the bad weather and global warming! Yes, the sun is to blame for my unemployment!

Well…whatever it is, it's got to be greed! Somebody is behaving unethically here!

---

[8] The Occupy Wall Street image comes from Kari O'Conner, "Saying A Lot With A Little: Occupy Wall Street Signs, Part 1." Postconsumers.com (November 9, 2011). http://www.postconsumers.com/education/saying-a-lot-with-a-little-occupy-wall-street-signs-part-1/

As it turns out, the instincts of the mob were right: the cause was greed. However, they pointed their fingers in every direction but the right one.[9]

The economic chaos wasn't caused by wealthy landowners, corporations, overpaid CEOs, or private businesses. It wasn't caused by politicians, overseas competitors, or the weather.

It was caused by the Masters of money—the people who produced and controlled the currency that everyone used.

---

[9] The image of the Federal Reserve Bank comes from Derrick Broze, "World Bank Warns Developing Nations On Federal Reserve Interest Rates." Truth in Media. (September 17, 2015). http://truthinmedia.com/world-bank-warning-developing-nations/

Since this secret was largely kept, the Masters of money went on to invent *paper* tokens, making it even easier to produce, borrow, and spend. They also realized that the Gold Family was doing a whole lot of nothing, so they sold most of the clan to overseas buyers. Now the paper money in circulation couldn't even be redeemed for something valuable; the only value it had was public confidence that it had value! If the public simply stopped believing that the fake money had any real value, then it wouldn't—at least in cases where people could use other currencies.

The Masters went on to legalize other private banks to commit fraud on their already fraudulent banking scheme. When the central banking Masters printed paper money, they didn't just spend it or loan it to people; they loaned it to *other banks*, who held on to a fraction of that money and then loaned out 10 times as much as they had in their reserves just by pushing a button on a keyboard. Now inflation would really get going![10]

Just when you think it couldn't get more inflated, the Masters created even more money out of thin air—this time *with no physical representation at all.*

---

[10] The image of fractional reserve banking comes from "What is Fractional Reserve Banking?". Hot Paper Money. http://hotpapermoney.com/spot-price-of-gold/fractional-reserve-banking-system/

If paper money is represented as digital numbers in banking computers, why not just create money by typing on a keyboard? Genius!

It was another step in the giant financial pyramid: digital bank deposits that represented (a fraction of) paper money that represented a (fraction) of real money—that no longer existed in the bank's vaults. It was a layer of fake money and fraud on top of *another* layer of fake money and fraud on top of *another* layer of fake money and fraud.

"Money" at this point had never been more easy to obtain! The cost of borrowing (interest) was an effective 00.0000%. Banksters—well I mean *bankers*—were overwhelmed with joy because of how easily they could sell their services, which were in such high demand.

Here, our story enters another major twist that merits attention.

Banks weren't the only beneficiary of the central bank. The government itself—the Treasury Department and Congress—benefited perhaps as much or more than anything else. After all, *how are politicians going to get re-elected if they have no money to spend on the things that the people and businesses who elect them enjoy?* Campaign fundraising and tax increases are a pain; it's so much easier to just borrow money from a central bank—with no intention of paying it back—so Congress can spend it on its biggest fans.[11] Having a generous friend with unlimited money has some serious perks![12]

---

[11] Cf. Von Mises, *Human Action,* 313.

[12] The image of Federal Reserve Chairman (Ben Bernanke), Chairwoman (Janet Yellen), and President Barak Obama comes from David Jackson, "Obama Nominates Yellen as Fed Chair." *USA Today.* (October 9, 2013)
http://www.usatoday.com/story/news/politics/2013/10/09/obama-yellen-bernanke-federal-reserve/2953189/
The (MIT commencement) image of Federal Reserve Chairmen (Ben Bernanke) and President George W. Bush comes from MITadmisions.org. "Bernanke to speak at Commencement!" (December 14, 2005).
http://mitadmissions.org/blogs/entry/bernanke_to_speak_at_commencem

So the central bank was naturally happy to loan trillions of paper dollars to the government, which in turn spent the money on regulations and subsidies that favor certain corporations (those promising support for certain candidates), and other things like "public works" and, let's not forget the big one, *war.*

War is the ultimate political drug. Wars trick the citizenry into thinking that anything that the elected want to do is allowable—so long as "national security" is the ultimate purpose. This is for the obvious reason that wars create a unified atmosphere of collective desperation, survival, confusion and vulnerability—all of which generates an opportunity for unbounded trust, and therefore unbounded control.[13] More intoxicating is an *eternal* war with an *unbeatable foe*. In that case, the state is effectively permanently unshackled from any public or legal limit on power. (It is no surprise then, to find governments *creating* their own foreign enemies to enable and control such wars in the first place.)

Wars, however, are extremely expensive, and they have to be paid for somehow. Some of these costs could be offset by borrowing money (selling bonds to the public). But the real providers are, once again, the Masters of money.

In the end, whether politicians (senators, representatives, and presidents)[14] need money to buy their voters, or whether obscure administrators are seeking more control (and need an excuse—a war—to get it), there would have to be someone willing to pay if any of this is going to happen. Here, the central banking money masters are readily available.

The government doesn't get all this (fake) money for free, however. The government would have to give up something of its own—assets, control, or at least make a promise of security.

And that's exactly what the government gave to the Masters—*legal security to remain the sole producer of money*. If anyone else was allowed to print money,

---

[13] "The great Randolph Bourne realized that 'war is the health of the State.' It is in war that the State really comes into its own: swelling in power, in number, in pride, in absolute dominion over the economy and the society. Society becomes a herd, seeking to kill its alleged enemies, rooting out and suppressing all dissent from the official war effort, happily betraying truth for the supposed public interest. Society becomes an armed camp, with the values and the morale—as Albert Jay Nock once phrased it—of an 'army on the march.'" Murray Rothbard, *Egalitarianism as a Revolt Against Nature and Other Essays*, R.A. Child, Jr., Ed. (Auburn: Mises Institute, 2000), 115-132. Cf. Rose Wilder, *The Discovery of Freedom* (New York: John Day Company, 1943), ch 5, "War."

[14] I point this out because there is no meaning in speaking of, much less criticizing (as often is the case), abstract, theoretical "politicians." There are only government workers and elected senators and representatives. *These* constitute "politicians" and "the government," whether one is comfortable making that identification or not.

and if anyone else was allowed to force the people to use *their* currency, the economic monopoly would come to an end. Once again, the state's monopoly on force complemented the central bank's monopoly on money.

The government would also have to pay interest on the money that they borrowed. Printing money isn't *entirely* free. So the Masters of money charged the Treasury for borrowing the money—just like a bank charges interest on a loan. The central banking masters, then, would *profit* from printing its "notes" and lending them out.

Eventually, the Masters came to realize the same thing that the politicians did: war is not bad, war is good. Only instead of giving power to politicians, wars would *directly profit* the Masters of money. It doesn't matter who wins. It doesn't matter who fired first. And it doesn't matter the ethnicity, religion, or nationality of either side. As long as bullets are being fired, buildings are being destroyed, and debts are being accrued, the banking business is booming. *Banks win every war.*

At the same time this was happening, the government was realizing something equally profound: *inflation is a way of paying debt.* Printing money is handy in and of itself—but it also depreciates, dilutes the currency so it becomes more worthless. So, while inflation is bad to savers (recall the inflation monster above), inflation is "good" for debtors. In theory, with enough inflation, debts will never have to be paid back! Debt can just be "inflated away."

The final step in the story of money is that this entire arrangement would evolve from the national level to the *international* level. The Masters of money had connections across the ocean—people who were conducting their own money-making schemes. (Fake money and fraudulent banking had proven profitable elsewhere.) Plans between masters proposed a new *world* bank, *international* monetary fund, and international currency.

This was a step that completed the journey of money's adventures through time, and concludes our brief tale:

1. *Nationalized mint:* the state coins money.
2. *Debasement:* stamped at a greater face weight than physical weight.
3. *Legal tender laws:* money is counted at its stamped value, not weighted value.
4. *Fractional-reserve banking:* tokens are easily created that represent more gold than possessed. Risky banking and unlimited money are simultaneously born.
5. *Fiat paper money:* tokens are irredeemable and are easily mass-produced.
6. *State annexation of banks:* government controls banking sector, where paper money exceeds all tokens/coins; digital currency (deposits) exceed paper money.
7. *Global consolidation of financial system:* world bank, universal fiat currency.[15]

Changing Gears

I hope you enjoyed this brief tale because, as you have already realized, it is not make-believe. We will now shift from our illustrated world of myth into the academic world of history, telling the same basic story in a more precise, American context. We will also switch to a less colloquial tone.

But first, a few introductory notes.

In the story below, you will inevitably draw many connections without help so it is hardly necessary to draw them myself. Likewise, there are referents to the earlier story that you won't find in the narrative below, and vice versa. There is not a one-for-one correspondence, there is no need to find it. My goal is more general: now that your interest has been sparked, perhaps you will find the subtitle of this essay more plausible than implausible.

Finally, I have chosen to implement many first-person, eye-witness accounts of hyperinflation because of the popular myth that inflation could not and does not possibly lead to genuine human suffering.

---

[15] See Block, *Defending the Undefendable,* 107.

Paper Money in the Early U.S.

The first several steps of the debasement of money have already been outlined above (e.g., stamped vs. weighed values).[16] So we will begin our journey at the first use of paper money in America, eventually making our way into central banking and the current scene.

Paper money came to America in 1690 when the Massachusetts Bay ran into a bit of a pinch. There was a war against Quebec and, as we learned already, war is expensive. Since easy money was not available, fiat paper was printed to pay the soldiers. It was supposed to be a one-time printing of notes (printing IOUs is risky, afterall) redeemable for specie after three years. But within months, the paper notes continued to be printed—taking not three, but *over 35 years* for soldiers to get their money back.[17] £40,000 worth of paper money was printed and depreciated by a staggering 40%. This caused the regular economic chaos associated with inflation (more on this below).

Apparently without remorse, two years later the "government moved against this market evaluation by use of force, making the paper money compulsory legal tender for all debts at par with specie, and by granting a premium of 5 percent on all payment of debts to the government made in paper notes."[18] Because of this forced inflation, high prices decreased exports from the colony and effectively drove real money (e.g., silver) out of the area.

Another printing of £500,000 in 1711 (for another failed expedition against Quebec) depreciated the currency 30% against silver.[19] Despite the economic harm done to the colonists, "Depreciation proceeded in this and other colonies despite fierce governmental attempts to outlaw it, backed by

---

[16] For a study of how Christians rejected the debasement of money throughout history, see Samuel Gregg, *For God and Profit: How Banking and Finance Can Serve the Common Good* (New York: Crossroads, 2016).

[17] Rothbard, *A History of Money and Banking*, 52.

[18] Ibid.

[19] Ibid. 54

fines, imprisonment, and total confiscation of property for the high crime of not accepting the paper at par."[20]

In 1716 Massachusetts's government created a "land bank" that issued £100,000 to be loaned on real estate in various counties. Unsurprisingly, inflation simply moved from one sector of economy to another; land prices skyrocketed. The notes printed by this land bank were redeemable for silver—until a competitor, a silver bank, came to the market. In an act of desperation, the land bank issued over £49,000 in *irredeemable* notes—notes not backed by anything.[21] The public wisely began to refuse these notes.

These unreasonably high prices and fraudulent practices—combined with Maryland literally giving £30,000 away to the public in 1733 to universalize the currency[22]—led to the King himself finally stepping in during the early 1740s. The British authorities shut down both the land bank and silver bank, and "tried intermittently to reduce the bills in circulation and return to a specie currency, but were hampered by its assumed obligations to honor the paper notes at par of its sister New England colonies."[23]

Such inflation benefited wealthy landowners and merchants who had debts to pay, since inflation reduces the amount of real debt that needs to be paid back. But this royal loyalty proved costly to everyone else:

> In 1744, another losing expedition against the French led Massachusetts to issue an enormous amount of paper money over the next several years. From 1744 to 1748, paper money in circulation expanded from £300,000 to £2.5 million, and the depreciation in Massachusetts was such that silver had risen on the market to 60 shillings an ounce, ten times the price at the beginning of an era of paper money in 1690.[24]

---

[20] Ibid.
[21] Ibid., 58.
[22] Cf., "helicopter dropping" money.
[23] Ibid.
[24] Ibid.

	MA	CT	Carolinas	RI
Inflation in 1740s-50s (paper to specie ratio)	11:1	9:1	10:1	23:1

By the 1740s, all of the colonies were using paper currency except Virginia (which capitulated later due to the French and Indian War). This hurled the economy into a predictable, but no less detrimental, boom-bust cycle of high prices and recessions.[25]

After King George's War in 1748, the British government required the American colonies to retire paper money, return to real money (and thus reality). This legislation began in the early 1750s and extended to 1764, whereupon all colonies were prohibited from issuing new paper money. Although it was a shock at first, silver quickly returned to the market, prices stabilized (including the foreign exchange rate), and the economy flourished.[26]

This stint of stability was short lived, however.

The redcoats were coming.

Money and Banking During the Revolution

To "fund" the Revolutionary War, Congress issued the paper Continental dollar. Between 1775-1777, it issued $225 million of these notes when there was initially $12 million of real money. In the end, the value of the Continental dollar dropped an abysmal 42 to 1 in relation to specie.[27] Since these economic conditions came home to roost in the form of austerity, the government had to once again resort to violence: price controls and

---

[25] See Donald L. Kemmerer, "Paper Money in New Jersey, 1668–1775," New Jersey Historical Society, *Proceedings* 74 (April 1956): 107–44. Cited in Rothbard, *History of Money and Banking*, 55.

[26] See Roger W. Weiss, "The Colonial Monetary Standard of Massachusetts," *Economic History Review* 27 (November 1974): 589. Cited in Rothbard, *History of Money and Banking*, 56.

[27] Rothbard, *History of Money and Banking*, 59-61.

compulsory par laws came into action, forcing the masses into even more poverty.

As we already learned from Massachusetts in 1690, the first people to get conned by the government's monetary policies are its own employees. The Continental Congress did not pay their soldiers in real money but rather a money substitute—the worthless Continental dollar. And since no business would accept this counterfeit—general stores, grocers, farmers, etc.—soldiers and others suffered terribly during the most crucial parts of the war. Eventually, the army was so fed up that the quartermaster issued $200 million of its own paper "certificates," which depreciated ("hyper-inflated") to virtually nothing. In another act of desperation, Congress created loan certificates, "notes issued by the government to pay for supplies and accepted by merchants because the government would not pay anything else."[28] Predictably, the certificates depreciated 24 to 1 in relation to specie by 1779. Many or most of these notes remained part of the permanent peacetime federal debt.

All of this is a summary. Since it is misleading to cite economic figures and numbers without exploring the concrete realities behind them, it is necessary to unfold this drama more thoroughly. As it should become clear, inflation is not a neutral economic term; it indicates the *horrifying* reality of currency depreciation, which creates poverty where there was once prosperity, and forces those who were already poor into calamitous suffering.

There is a particularly sinister and provocative title given to a 1777 letter in Steele and Morris's tome *The Spirit of Seventy-Six:* "More to fear from Paper Money than from British Generals." The Letter is written by Joseph Eggleston Jr. in Delaware to his father in Amelia County, Virginia. Eggleston. recounts specific examples of how "goods are 200% dearer than they were in Virginia when I left," such as paying "18 dollars for [a hat] of an inferior

---

[28] Ibid., 61.

kind," and "Rum…20/the quart."[29] He goes on to conclude that "it is my fixed opinion that America has much more to fear from the effects of large quantities of paper money than from the operations of Howe and all the British generals."[30]

Perhaps this was an exaggeration. Or was it? One must ask: what is worse, threats of war and foreign enemies, or starving to death unclothed in one's own home? Are bad guys with weapons genuinely more threatening than monetary inflation?

Some economic historians answer this question directly as it relates to the Revolution:

> The havoc wrought in the United States by the distortions, inequities, currency breakdowns, shortages, and depreciation caused by the central state, and local government policies of wild inflation and price control, was far greater than that imposed by the British troops during the war. This is to say nothing of the maleficent heritage of the public debt that remained for the future economic and political life of the country.[31]

Hyperinflation[32] *really can* be a greater threat than foreign enemies, for a broken economy can produce just as much starvation, violence, and death as the bloodiest of wars—as history would repeatedly go on to show.

According to another historian, by May of 1779,

> …a bushel of wheat sold for forty times what it had fetched two years earlier…Sometimes farmers would sell their goods to the British, who paid

---

[29] Henry Steele Commager and Richard B. Morris, *The Spirit of Seventy-Six* (Boston: De Capo Press, 1995), 791.

[30] Ibid.

[31] Murray Rothbard, *Conceived in Liberty* (Auburn: Ludwig Von Mises Institute, 2011), 1493.

[32] "Hyperinflation" is defined in different ways by different economists. Shared among them is the concept of accelerated inflation. According to the International Accounting Standard of IAS 29, a rate of inflation more than 26% annually (or 100% per three years) qualifies as hyperinflation.

in sound currency…America's financial woes were the greatest impediment to an adequate military supply system and a vigorous prosecution of the war. General Washington was learning what soldiers and statesmen discovered since the days of Cicero, who had proclaimed that the 'sinews of war [are] unlimited money.' The root of America's fiscal troubles was that too much paper money had been issued without adequate provision for its redemption.[33]

Thus, employers and businesses referred to the Continental dollar as "rebel money."[34] One Virginian spoke of "This monstrous…depreciation of the paper Money."[35] Others cursed the "wicked paper."[36]

C. PRICES RISE FANTASTICALLY AS PAPER MONEY SHRINKS IN VALUE

Quantity of Certain Staples That Could Be Purchased in Pennsylvania for £100 in paper currency.

April	Flour cwt.	Sugar cwt.	Iron cwt.	Beef bbl.
1774	105.9	36.4	76.9	36.4
1775	133.3	39.5	77.9	33.3
1776	143.3	30.8	74.8	26.7
1777	83.8	8.89	40.0	10.5
1778	63.2	2.75	11.8	9.78
1779	6.67	0.84	2.65	1.82
1780	1.15	0.30	0.88	0.22
1781	0.71	0.21	0.52	0.11

cwt. = 112 lbs.; bbl. = 225 lbs.

---

[33] John Ferling, *A Leap in the Dark: The Struggle to Create the American Republic* (New York: Oxford University Press, 2004), 218.

[34] Commager and Morris, *The Spirit of Seventy-Six,* 791.

[35] Ferling, *Leap,* 220. The table of prices comes from Commager and Morris, *The Spirit of Seventy-Six,* 789.

[36] Cited in John Witherspoon, *On Money and Finance* (Powder Springs: American Vision, 2010), 17.

Perhaps nothing is more honest than the inner folds of one's personal diary. The following entry comes from November of 1777 by 16 year-old Robert Morton of Philadelphia:

> None of the large ships have yet come up. A contest has subsisted in this city since the arrival of the fleet, concerning the legal paper currency. The English merchants that came in the fleet will not dispose of their goods without hard money, alleging that no bills are to be bought, no produce to be obtained, and no method can be adopted by which they can send remittances. Numbers of the most respectable inhabitants are using all their influence to support it, and numbers of others who have no regard for the public good are giving out the hard money for what they want for immediate use, thus purchasing momentary gratifications at the expense of the public, for if the circulation of this money should be stopt, many who have no legal money but paper and have no means of obtaining gold and silver, will be reduced to beggary and want, and those who are so lost to every sense of honor, to the happiness of their fellow citizens, and eventually their own good, as to give out their hard money, either for the goods of those who are newcomers, or in the public market where it is now exacted for provisions, will, by their evil example, oblige those who possess hard money, to advance it and ruin the credit of the other money for the present. The consequence of which must be that we shall be shortly drained of our hard cash, the other money rendered useless, no trade by which we can get a fresh supply; our ruin must therefore be certain and inevitable.[37]

The hopelessness in Morton's voice is evident, as is his inner disturbance by what such a faulty economy was doing to so many peoples' lives. Inflation led to forced-famines and a loss of human dignity (in Morton's words, "every sense of honor").

Perhaps this, too, was just an isolated exaggeration. Certainly nothing as benign as paper currency and federal debt could actually result in people starving to death.

---

[37] Commager and Morris, *The Spirit of Seventy-Six*, 792.

But Congress, too, made the same kinds of observations in the same year:

> Paper currency…is multiplied beyond the rules of good policy. No truth being more evident, than that where the quantity of money…exceeds what is useful as a medium of commerce…the consequences to be apprehended are equally obvious and alarming. They tend to the depravity of morals,— decay of public virtue,—a precarious supply for the war,—debasement of the public faith,—injustice to individuals, and the destruction of honour, safety, and independence of the United States.[38]

One shouldn't miss the powerful point being made in this quote: *fake money leads to immorality and injustice.* It is evil because it constitutes systematic dishonesty and misallocation of resources.[39]

Even the elite and wealthy (who still traded in real gold and silver) were affected by the plague of hyperinflation:

> Numerous delegates moved to less expensive lodgings, shared quarters with a colleague, or dined at common tables in boarding houses. Every congressman had a friend who had been compelled by financial necessity to quit public service. Yet most congressmen were considerably more affluent than the artisans and laborers in urban America. After nearly five years of war, ordinary workers were severely pinched. Prices in 1779 were eight times greater than when the war began. Wages had seldom kept pace. Widows, orphans, and clergyman, and salaried officials were especially hard hit.[40]

As one might expect, some people took advantage of this desperate situation. Robert Morris was "the former congressman who had been lukewarm toward independence in 1776, and who had become perhaps the

---

[38] Cited in Edwin Vieiera, Jr., *Pieces of Eight: The Monetary Powers and Disabilities of the United States Constitution,* 2 vols, 2nd ed. (Fredericksburg: Sheridan Books, 2002), 84.

[39] Cf. Gregg, *For God and Profit.*

[40] Ferling, *Leap,* 221.

wealthiest man in America in the course of the war."[41] He became the Superintendent of Finance for Congress in 1781 and went on to create the first and second central bank in U.S. history.[42] Prior to these events, Morris financed various groups—at one point even personally paying £10,000 towards troops under Washington.

We will return to Morris in a moment. For now, it is sufficient to summarize by saying that the economic conditions were catastrophic. (Even Morris conceded, "We have already calamities sufficient for any country."[43]) In April 1779, George Washington himself complained, "A wagon load of money will scarcely purchase a wagon load of provisions."[44] One Englishman from London remarked, "The Congress are fallen into general contempt, for their want of credit and power; the army is absolute and has declared it will not submit to a peace made by Congress; the people grumble, but are obliged to surrender one piece of furniture after another, even to their beds, to pay their taxes."[45] This is economic desperation if there ever was such a thing.

During all of this chaos, many of the American people couldn't pinpoint who or what exactly was behind all of the woe. But they had some good hunches, and someone had to be brought to justice. A perusing of titles in Commager's *The Spirit of Seventy-Six* is sufficient to get a sense of the energy: "Monopolizers are our Worst Oppressors"; "That 'Pernicious' Practice of

---

[41] Ibid., 222.

[42] While a military coup was on the verge of happening (the "Newburgh Conspiracy"), "To whipsaw Congress, Robert Morris had submitted his resignation at the end of January. This sudden and surprising move hit the Congress with the force of a thunderclap. It was an arrogant attempt at blackmail, for his resignation was to take effect at the end of May, *unless* Congress had by then established a system for the permanent funding of the public debt." Rothbard, *Conceived in Liberty*, 1520.

[43] Robert Morris in *Congressional Series of United States Public Documents*, Volume 2585 (Washington D.C.: Government Printing Office, 1889), 235.

[44] Cited in Albert Bolles, *The Financial History of the United States* (New York: D. Appleton and Company, 1879), 132.

[45] Benjamin Talmage (November 6, 1780), cited in Commager and Morris, *The Spirit of Seventy-Six*, 795.

Engrossing"; "The Spirit of Avarice Threatens the Liberties of America"; "Washington: 'Hunt Them Down as Pests of Society'"; "Young Hamilton Denounces the War Profiteers", etc.

So the mob held a sort of "Occupy-Wall Street" movement:

> Public meetings were held, attended by thousands of desperate and angry residents. At one such gathering in May [of 1779], General Daniel Roberdeau, a militia commander and former congressman—John and Samuel Adams had briefly lodges in his house in 1777—told an excited crowd that unscrupulous businessmen, who were "getting richer by the blood," of their countrymen, were "the greatest cause of our present calamities."[46]

Unfortunately, this particular meeting elected committees to do the worst thing it could have done: centrally control prices goods and services.

As basic economics has shown since the field's founding in the late 1800s, determining prices by decree—instead of letting supply and demand determine prices—virtually always results in either overproduction (and thus wasted resources), or underproduction (and thus shortages). This is true regardless of what is considered "fair," regardless of an intent to help the poor, and regardless if (for example) a selfish, wealthy corporation or CEO is on the supply side. (Hence, the "*laws*" of supply and demand.) Consequently, when these laws are challenged—as when gravity is challenged, the result is typically painful.

> ...the proponents of price controls had no economic arguments. Their views were purely superficial and ad hoc: 'Prices are going up, they shouldn't, ergo outlaw price rises,' was the argument in form.[47]

---

[46] Ibid. Cf. Commager and Morris, *The Spirit of Seventy-Six*, "The Profiteers and Profiteering," 802-814.

[47] Rothbard, *Conceived in Liberty*, 1492.

A sad case of this economic failure occurred in Philadelphia, leading not only to increased suffering for the poor and needy, but also to mob of violence on the doorstep of a prominent politician. In this case, that doorstep was the house of James Wilson, a signer of the Declaration of Independence and (later) Supreme Court Justice.

> As the soldiers drew up before Wilson's house, gunfire rang out. It has never proven which side fired first, but the shots set in motion a battle that lasted ten minutes. It ended only when Joseph Reed, Washington's former aide who now was the chief executive of Pennsylvania, arrived on horseback with a small force of calvary. When order was restored, it was discovered that nearly two dozen men had been killed and wounded. There were casualties on both sides. More than a score of militiamen were arrested. Neither Wilson nor any of his comrades in the citadel-house were taken into custody.[48]

This was the extent of success when it came to price-controls.

It is no wonder that America's first economist, Peletiah Webster, framed the situation in the following terms:

> Perhaps this whole transaction affords the most striking proof conceivable, of the absurdity of all attempts to *fix the value of money by a law*, or any other methods of *compulsion*.[49]

---

[48] Ferling, *Leap*, 223-225.

[49] Peletiah Webster, "Remarks on the Resolution of Council Of the 2d of May, 1781, for raising the Exchange to 175 Continental dollars for 1 hard," *Political Essays On the Nature and Operation of Money, Public Finances and Other Subjects* (New York: Burt Franklin, 1969 [1791]), 502.

Post-Revolution Responses to the New Nation's
Monetary Crisis

Robert Morris and other businessmen were understandably against price controls. It hurt their profits. But others were against price controls because it hurt those who needed help the most. Indeed, price controls are harmful for all parties involved, producer *and* consumer.

Webster was not alone in recognizing this fact. John Witherspoon, a Christian pastor, signer of the Declaration of Independence, and President of what would later become Princeton University, also denounced the absurdities of such economic regulations.

> Witherspoon…accurately and prophetically warned Washington that the army's severe price and wage controls on the commodities and services it purchased would only aggravate the shortages and lead to starvation for the army. No man, declared Witherspoon, can be forced to supply goods in the market prices he considered unreasonable…[the market price that] clears supply and demand can only be set on the market by the voluntary interactions of buyers and sellers, not by any outside politician or government official, it being impossible for any authority to know all the nuances and variations that enter into supply and demand and hence into price.[50]

In July 1779, ten Philadelphia workers made this very argument, as price controls made it impossible for them to keep making shoes:

> If [the system of price controls] is absurd and contrary to every principle of trade…It will destroy every spring of industry, and will make it the interest of every one to decline all business…Trade should be free as air, uninterrupted as the tide, and though it will necessarily like this be sometimes high at one place and low at another, yet it will ever return of

---

[50] Rothbard, *Conceived in Liberty*, 1492.

itself sufficiently near to a proper level if…injudicious attempts to regulate it, are not imposed…[51]

Witherspoon was so adamant about the inherent evil of fake money and price controls that he wrote an entire book on it entitled, *An Essay on Money as a Medium of Commerce*. In one place the books reads,

> No paper of any kind is, properly speaking, money. It ought never to be made a legal tender…the increase in currency in any nation by paper, which will not pass among other nations, makes the first cost of everything they do greater, and of consequence, profit, less…Those who refuse doubtful paper—and thereby disgrace it or prevent its circulation—are not enemies, but friends to their country.[52]

U.S. Congresses throughout history have never taken these words of Witherspoon seriously.[53] More alarmingly, if an elected official today were to do exactly what Witherspoon advised—disgrace paper dollars and prevent its circulation—that Senator or Representative would be officially considered an enemy of the state and would be prosecuted to the full extent of the law.[54]

Not everyone agreed with Witherspoon and Webster's position on paper cash, however:

---

[51] Cited in Rothbard, *Conceived in Liberty*, 1491.

[52] John Witherspoon, *An Essay on Money as a Medium of Commerce* (Philadelphia: Young, Stewart, and M'Culloch, 1786), 76.

[53] Ever since 1933, in fact, it is *illegal* to use gold as a medium of exchange. A person can buy and sell it as a commodity, but it is not considered "money" or "legal tender."
Witherspoon's summary above is also prophetic in its observation that the devaluation of a currency "will not pass among the nations." Since "QE3" forward (quantitative easing policies enacted by the U.S. Federal Reserve in 2013), China (among others) has wisely become increasingly hesitant to purchase U.S. debt. The result is that the U.S.'s own central bank—and not the Chinese government—has become the larger holder of U.S. bonds.

[54] As with so many things, what America's founders declared necessary, today's American Congress has declared criminal.

[Morris] recognized that the paper would depreciate, but he looked forward to this as a tax; the obvious inequity of the tax's falling hardest on the lowest-paid and the most exploited group in the country, the soldiery, caused him only fleeting regret. These men would simply have to sacrifice their pay as well as their lives to the national effort…Benjamin Franklin hailed paper as a 'wonderful machine'…In 1779…John Jay prepared an apologia for the depreciating Continental paper.[55]

Despite this disgreement, it is important to note the larger context of Witherspoon's criticism from 1786. It arose partly from the founding of America's first central bank four years earlier. Ever since the riots during the Revolution, Robert Morris learned that the best way to make and control money is to literally *make and control money.* Enter the world of centralized, monopolized banking.

Around the time Continental currency was leaving circulation, the Bank of North America was established (1782). It was privately owned,[56] utilized fractional reserves, and was given the exclusive right to bank with the U.S. federal government. It was the depository of all congressional funds.[57] "By the end of 1783, all the wartime state paper had been withdrawn from circulation."[58]

But the bank came to an end as the people who witnessed the revolution knew quite vividly how much destruction could come from paper money and its inflationary tendencies. As is true today, no currency can survive without public confidence. That was the case with the Bank of North America. Morris created his own currency in response ("Morris notes"). But this project did not last either. Around this time, James Madison in "Federalist No. 10" made

---

[55] Rothbard, *Conceived in Liberty,* 1493.

[56] Contrast with Hamilton's earlier plan of 50/50 bank ownership in 1780. See Commager, *The Spirit of Seventy-Six,* 798-99.

[57] Rothbard, *A History of Money and Banking,* 63.

[58] Rothbard, *Conceived in Liberty,* 1497.

reference to those with "a rage for paper money," which Madison aptly christened a "wicked project."[59]

Apparently undeterred by public sentiment, in 1790 Alexander Hamilton urged the formation of another central bank. This time the government would own 1/5 of the shares. Thomas Jefferson criticized the project, but President Washington was persuaded by Hamilton's defense and signed the bank bill into law within 36 hours. The "Bank of the United States" opened in 1791, had a 20-year charter, and was led by its President, Robert Morris.

The government soon borrowed $6.2 million in 1796 resulting in a wave of inflation; a 76% rise in prices caused its regular economic chaos. But for bankers, business was booming, as eighteen new banks were created in five years.[60]

The Jeffersonians continued to argue that this whole central-banking business was unconstitutional, but the Hamiltonians claimed it could be legitimized under the implied powers of the Constitution. Hamilton's position was eventually upheld in *McCulloch vs. Maryland* in 1819.

Amazingly, when the time came to renew the charter in 1811 the bill failed by one vote in the Senate and one vote in the House. All eyes were watching: would this be the end of fake money and fraudulent banking in America?

The answer would become clear: not when there's another war to fight.

Money and Banking in 19th Century America

War broke out in 1812, extending as far as the U.S. President's house (which was burned in 1814 and rebuilt as "the White House"). There was no central bank at this time. However, there were plenty of state banks making easy loans and funding the war. In 1815, real money was at $5.4 million while

---

[59] Cited in David Boaz, ed., *The Libertarian Reader* (New York: Simon and Schuster, 2015), 23.
[60] Rothbard, *A History of Money and Banking*, 68.

the notes issued by banks were at $11 million.[61] The federal government issued treasury notes that could be used as currency, causing even more inflation. Prices increased 35% from 1811 to 1815. People started pulling their money out of the state banks, as did other New England banks, which sought to redeem in specie. The run quickly revealed that the banks didn't have enough money to go around, and the fraud behind "fractional-reserve banking" was laid bare.

But then, the unthinkable happened. The federal government didn't take the state banks to court, and the banks didn't declare bankrupcy and liquidate. (This is what would typically happen if any other business in the market broke its contractual promises.) In August of 1814, the government *allowed banks to continue operating without legal recourse.*

> In short, in one of the most flagrant violations of property rights in American history, the banks were permitted to waive their contractual obligations to pay in specie while they themselves could expand their loans and operations and force their own debtors to repay their loans as usual.[62]

This bank run revealed the disturbing nature of the modern banking system and foreshadowed the events of the 20th and 21st centuries:

1. The system itself is fraudulent; contracts are made that cannot be honored.
2. Times of crises (e.g., war) are the greatest opportunities for profit; immoral profit-making can always be glossed over with patriotism.
3. War means prosperity for certain members of the wealthy, but austerity for the people and death for the soldier.
4. Banks are therefore incentivized to instigate conflict.

---

[61] Ibid., 73.

[62] Ibid., 75.

5. Banks are granted a special status with the government and will not be treated like any other business; this is because banks and paper money are the blood that keeps the government deficit machine running.

"It thus became clear to the banks," continues Rothbard, "that in a general crisis they would not be required to meet the ordinary obligations of contract law or of respect for property rights…" In other words, large-scale theft and fraud was now legalized.

But, surely this is not really "fraud" and "theft"? There would be riots in the streets and a coup. Isn't banking just a morally neutral practice? Perhaps it is important to briefly review this aspect of law and political theory:

> Fraud is equivalent to theft, for fraud is committed when one part of an exchange contract is deliberately not fulfilled after the other's property has been taken. Banks that issue receipts to non-existent gold are really committing fraud, because it is then impossible for all property owners (of claims to gold) to claim their rightful property. Therefore, prohibition of such practices would not be an act of government *intervention* in the free market; it would be part of the general legal *defense* of property against attack which a free market requires.[63]

If this is true, or at least compelling, one is left asking: How could this possibly happen in America? How could state banks just reject private property rights and steal huge sums of cash while Congress looks on? This was more or less the question economist David Ricardo asked Senator Condy Raguet years later in 1821, and here is how Raguet responded:

> …the difficulty is easily solved. The whole of our population are either stockholders of banks or in debt to them. It is not the *interest* of the first to press the banks and the rest are *afraid*. This is the whole secret. An

---

[63] Rothbard, *America's Great Depression,* 27.

independent man, who was neither a stockholder nor debtor, who would have ventured to compel the banks to do justice, would have been persecuted as an enemy of society.[64]

Thus, American culture at large had become complacent and corrupt.

But there was still a remnant, and it would continue fighting. The Old Republicans and Federalists insisted that the banks revamp and return to real money. However, in 1816, the Democrat-Republican establishment became fixed on the idea of another central bank. (Maybe things would be different this time?) This political establishment ultimately won, and in 1817 the Second Bank of the U.S. opened its doors with a 20-year charter.

The government owned 50% of the central bank's shares. What that would mean in making decisions was not entirely clear. More challenging, of course, was controlling the moral hazard that emerged from the notorious state-bank run years earlier. That hazard was about to produce another episode: having already swindled the American people below them, the state banks were on track to swindle the new bank above them.

Money supply increased $19.2 million as the Second Bank of the U.S. maintained a .11 reserve ratio.[65] The state banks borrowed from the central bank interest free and generally had no intention of repaying it back. After all, since the federal government would allow them to defraud the American people, it probably wouldn't care if the state banks defrauded the government's new central bank itself.

This approach overestimated Congressional stupidity. When the new central bank was on the verge of bankruptcy in 1818—and during the birth of countless new fraudulent schemes in the financial system[66]—the Second Bank actually contracted credit and redeemed the branch banks on par. Debtor banks were forced to redeem in real money.

---

[64] Cited in Rothbard, *A History of Money and Banking*, 82.

[65] Ibid., 86.

[66] Ibid., 87-88.

These heroic actions, along with the ouster of bank President William Jones, managed to save the Bank of the United States, but the massive contraction of money and credit swiftly brought the United States its first widespread economic and financial depression. The first nationwide 'boom-bust' cycle had arrived.[67]

The contraction was a violent 47% in one year. From 1819 to 1822, over 70 of the 340 banks in America closed doors. Land sales went from $13.6 million in 1818 down to $1.7 million in 1820. The monetary conditions were so bad that people bartered with corn and whiskey. In the words of William Gouge in *A Short History of Paper Money and Banking in the United States*, "the Bank was saved, and the people were ruined."[68]

Fake Money and Fraudulent Banking Stops; Economic Prosperity Begins

"The bank is trying to kill me, but I will kill it!"
—Andrew Jackson

The new nation had had enough. The financial memory and collective consciousness of food shortages, shrinking living standards, death, social instability and so many other things had accumulated to a new high. Every central-banking and paper-currency experiment since the days of the colonies resulted in little more than unnecessary debt and economic woe. Politicians made decades of unfulfilled promises as each "new" solution produced austerity and financial chaos. The time was ripe for a monetary reformation.

And it came. The "Jacksonians" were the closest thing to modern-day "libertarians." They clung to the basic ideas of minimal government and

---

[67] Ibid., 89.

[68] William Gouge, *A Short History of Paper Money and Banking in the United States* (New York: Augustus Kelly, 1968), 110.

economic freedom. This was immediately manifest in their opposition to Whig infrastructure stimulus programs (e.g., new railroads) and, in the monetary world, their opposition to fake money and fraudulent banking.

With sound Ricardian, economic convictions, the Jacksonians insisted on real money (not paper), 100% reserve banking (not fractional-reserve), and decentralized banking (no single centralized bank). After vetoing the central bank charter renewal in 1831 and distributing the deposits to 91 state banks in 1836, the economy began to be cleansed of its artificial prices, disequilibrium, inflation, fake money, and shoddy contracts.[69]

At first, prices increased 52% from 1834-1837, which was due to the expansion of the money supply from $109 million in 1830 to $159 million in 1833. After this temporary bubble, the time-lagged effects of the monetary reformation began to bear fruit. Prices fell a staggering 42% in 1839 as 23% of banks closed. By 1841, the Second Bank of the United States was nonexistent.

The ultimate result of this unshackling was one of the most prosperous economic periods in American history.[70] Deflation and cheaper prices proved to be a friend—not an enemy—-to economic health. Within the same 4-year period, the money supply dropped 34%, real consumption increased 21%, and real Gross Net Product a whopping 16%.[71] More people were able to hold on to more of their income because of cheaper goods and services. This left-over income could be spent in other areas or put in banks as savings— all of which created more production and wealth. Businesses did not have to worry about falling prices because the increase in volume resulting from lower prices compensated losses from cheaper prices.[72] Their input prices— cost of materials and other capital—were now cheaper as well, allowing them to make a profit at lower prices. Furthermore, business owners' own savings

---

[69] Rothbard, *A History of Money and Banking,* 92-96.

[70] As the saying goes, "short term pain, long term gain."

[71] Ibid., 103-104.

[72] If Walmart today doubled their prices, it would not double their profits!

from cheaper prices allowed them to invest or save in their business or in others'.

In a word, sound economic principles—(a) that savings is good and leads to production, growth, and stability; (b) that manipulation of prices lead to negative economic effects[73]; (c) that banking should be treated like any other business in the free market[74]; (d) that real money and a stable currency provides the basis for real economic growth and a stable economy—were generally vindicated during this period.

More War, and the National Banking System

As happens so often, war destroys interludes of peace and prosperity. Whatever gains had been made in the two decades prior were lost during the Civil War.

A new paper money called "greenbacks" were issued in 1862 to help fund the destruction. These Legal Tender Acts (1862) promised to be the first and last emergency printing of paper notes,[75] and a massive bond of $150 million was ultimately offered to the largest banks in America.

But, just as there is nothing more permanent than a temporary government program, there is nothing more infinite than a one-time political promise. Another $150 million were printed in July, and another $150 million in 1863. Eventually, there were well over $400 million greenbacks in circulation.[76] The Treasury began to get rid of its gold as greenbacks

---

[73] The Jacksonians weren't *completely* opposed to manipulating prices. Instead of abolishing the value ratio of gold to silver and letting the market decide how valuable each was, they merely readjusted it in the Coinage Act of 1834 (in that case, to overvalue silver instead of overvaluing gold).

[74] Note that following Jackson, President Martin Van Buren fought against efforts to confer special privileges to banks through the Independent Treasury System.

[75] Rothbard, *A History of Money and Banking*, 122-123.

[76] Ibid., 124.

continued to fly off the printing press. By the wars end, the money supply increased 92% and sent prices up an abysmal 110%.[77]

Meanwhile, various bills and legal battles determined the value and use of greenbacks. It was a period in American financial history that tried to get a grip on the modern monetary paradox: paper money isn't real money, but it can be exchanged for real money, like gold. So governors, lawyers, and politicians inquired, are greenbacks *really* as "good as gold," and are the people—along with states, businesses, and courthouses—forced to recognize their value (or worthlessness)? To note but one case study, the Supreme Court of California "ruled in 1862 that greenbacks could not be accepted in state or county taxes, since the state constitution prohibited any acceptance of paper money for taxes. The state of Oregon was quick to follow California's lead."[78] All of this introduces a dimension that we don't have time to discuss: the havoc wreaked in legislation and law systems when fraud becomes legal.

During the war, a banker and shrewd salesman by the name of Jay Cooke made a hefty profit selling bonds. He ultimately wanted to monopolize all debt underwriting to increase his profits. But this would require a unified banking system. So Cooke made friends with Treasury Secretary Salmon Chase and Senator John Sherman, who eventually forged the National Banking System in the National Banking Act of 1863 and 1864.

The National Banking System was an effort at monopolizing the banking system through (a) nationalization (recognizing only "approved" banks); (b) establishing an interdependent, web-like organization of "branch" banks; (c) a close partnership with the federal government; and (d) sharing the same pool of reserves. In this model, the New York Bank was the primary hub.

Although this arrangement did not technically implement a "central bank" that regulated all the others and coordinated inflation, national banks

---

[77] Ibid., 130.
[78] Ibid., 129.

did require specie redemptions from smaller banks for national bank deposits, and with shared reserves,

> The whole nation is able to inflate uniformly and relatively unchecked by pyramiding on top of a few New York City banks.
>
> ...not only did the national banking system allow pyramiding of the entire banking structure on top of a few large Wall Street banks, but the very initiating of the system allowed a multiple expansion of all bank liabilities by centralizing a large part of the nation's cash reserves from the individual state banks into the hands of the larger, and especially the New York banks...Every bank could only issue notes if it deposited an equivalent of U. S. securities as collateral at the U.S. Treasury, so that national banks could only expand their notes to the extent that they purchased U.S. government bonds. This provision tied the national banking system intimately to the federal government, and more particularly, to its expansion of public debt, and the more the banks purchased that debt, the more the banking system could inflate.[79]

State banks resisted at first, but in 1865, Congress placed a 10% tax on bank notes. This effectively outlawed all notes issued by banks and gave a monopoly on notes to the national banks.

In 1867, the topic of greenbacks and payment re-emerged in the Supreme Court case of *Hepburn vs. Griswold.* It was decided that greenbacks weren't constitutional and that gold would have to serve as base payment. This was reversed in 1871 with *Knox vs. Lee* and *Parker vs. Davis*, permanently legalizing the plague of paper money in the U.S.[80]

As one would predict, a number of vicious cycles—monetary expansions and contractions, booms and busts, financial panics and recoveries—afflicted the following decades. 1873, 1884, 1893, and 1907 serve as distinguished episodes of chaotic bank runs and financial ruin. In the vast majority of cases,

---

[79] Ibid., 138.
[80] Rothbard, *A History of Money and Banking,* 152-53.

the banking system did not default and bankers did not go to court for their crimes since fake money and fraudulent banking had become "business as usual."

As we already learned during our survey of the Revolutionary period, such "business as usual" affected the day-to-day lives of the average person— creating inhumane conditions and severe disruption to society. To drive home that particular point again, I want to provide a never-before published eye-witness account of the financial panic of 1907.[81]

My friend Ferris Bauman (of Kadoka, SD) is the grandson of Frank L. Bauman, who was attending business school in Nebraska when the bank run occurred. What follows is the full text of a letter Frank sent to his parents (preserved today in Ferris's personal archives)[82]:

Grand Island, NE
October 1, 1907

Dear Parents,

I will have to write to you and tell you my bad luck. The bank that I had my money is busted and I have got just 15 cents in my pockets. I have to pay my room and board tomorrow. That will take $5.75. I asked Hargis what to do and he said that he thought I would get all my money in a few days, but it might be a month.

He said he would loan me $10.00 until I got mine. I may get it all and I might not. I had $50.00 in the bank when it busted, all the banks are closed and they won't cash a draft check or anything else.

---

[81] For a full historical account of this event, see Robert Bruner and Sean Carr, *The Panic of 1907* (Hoboken: John Wiley and Sons, 2007).

[82] I accessed the archives to transcribe this letter on April 27th, 2016, in Rapid City, SD, where Ferris was living at the time.

I will not need any more money until after Christmas if I get that or part of it. Hargis told me not to worry for I would get it all but a couple dollars anyway, but there are three banks here and the county attorney teaches law here and said that the bank I had my money in was the safest of them all. Everybody is looking for the others to break up.

It is going to be a hard time here. Several students had to quit school and go to work already for nearly all of them had their money in that bank. I was awful surprised on hearing of Jim getting hurt and hope he is doing better.

You had better not send me any money yet. I can get that of Hargis and if you sent me some I would not know what to do with it, as none of the banks are safe and I don't want to keep it in my trunk.

I bought a fountain pen and paid $1.75 for it. I would not have done it if I had of known that that bank was going to bust. But I guess it would have been better if I had spent it all. I was feeling pretty blue today noon, but Hargis made me feel better, but I have my doubts whether I will get my money or not.

Say, if you have got any money in the bank you had better get it out for the lawyer told us that he thought about one fourth of the banks will go to pieces. This is what a fellow gets for being in town. I had ought to stayed home and then I wouldn't have lost all of that money.

But I'm getting better grades along and am ahead of all the started with me in my books. Writing and spelling bothers me the most.

I guess this is all this time, I will write more later when I have more time and got my wits about me, for now I am all shook to pieces over that blamed old bank. All that I hear now is 'bank, bank, bank' for nearly everybody had money in that one and those that had money in the others can't get it so it is all the same.

From your unlucky son,

Frank

[Archive note from son:] After graduating from Business College Dad worked in a bank in Fairbury, but wasn't satisfied there; he liked the country and fresh air.

The Federal Reserve System

Rothbard sets the stage for the early 20th century:

By the turn of the century the political economy of the United States was dominated by two generally clashing financial aggregations: the previously dominant Morgan group, which had begun in investment banking and expanded into commercial banking, railroads, and mergers of manufacturing firms; and the Rockefeller forces, which began in oil refining and then moved into commercial banking, finally forming an alliance with the Kuhn, Loeb Company in investment banking and the Harriman interests in railroads. Although these two financial blocs usually clashed with each other, they were as one on the need for a central bank. Even though the eventual major role in forming and dominating the Federal Reserve System was taken by the Morgans, the Rockefeller and Kuhn, Loeb forces were equally enthusiastic in pushing, and collaborating on, what they all considered to be an essential monetary reform.[83]

Industrialism and capitalism were in full swing. The two major sources of entrepreneurial power in America sought the benefits of a newly designed centrally-controlled banking system. But to get there, it needed an army—a tool of force—to make it all happen. The U.S. federal government was the tool of choice.

Congress and the federal government were under greater influences than the age-old desire to profit. Uncanny human optimism, naïve foundationalist

---

[83] Rothbard, *A History of Money and Banking*, 188.

epistemology, chronological snobbery, confident claims of finality and triumphalism, trust in the powers of top-down central planning, megalomania empire-building, the superiority of certain kinds of language, ethnicities, methods of knowledge (e.g., empiricism), and a whole host of other features and attitudes that characterized "Modernism" filled the atmosphere of the early 1900s. The utopian dreams of everything from Zionism to Marxism to Leninism to Fascism to the incomparable architecture plans of Albert Speer in the Third Reich saturated the Western ethos of the age. And, curing millions of disease with new vaccines, harnessing the power of electricity, and having built such structures as the Brooklyn Bridge, was it really so unreasonable to think that these utopian dreams couldn't come true?

Globalism also made for a smaller, manageable world. The age for a new kind of humanity had begun. Mastery over the raw materials of nature was not just possible; it was *inevitable*.

Thus, Modernism gave birth to countless command-and-conquer, architectural, and centralization projects in a whole host of different contexts. (Two world wars are relevant here.) In the economic world, this included such things as control of property and food supply in Russia, control of global currencies by U.S. Congress,[84] and control of the banking system by the Federal Reserve. This subsection focuses on the last of these.

Picking up from Rothbard's quote above, the central banking and Rockefeller/Morgan constituency held a commission in New York in March of 1906. "The commission used the old Indianapolis questionnaire technique: acquiring legitimacy by sending out a detailed questionnaire on currency to a

---

[84] See the Philippine Currency Bill (1903), The Mexican Currency Reform Act (1905), and Roosevelt's three-person Commission on International Exchange in 1903, which was aimed at reforming the money-system of Mexico, China, and the rest of the world that used silver. The U.S. confronted the Dominican Republic in 1905 and Nicaragua in 1912. The goal of these efforts was to establish a gold-exchange standard (not to be confused with a "gold standard"), which tied silver to U.S. gold.

number of financial leaders."[85] The goal was to legitimize (and create) the demand for a new central bank. The commission issued a "Currency Report" in October that called for a "central bank of issue under the control of the government" and "centralization of financial responsibility."[86] This second requirement is particularly ironic given that the Federal Reserve that resulted from these meetings has *never* been audited.

In any case, the American Bankers Association in 1905-6 held conventions calling for "emergency assets currency which would be issued by a federal commission, resembling an embryonic central bank."[87] The bank run in 1907 (refer to Bauman above) seemed to galvanize the need for such "emergency" funds.[88] Frank Vanderlip of National City Bank of New York argued that the U.S. should follow other "great" nations in the task of using scientific principles for centralization. Paul Warburg of Loeb Company added that "small banks constitute a danger,"[89] and "the entire idea of a free and self-regulating market was obsolete, particularly in the money market. Instead the action of the market must be replaced by 'the best judgment of the best experts.'"[90] Finally, two academic societies, the American Academy of Political and Social Science (AAPSS) and the Academy of Political Science (APS), provided "expert testimony" in making a case for a new monetary system.

By 1911, a plan for the new bank had been drafted for approval of U.S. Congress. Senator Aldrich and the bankers left for a private club co-owned by J.P. Morgan on a distant island off the coast of Georgia.[91] There, on Jekyll

---

[85] Rothbard, *A History of Money and Banking,* 236.

[86] Cited in ibid., 236.

[87] Ibid., 237.

[88] In response to the panic, the National Monetary Commission was established, which ultimately lent support to the Federal Reserve Act of 1913.

[89] Paul Warburg cited in ibid., 243.

[90] Rothbard in ibid., 250.

[91] The conference included the following members: Senator Aldrich; Frank Vanderlip (President of National City Bank, New York); Piatt Andrew (assistant Secretary of the

Island, "the attendees addressed each other only by first name, and the railroad car was kept dark and closed off from reporters and other travelers on the train."[92] The plan would have passed in 1911 but Aldrich lost his place in Congress and the Democratic majority that came to power didn't favor the bank bill. During this interim, the American Bankers Association gave support for the new plan. Aldrich's (Republican) name also fell off the bill in order to appeal more easily to the Democrats in power.

By fall of 1913 enough support had been garnered to give the bill another run. A. Hepburn of Chase National Bank shamelessly spoke at the Bank's annual meeting in August, "The measure…will make all incorporated banks together joint owners of a central dominating power."[93] Finally, two days before Christmas in 1913, the Federal Reserve Act became law.

> The financial elites of this country, notably the Morgan, Rockefeller, and Kuhn, Loeb interests, were responsible for putting through the Federal Reserve System, as a governmentally created and sanctioned cartel device to enable the nation's banks to inflate the money supply in a coordinated fashion, without suffering quick retribution from depositors or noteholders demanding cash.[94]

Treasury by President Taft); Paul Warburg (partner of Kuhn&Loeb); Henry Davison (business partner of Morgan's); Benjamin Strong (Head of the Bankers Trust); Charles D. Norton (President of First National Bank, New York). Thus, "two Rockefeller men (Aldrich and Vanderlip), two Morgans (Davison and Norton), one Kuhn, Loeb person (Warburg), and one economist friendly to both camps (Andrew)." Rothbard, *A History of Money and Banking*, 253.

[92] Ibid., 253. For additional accounts of this major event in banking history, some better than others, see Roger Lowenstein, *America's Bank: The Epic Struggle to Create the Federal Reserve* (New York: Penguin Books, 2015), Peter Conti-Brown, *The Power and Independence of the Federal Reserve* (Princeton: Princeton University Press, 2016), G. Edward Griffin, *The Creature from Jekyll Island* (Westlake Village: American Media: 2010), and Mark Toma, "The Founding of the Federal Reserve System," in Randall Parker and Robert Whaples, eds, *The Handbook of Major Events in Economic History* (London: Routledge Publishing, 2013), 67-76.

[93] Ibid., 259.

[94] Ibid., 258-59.

In other words, the Federal Reserve was a central bank *par excellence.*

In a way, the Federal Reserve system hierarchicalized and centralized the branch-structure of the National Bank system, bringing a whole new level of functionality and control. Revisions to the Acts in 1918 also enabled the Federal Reserve to impose substantial regulations on member banks through the Open Market Committee (more on this below). [95]

The Fed Pyramid

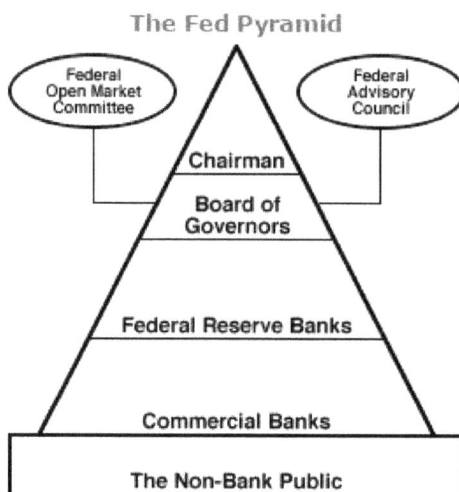

One person chairs the entire "Fed." The Board of Governors, which includes the chairperson, compromises 7 members (usually economists). The 37 Federal Reserve Banks include the 12 regional/district banks[96] (each with a president) and 25 branch banks. Finally, the commercial ("private") banks include over 20,000 institutions; all "national banks" in this pool are federal reserve banks.

The Federal Reserve itself is "owned" by the "private" member-banks. The twelve regional banks give stock to the member banks that yields a fixed

---

[95] "The Fed Pyramid" image comes from amosweb.com.

[96] Missouri is the only state to have two Federal Reserve banks.

6% dividend.[97] The Fed as a whole profits by its printing of "Federal Reserve Notes" ("dollars"), which are given to the banks (or to the U.S. Treasury) at a cost. If it sounds a bit wild, that's because it is: *the Fed ultimately prints dollars from nothing and (a) loans it out on interest and (b) buys the government's debt with it.* The banks and government then turn around and spend those "Federal Reserve Notes" on anything they wish, since it is privileged to be the official currency of the whole nation.

The major points about the Fed can be summarized as follows:

1. The Federal Reserve has a monopoly on money (its production, regulation, distribution, etc.) because it has an exclusive partnership

---

[97] "Shares of the capital stock of Federal reserve banks owned by member banks shall not be transferred or hypothecated. When a member bank increases its capital stock or surplus, it shall thereupon subscribe for an additional amount of capital stock of the Federal reserve bank of its district equal to 6 per centum of the said increase, one-half of said subscription to be paid in the manner hereinbefore provided for original subscription, and one-half subject to call of the Board of Governors of the Federal Reserve System. A bank applying for stock in a Federal reserve bank at any time after the organization thereof must subscribe for an amount of the capital stock of the Federal reserve bank equal to 6 per centum of the paid-up capital stock and surplus of said applicant bank, paying therefor its par value plus one-half of 1 per centum a month from the period of the last dividend." [12 USC 287. As amended by act of Aug. 23, 1935 (49 Stat. 713).]

with the government that has the greatest monopoly on force in the world.[98]

2. The parameters of this partnership are not clearly defined. What is clear, however, is that the Federal Reserve has no legal accountability.[99] The Fed has successfully resisted all attempts at being audited ever since its founding in 1913.

3. The Federal Reserve is, nevertheless, "privately" owned and through interest earns a profit for every note it prints and issues. Thus, "Federal" Reserve is a misleading title.

4. The Federal Reserve can control the supply and flow of money (i.e., the availability of credit) for the bulk of the U.S. economy. Other than monopolizing currency, it does this by three manipulations:

   a. increasing/decreasing *reserve requirement* (how much cash reserves that member-banks must maintain);

   b. increase/decreasing *discount rate* (the rate at which member-banks can borrow money from the Federal Reserve);

   c. conducting *open market operations* (buying and selling bonds, securities, and other "investments" with its printed notes).

These three tools enable economy-wide credit bursts and credit contractions—and economy-wide *crashes* like never before (see "the Great Depression" and "The Great Recession" below).

---

[98] It is interesting, as noted by Griffin and others, that the Seal of the United States is an eagle (a fierce predator) protected by the U.S. striped shield (representing the American government). This image appears on all Federal Reserve Notes.

[99] "The Federal Reserve is an independent agency, and that means, basically, that there is no other agency of government which can overrule actions that we take. So long as that is in place and there is no evidence that the administration or the Congress or anybody else is requesting that we do things other than what we think is the appropriate thing, then what the relationships are don't, frankly, matter." Alan Greenspan (Federal Reserve Chairman, 1987-2005) "Greenspan Examines Federal Reserve, Mortgage Crunch Interview with Jim Lehrer," *PBS News Hour* (September 18, 2007). http://www.pbs.org/newshour/bb/business-july-dec07-greenspan_09-18/

5. The paper notes issued by the Federal Reserve end up in the hands of the citizenry and function as the nation's exclusive currency.

6. The paper notes also function as the *reserves* of other banks—including those outside the U.S. Thus, the dollar is said to be the world's "reserve currency." So instead of gold reserves backing fiat currency (pre-1971), fiat currency backs fiat currency.

This is my own summary. Economists, historians, and politicians will undoubtedly have their own way of assembling these major points.

The Federal Reserve certainly does.

Here is a modern-day description of the Fed by the Minneapolis Federal Reserve bank website:

Nearly every country around the world, and certainly every developed industrial nation, has a central bank. Most serve one or more of the following functions: acting as a bank for bankers, issuing a common currency, clearing payments, regulating banks and acting as a "lender of last resort" for banks in financial trouble. The one thing they all do is serve as banker to their own governments.[100]

Notice immediately the association of economic prosperity with central banking. It is subtly suggested that, if a nation is going to be "developed," it had better have a central bank.

Some questions that come to mind in reading this summary might include, "is the Fed really necessary for a 'common currency' and, is that even desirable?," "if the Fed regulates banks, who regulates the Fed?," "why would banks end up in financial trouble to begin with?", and, "why do governments need a central bank—and why does it have to be the bank that I *must* serve

---

[100] "A History of Central Banking in the United States." The Federal Reserve Bank of Minneapolis. https://www.minneapolisfed.org/community/student-resources/central-bank-history/history-of-central-banking

and obey as well?" These are important questions that are typically not asked, and therefore not answered.

The article continues by re-writing banking history in the most unbalanced fashion. The Federal Reserve website strangely fails to mention the starvation, austerity, depravity and injustice, countless riots, violence, and the repeated, indescribable suffering experienced by Americans at the hands of bank monopolies for over a century of America's history.

Public perception of the Fed is regularly deceptive. Consider a 2016 article from the Sioux Falls *Argus Leader*, which includes interview responses by a newly appointed member of the Fed's Federal Advisory Council:

> "PayPal has billions of dollars in deposits. And really behind the curtain of PayPal, you won't find much. So the Fed asked is there systemic risk we bankers see in the shadow-banking arena," Karels said. "Then you get into Bitcoin where money is recorded but not really there, and there really is a lot of risk there."[101]

The irony is astounding: a Fed representative that supports printing money from thin air (not backed by gold) is criticizing other currency and payment methods for being backed by nothing. Additionally, "systemic risk" is the concern of one who represents a system that has led to every systemic failure imaginable—the Great Depression, the Great Recession, the phenomena of wide-spread bank runs, global economic instability, etc. (If banking with FDIC and Federal Reserve member banks wasn't risky, there would be no reason to pull money from banks in a panic, much less *insure* such banks!)

The general point is also clear: competition is not welcome when it comes to money and the exchange of money. The public is encouraged to believe that PayPal and Bitcoin are the villains who pose a threat to stability,

---

[101] Ken Karels in Jodi Schwan, "Great Western Leader has Federal Reserve's Ear," *Argus Leader* (June 12, 2016), 11A.

and not the Fed. This is pure deception. Just who is it who is hiding behind a curtain?

The Great Depression:
The Federal Reserve's Maiden Voyage

In 1921, the economy entered a recession. This was largely a response to the end of WWI and the Fed's quick increase of interest rates (from 4.75% in 1919 to 7% in 1920). Although painful, this correction rebalanced the economy into peace-time equilibrium and paved the way for some of the genuine productivity of the "roaring 20s." But since recessions are typically viewed as undesirable instead of cleansing to an economy, expectations of response came to the fore. Being a bit "gun-shy" (and slow to act), the Federal Reserve and the federal government ultimately did very little to help. As a result, conditions were restored about a year later—before plans of intervention came to fruition. There was no austerity, no multi-year depression, and no massive unemployment.

But the Fed lost its bashfulness and soon put on the modern deity of omnipotence and omniscience. With utopian dreams in view, it was time to test the full capacities of the new Federal Reserve banking system on the American economy. "Money" was therefore printed. The expansionary cycle lasted across 1921-1929; the discount rate of commercial paper went down from 7% in 1920 to 4% by 1928. $339 million in bonds were issued in 1923 alone.[102] By the end of this eight-year period, the money supply had gone up whopping 62%. (Or 7.7% annual inflation.) The "roar" of the "roaring twenties" was now loud as ever.

But why exactly did this expansionary cycle occur? There was no war in the 1920s; in fact, WWI had just ended.

There are a number of reasons—and a more "full" recovery from WWI was one of them. Another reason was that the doctrine of central banking

---

[102] Rothbard, *America's Great Depression*, 114.

welfare was fully resurrected. Paper currency was intended for the *public good*. As the Federal Reserve's own annual report of 1923 states, "The Federal Reserve Banks are the…source to which the member banks turn when the demands of the business community have outrun their own unaided resources. The Federal reserve supplies the needed additions to credit in times of business expansion and takes up the slack in times of business recession."[103] In good times and in bad, your shiny new friend, the Fed, is there to help.

President Coolidge was explicit in 1924: "It has been the policy of this administration to reduce discount rates."[104] His Treasury Secretary, Andrew Melon,[105] was even more plain: "There is an abundant supply of easy money which should take care of any contingencies that might arise."[106] Notice that these statements about central banking come from the White House, not the Federal Reserve; the marriage between monopolized force and central banking is shamelessly public. At any rate,[107] low interest and easy money were politically helpful to certain special-interest groups, like farmers. New England, which was in financial trouble in the 1920s, also benefited from these monetary policies.

A fourth reason for the expansionary cycle was the contemporary economic ideology about "stable prices." Modernism's deification of the state involved not only omnipotence and omniscience, but immutability as well. Unchanging prices were considered ideal.[108] This goal is obviously

---

[103] Cited in ibid., 120.

[104] Ibid., 121-125.

[105] Oddly enough, a foundation was named after Melon that (according to the website mellon.org), "endeavors to strengthen, promote, and, where necessary, defend the contributions of the humanities and the arts to human flourishing and to the well-being of diverse and democratic societies."

[106] Ibid., 125.

[107] No pun intended.

[108] "A perfectly even flow of economic activities is not practically attainable, but an increasing degree of economic stability is undoubtedly the goal toward which the world is now working." Arch W. Shaw, "Planning and Control of Public Works: A Report of the Committee on Recent

illogical in a market where prices are indicators of supply and demand. Supply and demand go up and down for countless reasons—production capacity, scarcity, new sources of input, varying rates of input, technological change, etc. Prices fluctuate because they *indicate economic states of affairs* (again, the "laws" of supply and demand), not simply because evil businesspeople are trying to make employees miserable or because workers have recently gotten lazy. As noted about the Revolutionary period, the controlling of prices always exhibits unintended, negative effects. Controlling the price of borrowed money (interest) follows the same economic laws.

It also should have been recognized that "Human action originates change. As far as there is human action there is no stability, but ceaseless alteration."[109] If a government or society wants utterly "stable" prices, it is going to have to be a society without human beings! "It is beyond the power of [humanity] to stop [change] and to bring about an age of stability in which all history comes to a standstill."[110]

Thus,

We may conclude that the Federal Reserve authorities, in promulgating their inflationary policies, were motivated not only by the desire to help British inflation and to subsidize farmers, but were also guided–or rather, misguided–by the fashionable economic theory of a stable price level as the goal of monetary manipulation.[111]

From 1920 to 1929, then, the American government and Presidential administration took the economy by the horns and expected beneficial results

---

Economic Changes of the President's Conference of Unemployment." (1929), xix. http://www.nber.org/chapters/c5505.pdf
[109] Von Mises, *Human Action,* 224.
[110] Ibid.
[111] Ibid., 181.

for the foreseeable future.[112] "The ultimate aim" writes the 1929 Report of the Committee, is "that employment may be more stable and adequate income more assured, [which is] the intelligent and reasonable stabilization of business, mainly by the business community itself, aided by public administrators."[113] With modern science and statistical analysis, it was now possible for central planners to "command and conquer" like never before. "We are a long way on the road to new conceptions," Hoover remarked.[114] His economic committee was even more optimistic: "research and study, the orderly classification of knowledge...well may make complete control of the economic system a possibility."[115] The utopia was coming true: "With rising wages and relatively stable prices we have become consumers of what we produce to an extent never before realized."[116]

These claims were galvanized by appeals to the actual, revealed God of the universe. The "social gospel" movement had made its mark[117] and Christians uncritically climbed onboard what appeared to be a program of moral, "social justice."[118] Catholics, Protestants, and others backed the

---

[112] "The changes affecting economic welfare were there described and, when possible, statistically measured. Now the most active and influential factors in that progress should be segregated and subjected to analysis, with the hope of contributing to a practical, workable technique designed to promote a reasonable balance of economics forces." Shaw, "Report of the Committee," xx.

[113] Ibid., xxviii.

[114] Ibid., 205.

[115] Cited in ibid., 207.

[116] Cited in ibid., 206. See it cited in the *Bismarck Tribune* (July 11, 1929).

[117] For a more detailed look at the social-gospel's founder, Walter Rauschenbusch, see Stanley Hauerwas, "Christian Ethics in American Time: Walter Rauschenbusch and the Saving of America," in *A Better Hope: Resources for a Church Confronting Capitalism, Democracy, and Postmodernity* (Grand Rapids: Brazos Press, 2000), ch 5.

[118] For more on capitalism, Christianity, and social justice, see the published works of Edmund Opitz. See also Jay Richard, *Money, Greed, and God: Why Capitalism is the Solution Not the Problem* (New York: HarperOne, 2010) and Robert Sirico, *Defending the Free Market: The Moral Case for a Free Economy* (Washington D.C.: Regnery, 2012). For a contrasting but thoughtful

government's controlling of prices, intervention, and especially its criticism of the "wicked" 12-hour work day of steel factories.[119] With God and the church on their side, how could the nation's official authorities possibly fail?

> President Herbert Hoover, on the eve of the Great Depression, stood ready to meet any storm warnings on the business horizon. Hoover, the 'Great Engineer,' stood now armed on many fronts with the mighty weapons and blueprints of a 'new economic science.' Unfettered by outworn laissez-faire creeds, he would use his 'scientific' weapons boldly, if need be, to bring the business cycle under governmental control. As we shall see, Hoover did not fail to employ promptly and vigorously his 'modern' political principles, or the new 'tools' provided him by 'modern' economists. And, as a direct consequence, America was brought to her knees as never before.[120]

It was less than a year after Hoover's bureaucracy finished bragging about prosperity that the boom turned into a bust. A small, upward shift in interest rates was enough to prick the bubble.[121] Major indicators in summer of 1929 indicated that a correction was on its way and, by October, the true state of affairs came home to roost.

On Monday October 24th, the Dow Jones Industrial Average dropped an incredible 12% by the day's end. On Tuesday it dropped another 11%. People began pulling cash from banks in a panic. Due to the fractional reserve system, only a fraction of people were able to retrieve their money, leaving the rest with nothing. Over 2,500 banks shut down from 1931-32; by 1933, the bank run had become so dire that Roosevelt, in his second day of office

---

perspective, see Hauerwas, *A Better Hope,* and Daniel Bell, *The Economy of Desire: Christianity and Capitalism in a Postmodern World* (Grand Rapids: Baker Academic, 2012).

[119] Rothbard, *America's Great Depression,* 202.

[120] Ibid., 207.

[121] "Between January and July 1928 the Fed raised the discount rate from 3.5% to 5%." Timothy Cogley, "Monetary Policy and the Great Crash of 1929: A Bursting Bubble or Collapsing Fundamentals?" *FRBSF Economic Letter.* (San Francisco: Federal Reserve Bank of San Francisco, 1999).

as President, decreed a shutdown of all banks in the country from March 6-13 ("Proclamation 2039").

In response to the downturn, the government (coupled with the Federal Reserve) conducted the most comprehensive series of interventions ever performed on the economy. A whole host of new government agencies, programs, departments were born. These included the CCC (Civilian Conservation Corps), FERA (Family Electric Rate Assistance), CWA (Civil Works Administration), AAA (Agricultural Adjustment Act), TVA (Tennessee Valley Authority), PWA (Public Works Administration), SEC (Security and Exchange Commission), FFB (Federal Farm Board), NCC (National Credit Corporation), RFC (Reconstruction Finance Corporation), and many more. In 1930 alone, public works spending amounted to over $900 million, including such massive projects as the Hoover Dam. The Federal Reserve also dropped rates from 4.5% to 2% in hopes of "stimulating" the economy.

Federal administration was so desperate that it reduced immigration by 90% and introduced bills to forbid short-selling on the stock market.[122] From 1931-1933, it even considered centrally-controlling all businesses with over 50 employees through the Federal Trade Commission, an arrangement resonant with contemporary communist Russia. This totalitarian "Swope" plan[123] was rejected in favor of a string of legislative interventions such as the "Employment Stabilization Act" (1931), "Revenue Act" (1932), Glass Steagall Act (1932),[124] the "Agricultural Adjustment Act" (1933), National Industrial Recovery Act (1933), the Smoot-Hawley Tarriffs (1930), and many others. "Total public relief in 120 of the nation's leading urban areas

---

[122] See Rothbard, *America's Great Depression*, 240-248.

[123] Gerard Swope, whom the plan was named after, was the President of General Electric at the time.

[124] The Glass Steagall Act "(a) greatly broadened the assets eligible for rediscounts with the Fed, and (b) permitted the Federal Reserve to use government bonds as collateral for its notes, in addition to commercial paper. The way was now cleared for a huge program of inflating reserves and engineering cheap money once again." Rothbard, *America's Great Depression*, 302.

amounted to $33 million in 1929, $173 million in 1931, and $308 million in 1932."[125] Hoover personally took it upon himself to criminalize short-sellers since that encouraged lower stock prices. These investigations focused on "sinister" and "systematic bear raids," "vicious pools…pounding down" prices, "deliberately making a profit from the losses of other people."[126] All of these laws, decrees,[127] and bureaucratic programs came to regulate prices and processes on everything from grain to electricity to wages to mortgages.

To top it all off, Hoover *insured and protected* fraudulent banking instead of outlawing it. From the Glass-Steagall Act forward, bank runs would be *backed* by federal insurance. So when the banks lost the money of its account holders, the government would step in to pay for a portion of the losses (e.g., "FDIC insured up to $250,000"). To think that this action embodied any form of justice is difficult to fathom.[128] In any case, the inherent riskiness of fractional-reserve, central banking was no longer a secret. It was now publicly and unashamedly acknowledged.

In a word, then, the government and Federal Reserve threw everything and the kitchen sink at the economy. The goal was to provide relief to the unemployed, stability in the financial system, and, of course, increase revenues so the government could continue to "helpfully" intervene.

None of these things happened. Instead, a severe recession became a severe depression. What could have been a one or two-year recovery (such as in 1921) evolved into an eight-year nightmare, earning the notorious title

---

[125] Ibid., 301.

[126] Citied in ibid., 316.

[127] Hoover's executive order count (968) remains the fifth highest in U.S. Presidential history. (Theodore Roosevelt, Calvin Coolidge, and Woodrow Wilson, ranked fourth, third, and second highest, respectively). This is considerable given that W. Wilson and T. Roosevelt served two terms as opposed to one. Hoover's successor, Franklin D. Roosevelt, retains first place (by a huge margin) at 3,522 executive orders. Roosevelt more or less continued Hoover's modernist, statist projects.

[128] It would be akin to a mother sending her son to go gambling and saying, "If you lose anything, don't worry, I'll pay for most of the losses."

"The Great Depression." As early as 1933, after the bulk of new policies and programs had been implemented, production was half of what it was in 1929. Unemployment soared to 25% of the labor force. The Revenue Act *decreased* tax revenues instead of increasing them. Price controls did nothing but create shortages and waste. To give but one example from agriculture, "By the end of the Hoover administration, combined cotton and wheat losses by the FFB totaled over $300 million."[129] These losses of food and basic supplies happened as women, children, and families nearly starved. The irony was appalling.[130]

Hoover, however, wasn't finished. His greatest plan was yet to unfold. A new enemy entered his mind, which was *money itself*. Presidential Executive Order 6102 came into effect April 5, 1933, which confiscated the gold of all American citizens and non-citizens. A person who owned gold was, after all, considered an immoral "hoarder" who threatened the economic stability of the nation. True citizens were those loyal to the paper notes printed by the Federal Reserve—notes which, of course, were given in exchange for the confiscated gold.[131]

The full text of the order includes the following threat:

> Section 9. Whoever willfully violates any provision of this Executive Order or these regulation or of any rule, regulation or license issued there under may be fined not more than $10,000, or, if a natural person may be imprisoned for not more than ten years or both; and any officer, director, or agent of any corporation who knowingly participates in any such violation may be punished by a like fine, imprisonment, or both.

---

[129] Ibid., 235.

[130] It is particularly ironic because it was future President Hoover who provided the starving Russians with aid via the American Relief Administration around 1921—a starvation that was largely (though not entirely; a drought had taken place) caused by precisely the same kind of price-controls and bureaucracy that antagonized the economic recovery in America during the 1930s. See Richard Pipes, *Communism: A History* (New York: Random House, 2003), ch 2.

[131] The image of the Executive Order is an actual photograph that can be found on Wikipedia.com

> # UNDER EXECUTIVE ORDER OF THE PRESIDENT
> Issued April 5, 1933
>
> ## all persons are required to deliver
> # ON OR BEFORE MAY 1, 1933
> ### all GOLD COIN, GOLD BULLION, AND GOLD CERTIFICATES now owned by them to a Federal Reserve Bank, branch or agency, or to any member bank of the Federal Reserve System.
>
> Executive Order

In addition to "hoarders" of gold, the government and federal administration (unsurprisingly) blamed speculators and wealthy corporations as the cause of the world's woe.

But the cause of the Great Depression wasn't any of these groups—as if "gold hoarders" and a small group of pernicious traders on Wall-Street could actually create the largest economic depression in history. If anything, it was greed of the "masters of money" from years earlier, coupled with the most powerful government in the world enforcing the most anti-productive economic policies imaginable.

The Boom-Bust Cycle Continues

"The U.S. government has a technology called a printing press (or today, its electronic equivalent) that allows it to produce as many U.S. dollars as it wishes at no cost."
—*Ben Bernanke* (2002)

The boom-bust cycle of easy money and expansion followed by a contractionary bust and recession continued throughout the 20th century. Fortunately, none were as severe as the Great Depression. During this mid-century period, the Federal Reserve Note became principally worthless when the gold standard was abandoned in 1971 under Nixon. The clock is still ticking as to when the dollar will become *practically* worthless as well.[132]

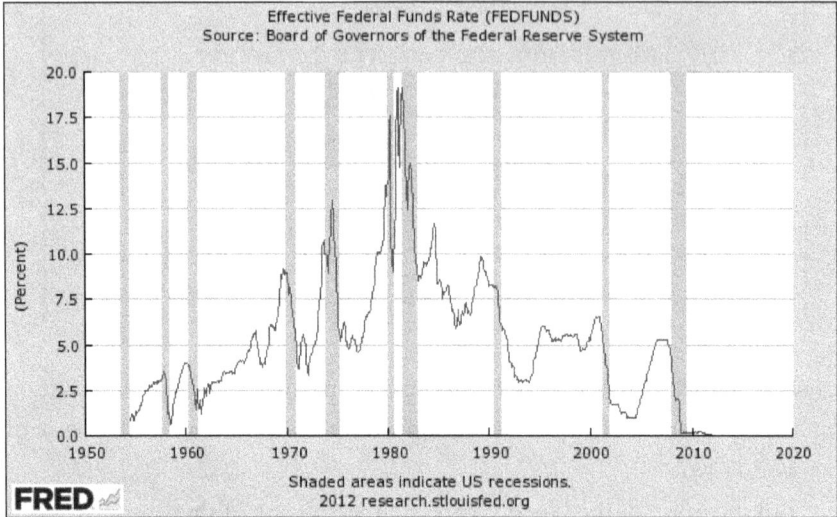

One author summarizes the deadly effects of 20th century central banking:

Congressman Buffet has…pointed out that the holders of government bonds lost more of their savings during 1950 by the process of government engineered inflation than the entire country lost in all the bank failures between 1921 and 1933. Holders of United States Savings Bonds in 1950 lost $3,600,000,000. All losses by bank depositors from 1921 through 1933 totaled $1,900,000,000. All of this has been justified by the federal government in terms of a dubious economics, the central thesis of which is that the way to prosperity is not by production but by political spending of what has been produced by those who work.[133]

---

[132] In the table from the Federal Reserve Economic Data (FRED), the vertical columns indicate recessions.

[133] Edmund Opitz, *The Libertarian Theology of Freedom* (Tampa: Hallberg Publishing, 1999), 135.

Location	Start Date	Equivalent Daily Inflation Rate	Currency
Hungary[1]	Aug. 1945	207%	Pengő
Zimbabwe[2]	Mar. 2007	98.0%	Dollar
Yugoslavia[3]	Apr. 1992	64.6%	Dinar
Republika Srpska†[4]	Apr. 1992	64.3%	Dinar
Germany[5]	Aug. 1922	20.9%	Papiermark
Greece[6]	May. 1941	17.9%	Drachma
China§[7]	Oct. 1947	14.1%	Yuan
Free City of Danzig[8]	Aug. 1922	11.4%	German Papiermark
Armenia[9]	Oct. 1993	5.77%	Dram & Russian Ruble
Turkmenistan††[10]	Jan. 1992	5.71%	Manat
Taiwan[11]	Aug. 1945	5.50%	Yen
Peru[12]	Jul. 1990	5.49%	Inti
Bosnia and Herzegovina[13]	Apr. 1992	4.92%	Dinar
France[14]	May 1795	4.77%	Mandat
China[15]	Jul. 1943	4.75%	Yuan
Ukraine[16]	Jan. 1992	4.60%	Russian Ruble
Poland[17]	Jan. 1923	4.50%	Marka
Nicaragua[18]	Jun. 1986	4.37%	Córdoba
Congo (Zaire)[19]	Nov. 1993	4.26%	Zaïre
Russia††[20]	Jan. 1992	4.22%	Ruble
Bulgaria[21]	Feb. 1997	4.19%	Lev
Moldova[22]	Jan. 1992	4.16%	Russian Ruble
Russia / USSR[23]	Jan. 1922	3.86%	Ruble
Georgia[24]	Sep. 1993	3.86%	Coupon
Tajikistan††[25]	Jan. 1992	3.74%	Russian Ruble

In addition to this peril "at home," nations overseas witnessed the currency collapse in over fifty cases of hyperinflation. The list above is a sample of these cases. [134]

---

[134] Steve Hanke and Nicholas Krus, "World Hyperinflations" in Randall Parker and Robert Whaples, eds, *The Handbook of Major Events in Economic History* (London: Routledge Publishing, 2013).

To take one example, if a person was living in Yugoslavia in the early 1990s and a gallon of milk on Monday cost 1 dinar, that same container of milk would cost 1.64 dinar on Tuesday, 2.69 dinar on Wednesday, and so on. As I type this essay, Venezuela is currently experiencing a 500% annual inflation rate (and 15% unemployment).

Many readers may wonder: *how long can the central banking system last in America, given the permanent system of growing debt and inevitability of hyperinflation?*

This is a common and fair question. Regarding the first part, the government and Fed sees the situation like this: as long as (a) inflation keeps up with growing debt and (b) someone buys its debt (bonds), growing debts will never have to be paid. (This is, in fact, the major reason why the term "inflation" is typically viewed *positively* by modern economists, instead of negatively). The idea of paying back debt to balance the books is considered an "ancient" and "outdated" idea. Today, in our "developed" and "scientific" society, debts can just be wiped out through currency debasement.

Regarding the second point, the U.S. dollar hasn't collapsed despite trillions of printed notes because, as we learned earlier, the federal reserve note is the reserve currency of the *world*. This is not the case for the other 50+ cases of hyperinflation in the 20th and 21st century. Because of this caveat, it is believed that the dollar *can't* hyperinflate; the amount of cash in circulation is just too massive to ever see an entire collapse of value.

Both of these positions represent a severe miscalculation of both the U.S. debt burden and the likelihood of world reserve currencies collapsing. First of all, world-reserve currencies do, in fact, collapse. They are said to have an average lifespan of a century (see image below).[135] This collapse may occur because of hyperinflation or because of other factors. There is no reason why, in principle, a reserve currency is somehow immune to the basic rules of economics that apply to other currencies. A debased currency is a debased

---

[135] I could not locate the source of the Global reserve currencies image; there appears to be many variants online. The specifics about each currency and period are addressed in a number of specialized articles but I have not been able to locate a systematic study.

currency whether it is used in one bank or a million. Just because the pool of the U.S. dollar is bigger than any other currency in history does not mean that it will never turn red as more and more drops of red ink are dumped into it. It might take longer than other cases, but the pool will probably turn red.

Global reserve currencies since 1450

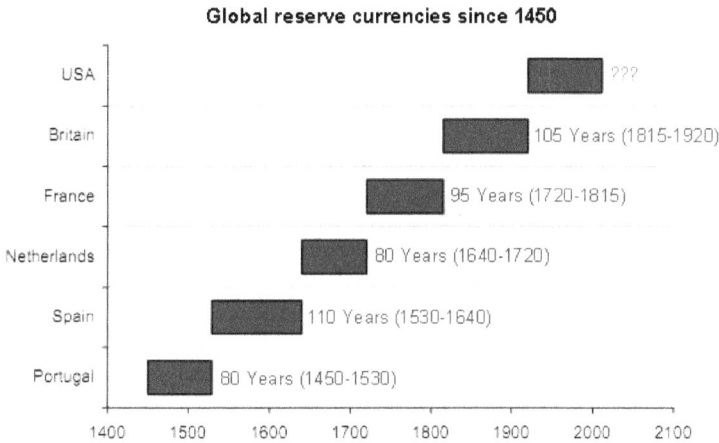

Second, the U.S. government is having trouble finding people to buy its bonds. China used to be hot on the market but now the Federal Reserve itself is the biggest purchaser of government bonds. This means that it must issue reserve notes to sustain the debt-buying machine, causing more inflation (see quote below). Furthermore, with over $20 trillion in debt, the interest payments have become almost unpayable. The Fed has kept rates below 1% to keep the U.S. government from going bankrupt on its own debt. The system is indeed, gridlocked. As one financial commentator accurately put it:

Hyperinflation happens when government debt is over 80% of GNP and the deficit is over 40% of government spending. The US is at or near these numbers, so the danger of hyperinflation is real. What happens is that the more the central bank prints money and buys bonds the less other people want to hold bonds. But the less other people hold bonds, the more the central bank has to buy them so the government has enough money to spend. You get a positive feedback loop or death spiral.[136]

The Fed's Second Great Feat: The Great Recession

"Housing markets are cooling a bit. Our expectation is that the decline in activity or the slowing in activity will be moderate, that house prices will probably continue to rise."
—*Ben Bernanke* (February 2006)

The point of no return was faced in "the Great Recession" of 2008. Both the federal government and the Federal Reserve were directly responsible.

The Great Recession was precipitated by a bubble in the housing market during 2001-2007 which burst in 2007-2008, sending a shockwave of defaults and bankruptcies across the financial sector. The defaults were largely due to "subprime mortgages," meaning "not very good mortgages; people should probably have never bought these homes (...good heavens who let people buy these insanely priced homes!?)."

How was the government responsible? Through "Fannie Mae," "Freddie Mac," and a string of legislations that go all the way back to the Great Depression. Fannie Mae is an abbreviation of "Federal National Mortgage Association" (FNMA), which was created during the Great Depression in 1938 to "help" with housing problems. "Freddie Mac" is an abbreviation of the Federal Home Loan Mortgage Corporation (FHLMC), which was created in 1970 to also expand home-debt. In a word, Freddie buys mortgages on the secondary market, puts them in a giant pool, and then sells parts of this pool as "mortgage-backed" securities to investors on the open market. It's similar, though not identical, to how farmers sell their grain, which mixes with everyone else's grain, and then gets sold in various bins and amounts to outside buyers. In the words of the current FHFA website:

---

[136] Vincent Cate, "Frequently Asked Questions on Hyperinflation." *Financial Sense* (October, 2012).

Fannie Mae and Freddie Mac were created by Congress. They perform an important role in the nation's housing finance system – to provide liquidity, stability and affordability to the mortgage market. They provide liquidity (ready access to funds on reasonable terms) to the thousands of banks, savings and loans, and mortgage companies that make loans to finance housing.[137]

Regarding legislation, various laws dealing with housing and mortgages paved the way for the 2008 crisis. The Community Reinvestment Act of 1977 began to take on drastic revisions in 1989, 1995, and 2005, which "put pressure on banks not merely to change their institutional 'outreach' to the 'underserved' population but to actually make more loans to them, even if this required 'innovative or flexible' lending practices."[138] In 1992, FHEFSSA (The Federal Housing Enterprises Financial Safety and Soundness Act) also required Fannie and Freddie to provide essentially subprime mortgages.[139] In 1999, certain provisions of the Glass-Steagall Act were repealed, which removed the separation between investment banks and depository banks in America. In 2003, the Dream Downpayment Act was passed, making homeownership for those in poverty and minorities even easier than before.

These federal efforts were meant to induce artificial growth in the housing market and the economy at large. It was "artificial" because they were aimed not at producing actual wealth, but producing a wealth *effect*—the *feeling* of being prosperous (and a phenomenon that is both politically useful and sometimes ideologically validating). These efforts were also combined with an expansionary cycle initiated by the Federal Reserve. Interest rates were drastically pulled from 6.5% in 2001 down to 1% in 2003.

All of this "easy money" was taken advantage of by those who "benefited" from the new laws regarding home-buying:

---

[137] "About Fannie Mae and Freddie Mac." FHFA. www.fhfa.gov
[138] Thomas Sowell, *The Housing Boom and Bust,* revised ed. (New York: Basic Books, 2010), 123.
[139] Ibid., 30.

> Ninety percent of subprime mortgage loans made by 2006 were adjustable rate mortgages. That same year, the average subprime borrower made only 5% down payment on a home...[Fannie and Freddie did this because they] had quotas set for them by the Department of Housing and Urban Development to buy mortgages that lenders had made with borrowers in what was called 'the underserved population'.[140]

Indeed, the notorious "subprime mortgages" were not only approved by the government, but systematically *mandated*.

Some of these mortgages didn't even require a down-payment. These "interest-only" mortgages increased as much as 66% in the San Francisco Bay area. Why bother with a 30-year, 50-year, or 80-year mortgage? Just go for eternity! In a remarkable twist of morals, all of these efforts (later referred to as "predatory lending" practices) were justified under the sentiment of "everyone should own a home." Part of the American dream, after all, is owning a big house with a nice white picket fence. In this way and others, nationalism naturally fed into the (pro-bank) debt-building machine.

As you might imagine, the boom during this period was astounding. The Down Jones Industrial Average went from 7,500 in 2002 to a whopping 14,000 in 2007. Housing prices doubled or even tripled in certain parts of the country. It seemed everyone was wealthy.

The wealth *effect* was successful because the feeling was there. But in reality, everyone was much *poorer* than they had ever been. Long-term debts enslaved a whole new generation—as did overvalued stocks that flew off the shelves. The economy became inverted from a structure characterized by current production to a structure characterized by current *debt* with the hopes of *future* production. The boom fell soon fell into a bust.

The Fed raised rates to 5.25% in 2006, pricking the bubble and sending the economy into a tailspin. All those home-flippers who bought properties

---

[140] Ibid., 18.

just to sell them later eventually found themselves in a trap: nobody wanted (or could afford) to buy their expensive houses. The default spree began, and by 2009 unemployment rose to 10% and the Dow Jones dropped to 7,500, cutting itself in half. Many American corporations found themselves bankrupt. Banks also found themselves in trouble because no more money was coming in. In fact, people were trying to pull it out.

Because the banking system was integrated, and because there was such a massive amount of mortgages that couldn't get paid for by either debtors or dwindling bank reserves, a chain reaction began to take place in the banking world. One bank was on the edge of its reserve limit, so it asked a commercial bank for a loan, but that bank didn't have enough money to bail out the first bank. This process of requests continued throughout all the branch banks. Because the entire financial system is based on the ability to borrow and that ability was no longer working, the whole financial system was headed towards a freeze.[141]

Practically, this meant that millions of credit-card users would be stiffed at the counter. A person would be checking out at the grocery store and their swipe would be rejected. There was simply no "credit" on the back end to make the transaction work. The same problem would plague home-buyers seeking a mortgage, investors and entrepreneurs seeking a loan, and so on. Again, because the "financial system" = the "debt system," the lack of credit (ability to borrow) means wide-scale financial collapse. Obviously, if a financial system and economy were based on savings-oriented payments and 100% reserve banking, there would be and could be no such crisis.

Although businesses suffered, the stock market tanked, and the mob took to the streets ("Occupy Wall Street"), the credit-system didn't ultimately collapse in the Great Recession. The Federal Reserve shined in the 2008 crisis

---

[141] On March 28, 2007, Fed Chairman Ben Bernanke carelessly remarked, "At this juncture, however, the impact on the broader economy and financial markets of the problems in the subprime market seems likely to be contained. In particular, mortgages to prime borrowers and fixed-rate mortgages to all classes of borrowers continue to perform well, with low rates of delinquency."

in its role as the "lender of last resort." Instead of merely providing more cash to commercial banks and lowering interest rates (which it did), the Fed purchased most of the toxic assets (e.g., defaulted subprime mortgages). This occurred in the $700 billion Emergency Economic Stabilization Act (2008), which was given structure in the Troubled Asset Relief Program (TARP). This bailout did nothing to prevent economic waste or the moral hazards that led to such a crisis, nor did it address any other fundamental problem. But it did prop up the banking system enough to keep the debt flowing. In a word, the American system of fake money and fraudulent banking had fallen into cardiac arrest, and the Fed gave it a jolt back into life.

Additionally, the federal government just couldn't help but intervene in a Hoover-like fashion to "restore" the economy. These interventions (predictably) worsened the problems just as they did for the Great Depression. A year after George Bush signed the bailout bill, President Obama signed the American Recovery and Reinvestment Act (2009), a $787 billion stimulus package aimed at "creating jobs." To offset the decline in home purchases and increase in foreclosures, Congress also "authorized an *increase* in the size of the loans that the Federal Housing Administration could insure—nearly doubling the mortgage loan limit from $362,500 to $719,000."[142] Not even a year had passed and Congress had already initiated the next housing bubble![143]

---

[142] Sowell, *The Housing Boom and Bust*, 71. Italic original.

[143] The foreclosure rate graphic comes from Bill McBride, "Fannie Mae Serious Delinquency rate declines, Freddie Mac rate increases." (January 31, 2012). *Calculated Risk*. http://www.calculatedriskblog.com/2012_01_01_archive.html

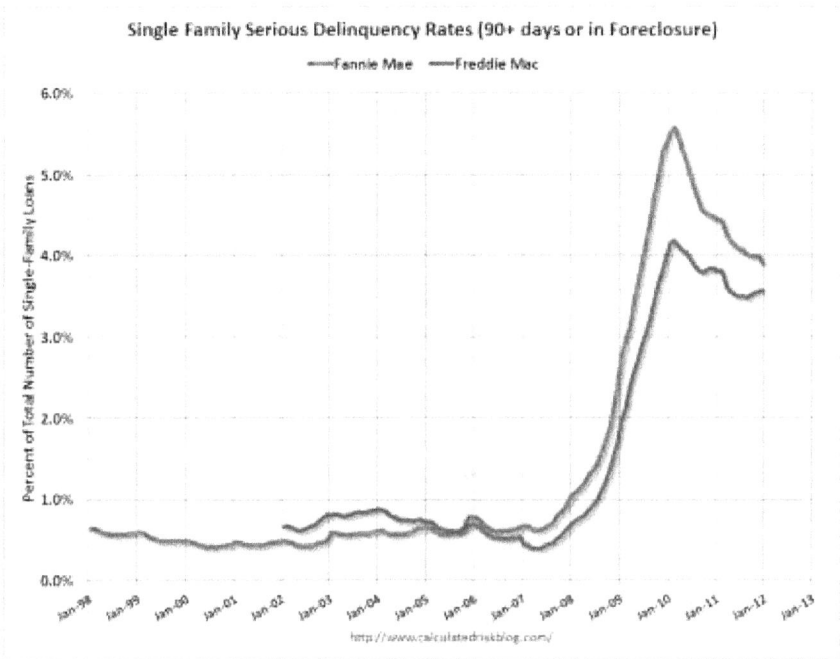

Single Family Serious Delinquency Rates (90+ days or in Foreclosure)

GDP dropped from $14.7 trillion in 2008 to $14.4 trillion in 2009 (the sharpest decline in nearly a half-century). In 2009, unemployment reached 9.7% and then 10.2% by the fall. Despite the stimulus efforts, the velocity of money dropped to a 50-year low.

As with any failed government intervention, the state's solution is *more* government intervention. So the Dodd-Frank Act ("Restoring American Financial Stability Act of 2010") came into effect July, 2010. This massive piece of legislation (2,300 pages) was dedicated to overhauling financial policies in the banking and mortgage industries. Its purpose was to "fix," in effect, the recession and prevent it from happening again. In particular, the Act was supposed to prevent "predatory" lending practices by banks (a term the Fed has never once defined), implement new underwriting standards and, among other things, authorize "regulation of the rating agencies—with a focus on their underlying conflicts of interests with issuers of asset-backed securities, as well as on the reduction of regulatory reliance on their ratings—in an attempt to increase the transparency of the credit risk of the underlying pool of loans."[144]

In reality, the law is just another piece of legislation that *amplifies* precisely those areas of action and policy that should be eliminated. Michael Nwogugu in the *European Journal of Law Reform*, for example, notes how the entire Act gives an incredible amount of power to the U.S. Secretary and Exchange Commission and the Federal Reserve.[145] Neither of these institutions, of course, should even exist. How much less should they be given additional measures of authority beyond the incalculable, detrimental influence they already have.

Post Great Recession

In the end, there was and has been no economic "recovery." The crisis of 2007-2008 is not limited to those two years, but continues to drag on in the measurable form of continually missed production projections, high inflation, exponentially growing debt,[146] and a fractional-reserve, centrally-controlled banking system that is headed for another heart-attack.

This general fact is now commonly acknowledged in an economic community that used to be so favorable towards government intervention and the Fed's monetary policies. One can find these concessions in mainstream graduate economic textbooks. Colander's 9th edition *Economics*,

---

[144] Matthew Richardson, "Regulating Wall Street: The Dodd-Frank Act." *Economic Perspectives* 36:3 (2012):86.

[145] Michael Nwogugu, "Unconstitutionality of the Dodd-Frank Act" *European Journal of Law Reform* 17:1 (2015).

[146] In 2016, the rate of increase of the national debt has reached 1 trillion per 6 months. Within two years, it is likely this rate will double or triple; a trillion-dollar monthly increase is approaching quickly. Eventually, of course, the rate will exceed the rate of financing and even printing, whereupon hyper-inflation will likely set in (defaulting is, from a Congressional view, less desirable).

for instance, frankly explains how things did not pick up after 2008 as expected. He dedicates a chapter to the Great Recession and the theory of "structural stagnation hypothesis."[147]

As far as the conditions that gave birth to the Great Recession, these have not changed. Virtually all have returned. "Subprime 2.0,"[148] complete with the same type of risky and/or interest-only loans, artificially low-interest rates set by the Fed, thousands and thousands of pages of federal financial law that no citizen has even read, along with various other factors have set up the economy for yet another bust.

Meanwhile, corruption behind the Great Recession continues to surface. It was discovered that the Office of Federal Housing Enterprise Oversight (OFHEO) caught Fannie Mae Freddie Mac with $11 billion worth of accounting errors in 2007.[149] It was also learned that at the peak of the housing boom in California, only 30 examiners "watched over nearly 5,000 consumer finance companies."[150] This is but a sample of the innumerable corruptions that characterized the time, and continue to be uncovered.[151]

The Fed was largely responsible for Great Recession just as it had been for the Great Depression. Remarkably, central bankers from this period have made it a new hobby to pat themselves on the back for saving the world. The

---

[147] David Colander, *Economics*, 9th ed. (New York: McGraw Hill, 2013), 616. While not entirely free-market oriented and rather uncritical of central banking, Colander also points out "government failures" and rarely hesitates to criticize economic policies that hurt precisely the people that they are supposed to help. The unquestionable academic consensus of "modern" and "scientific" economics is, perhaps, beginning to shift away from Hoover and Keynes and more towards Hayek and Von Mises, albeit gradually and in pockets.

[148] "Subprime 2.0" yields over 1,000 results in Google, all (from what I observe) refer to the continuation of the housing and mortgage crises in the Great Recession.

[149] Sowell, *The Housing Boom and Bust*, 49, 81.

[150] Ibid., 83.

[151] As another case in point, in 2016 Wells Fargo was fined $1.2 billion due to "reckless lending" practices under the Federal Housing Administration from the years 2001-2010. See Liz Moyer, "Wells Fargo to pay 1.2 billion in Mortgage Settlement." *New York Times* (February 3, 2016).

bravery, chivalry, and superb moral superiority of the central bank is publicized like never before in the Great-Recession autobiographies of Fed chairmen (2006-2014) Ben Bernanke and New York Federal Reserve President (2003-2009) and Secretary of the Treasury (2009-2013) Timothy Geithner.[152] Meanwhile, the "view from the ground" has also reached epic interest with the film *The Big Short* (2015), starring Brad Pitt, Ryan Gosling, Christian Bale, and Steve Carell.

As it stands today, the Federal Reserve is out of tricks. Manipulating discount rates, reserve requirements, and conducting almost every kind of open market operation imaginable have all been used to their fullest extent ever since 2008, exploding the Fed's balance with a staggering $4.5 trillion worth of assets.[153] As mentioned above, the economic fundamentals are not in place. In fact, they're about as far off base as the U.S. economy has ever been.

FRED — Federal Debt: Total Public Debt as Percent of Gross Domestic Product

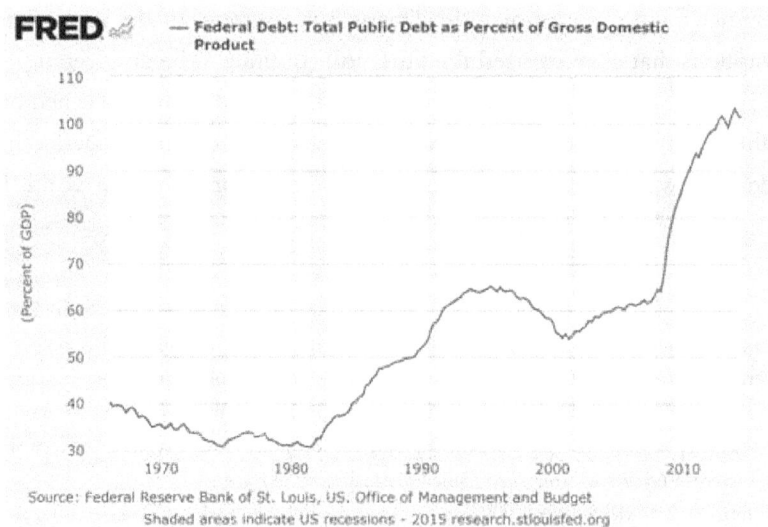

Source: Federal Reserve Bank of St. Louis, US. Office of Management and Budget
Shaded areas indicate US recessions - 2015 research.stlouisfed.org

---

[152] Ben Bernanke, *The Courage to Act: A Memoir of a Crisis and its Aftermath* (New York: Norton & Norton, 2015); Timothy Geithner, *Stress Test: Reflections on Financial Crises* (New York: Broadway Books, 2014).

[153] The image of the Federal Reserve balance sheet comes from nakedcapitalism.com, and the image of the debt to GDP chart comes from the Federal Reserve Bank of St. Louis (FRED).

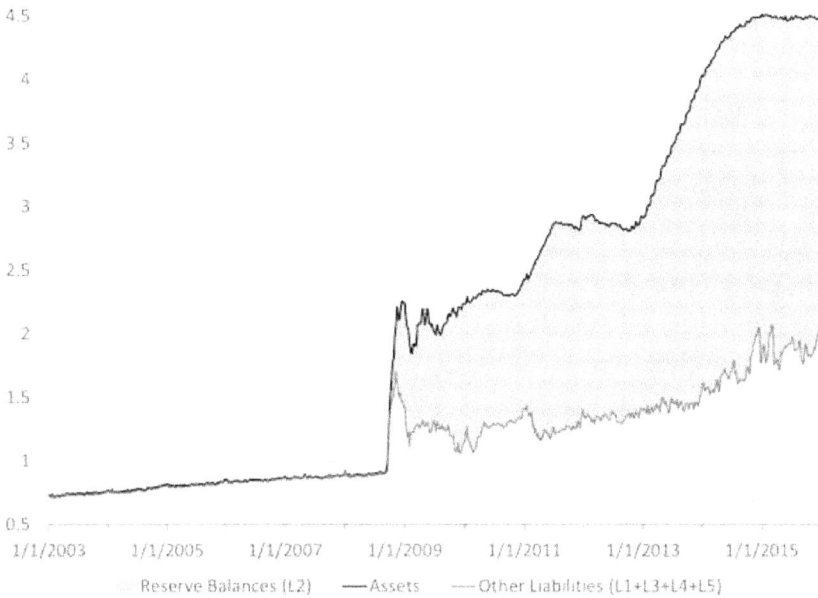

The only trick left is one of shear desperation: *negative* interest rates. If savings is bad and spending is good, then ultimately, banks (and even private account holders) will be penalized for saving. Indeed, there is good reason to believe that cash will be criminalized within the next decade.

One article from *The Toronto Star* summarizes the concept of negative interest and accurately rejects its legitimacy:

> In effect, this charges banks a penalty for keeping cash on hand instead of lending it out. The move is also meant to discourage consumers from saving, while encouraging them to spend....About a year and half ago, the European Central Bank cut its rate to below zero, and some individual countries have done the same thing. Since then, there hasn't been much growth. Consumers try to avoid fees. They hoard cash, which has the risk of theft and fire. They pay cash, and so avoid paying taxes. Anecdotally in Switzerland, where the rate is -0.75 per cent, the wealthy have been taking high-denomination Euro notes out of their accounts and putting them in

bank safety deposit boxes. It also nudges people toward more risky investments.

...A decade of ever-lower interest rates hasn't revived global growth. Canada is in better shape than most countries, and stimulus spending coming in the spring federal budget is a much better way to go than ever lower interest rates. Lower rates, including those below zero, are not something we need or want.[154]

Race to zero interest rates

Four European central banks have rates below zero. Others are close.

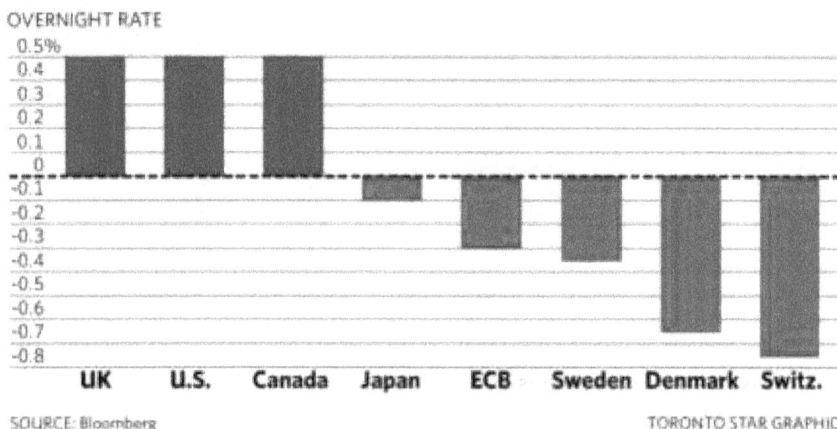

OVERNIGHT RATE

UK	U.S.	Canada	Japan	ECB	Sweden	Denmark	Switz.

SOURCE: Bloomberg

TORONTO STAR GRAPHIC

These negative interest rates could even take the form of negative mortgage rates. Simply taking on an 80-year mortgage, then, would be *profitable*. In 2016, a *Wall Street Journal* article featured a family that witnessed precisely that, as the title shows: "Negative Rates Around the World: How One Danish Couple Gets Paid Interest on Their Mortgage." These stories will likely become more and more common—until hyperinflation eradicates the principle, the interest, and any savings one might have.

---

[154] Adam Mayers, "Why they're talking about negative interest rates." *The Toronto Star* (February 3, 2016).

Conclusion

This essay has sketched but a few lines of thought regarding the history of money and banking in the U.S. Many things remain undiscussed, such as the role that gold and the gold-standard has played in the early 20th century, experiments in more private central banking, and recent efforts at auditing and/or shutting down the Fed.[155] The focus has also been on central banking and not on other economic factors that come into play—including such recent, important phenomena as globalism and world markets.

We have also not covered some of the more encouraging developments conducted in the private sector: decentralized digital currencies. Bitcoin, GoldMoney (formerly "BitGold"), currencies on the Ethereum platform, points and token systems within e-commerce, and other innovations are becoming more and more popular—especially in third world countries that need them the most, for they are the ones who have suffered the most from fake money and fraudulent banking.

Nevertheless, it should be evident just how important sound currency is to economic growth. Prosperity and peace are impossible without it. Fiat currency and government-insured fractional-reserve banking are destroyers of wealth, the fear of all who challenge poverty, and instigators of mass violence. There is no foreign army that can steal 50% of a nation's wealth without firing a single shot. There is no weapon, war-mongering dictatorship, or religious fanaticism that can annihilate the savings of an entire generation by thousands of legal transactions. There is no political party that can profit from wars regardless of the victor. These are unparalleled powers reserved for central banks alone.

Only when we realize this state of affairs will it be clear that fake money and fraudulent banking really are the greatest threats to American liberty.

---

[155] See Ron Paul, *End the Fed* (New York: Grand Central Publishing, 2009) and Thomas Woods, *Meltdown* (Washington D.C.: Regnery, 2009).

6

Christian Reflections on Privacy Rights and the Surveillance State

Jamin Hübner

Introduction

There is great room today for exploring the topic of "privacy rights." This applies not only to the United States, but to all countries. The topic is acute, however, in the U.S., due to the activities regularly conducted by the federal government—namely, mass surveillance and the automatic collection of personal communications data. The extent of this internal data-collection was largely publicized and popularized when the CIA contract worker and information systems analyst, Edward Snowden, leaked thousands of private documents that revealed the what and how of this surveillance operation. Since that time in June 2013, there has been increasing attention on the matter, but little critical reflection that transcends the hubbub of contemporary politics, agendas of the media and die-hard nationalists, and reductionisms of American legal scholars.

Much less are there Christian thinkers offering direction from a larger perspective that views the world as God's purposeful project and human beings as God's creatures. It is this kind of contribution that I hope to offer in this essay.

Framing Creation

As an explicitly Christian perspective on the topic of privacy rights, I want to move from broader theological assumptions to the particularities of privacy interactions.

It is a given in the Christian view of things that God made the world to exist within boundaries. The electromagnetic attraction of subatomic particles, the mass and energy ratios exhibited in the universe's aggregate material, the "fine-tuned" abilities of matter to form stars and so much more exist within clearly set (even quantifiable) margins.[1] As one surveys the solar system, the same phenomenon is witnessed. Too close to the black hole in our galaxy, and radiation destroys all life. Too close to the sun and the earth burns; too far away, and it freezes.[2] Life exists within boundaries.

The same goes for the earth. Too cold or too hot of temperatures, and creatures, plants, and cells lose life. Too much oxygen and not enough carbon dioxide—or vice versa—and all ecosystems collapse. Should the earth's core have been comprised differently, plate tectonics and all of its essential features for the carbon cycle would not exist. Life, again, exists within boundaries.

And the same is true for human beings—creatures particularly sensitive to all of what can be experienced in creation. The requirements for proper living conditions, food and hydration requirements, not to mention the capacity to see and hear and touch all that exists "out there," take place within defined ranges.[3] Within the right context, a person can live up to a century;

---

[1] See Robin Collins, "The Fine-Tuning Design Argument," in Michael Murray, ed., *Reason for the Hope Within* (Grand Rapids: Eerdmans, 1998).

[2] See Guillermo Gonzalez, *The Privileged Planet* (Washington D.C.: Regnery Publishing, 2004).

[3] Cf. Edmund Opitz, *The Libertarian Theology of Freedom* (Tampa: Hallberg Publishing, 1999), 67.

that same life can end simply by tripping over a log and bumping one's head in the wrong way. In that sense, the sheer contingency of life makes our human experience appear to be nothing and everything at the same time.

"Law" or "limitation," in this sense, *means life*. Without it, life cannot be. Perhaps it is less strange, then, when we read something like Psalm 1:2-3 in this framework: "their delight is in the law of the LORD, and on his law they meditate day and night. They are like trees planted by streams of water, which yield their fruit in its season, and their leaves do not wither." Law means life.[4]

Indeed, to live within God's revealed boundaries is to *flourish* as a human being. It is one thing to merely survive, another to live life with abundance. Boundaries not only provide the identifiable limitations and extremes within which life can exist, but also within *degrees* that correspond to the *abundance* of life lived.

There again, creatures witness the Creator's purpose, sovereignty and genius at work in creation. It is not simply true that our solar system is away from the dangers of the black hole we revolve around; it is placed in a "quiet" zone perfect for discovery and observation of the rest of the galaxy, away from the blinding luminance of star clusters and dust.[5] It is not only the case that the earth is the right distance from the sun for survival, but it is surrounded by other planets that through gravitation attract and consume catastrophic meteors that would otherwise have impacted the earth—as they have during earlier times in the solar system (thankfully, we were not around at that time!). And it is not simply the case that human beings have food to eat and objects to see, taste, and hear, but food that *tastes good*, plants and animals that are *pleasing* to the eyes, and sounds of birds, waterfalls, and crickets at night that are not merely audible, but within the range of our hearing, able to put a mind at ease. And as if that wasn't enough, looking up, both the universe *and* our planet's atmosphere happen to be remarkably transparent, functioning like a cosmic window for earth's inhabitants.

---

[4] Cf. Saunders in his article in this volume.

[5] Gonzalez, *Privileged Planet*, 166-67.

Various fields of human knowledge identify and elaborate on these boundaries and optimal ranges for different subsets of creation. In economics, for instance, certain "optimal" ranges within life get special attention. This is especially true for "praxeology," the study of human action. Such optimal ranges are so evident and so central to understanding life that they are commonly referred to as "laws," such as the "law of marginal utility" and "law of diminishing returns."[6] Human beings *act* within boundaries, tending to choose that which improves their condition as opposed to merely "getting by."[7] Human beings strive for the optimal—sometimes getting close, often missing the mark—so that they might enjoy life as "it was meant to be lived." This is true in both the broader sense of human nature and purpose and in the narrower sense of each individual's particular ideals.

The question now is, what are the boundaries within which human beings thrive in a self-knowing, self-aware community?

The concern for this essay is *privacy*, and that is an inherently epistemological subject, for it concerns the nature and extent of knowledge about others. Are there any boundaries that exist regarding what a human being(s) can and/or ought to know about others? If so, what might they be, and how can one tell?

Consider the Hermit

We might begin by identifying some theoretical boundaries on this topic: (1) *extreme isolation*—socially and epistemologically—from all other human

---

[6] See Ludwig Von Mises, *Human Action*, Scholar's Edition (Auburn: Mises Institute, 2008), ch 7; Murray Rothbard, *Man, Economy, and State*, 2nd Scholar's Edition (Auburn: Mises Institute, 2009), ch 1.

[7] Rothbard, *Man, Economy, and State*, 19: "All action is an attempt to exchange a less satisfactory state of affairs for a more satisfactory one."

beings,[8] and (2) *obsession with knowledge* of other human beings. Let us look more at each.

(1) Extreme Isolation. As a native of the Midwest, I have met many who I would describe as hermetic, whether by visiting remote parts of the Plains, camping in the Black Hills National Forest, or during travel across Montana, Wyoming, and South Dakota. A single individual, perhaps an older man with a beard (and a flannel shirt), finds it an improvement to live the "good life" in isolation. This may take place in a cabin in the woods or amidst the vast expanses of uninhabited prairie. Such hermits tend to purposefully ignore the whereabouts and activities of other people, for in the mind of the hermit, such knowledge only produces personal anxiety. People are weary creatures, always striving, never arriving and being satisfied.[9] Wars, violence, envy, suffering, greed, endless grief—would it not be better to shield one's mind from such realities altogether? Wouldn't it be more peaceful, at least internally? To hell with newspapers and Facebook.

Of course, the hermit exemplifies *intentional* ignorance. It is possible to be just as isolated epistemologically without intending to be so. Consider the powerful story of a Japanese soldier who had never learned that WWII had ended:

---

[8] The epistemological cannot be isolated from the social, and vice versa. See the discussion below.

[9] Cf. Blaise Pascal, *Pensees*, line 374: "Man's condition. Inconstancy, boredom, anxiety." Cf. line 172: "We never keep to the present. We recall the past, we anticipate the future…we are so unwise that we wonder about in times that do not belong to us…The fact is that the present usually hurts. We thrust it out of sight because it distresses us, and if we find it enjoyable, we are sorry to see it slip away. We try to give it the support of the future, and think how we are going to arrange things over which we have no control for a time we can never be sure of reaching. Let each of us examine his thoughts; he will find them wholly concerned with the past or the future. We almost never think of the present, and if we do think of it, it is only to see what light it throws on our plans for the future. The present is never our end. The past and the present are our means, the future alone our end. Thus we never actually live, but hope to live, and since we are always planning how to be happy, it is inevitable that we should never be so."

In 1974, Hiroo Onoda, a Japanese army intelligence officer, caused a sensation when he was persuaded to come out of hiding by a former comrade on the Philippine island of Lubang. Mr Onoda, now 83, wept uncontrollably as he agreed to lay down his rifle, unaware that Japanese forces had surrendered 29 years earlier. He returned to Japan the same year, but unable to adapt to life in his home country, emigrated to Brazil in 1975.[10]

Clearly, the lack of knowledge may not always lead to "the good life."

Whatever the case, intentional ignorance (often paired with apathy) undoubtedly has its advantages. Should negative memories be erased or prevented from coming into existence, then there is more hope for future enjoyment. Such ignorance also exists in harmony with an obvious anthropological limitation: *human beings are not meant to know everything.* King Solomon knew this well.

On the one hand, knowledge is worth more than gold (Prov 8:10), is accumulated by the wise (Prov 10:14), disseminated by the wise (Prov 15:7), can save lives (Prov 11:9), invokes intelligence (Prov 18:15; 19:25), and is hated by fools (Prov 1:7, 22, 29). On the other hand, "For in much wisdom is much vexation, and those who increase knowledge increase sorrow" (Eccl. 1:18, NRSV).[11] A more formidable challenge also comes in contemplating that which transcends creation; "Such knowledge is too wonderful for me," Solomon's father sang, "it is so high that I cannot attain it" (Ps 139:6). "Who has known the mind of the Lord?" writes Paul to the Romans centuries later

---

[10] Justin McCurry and John Oglionby, "60 years after the war ends, two soldiers emerge from the jungle," *The Guardian* (May 27, 2005).

[11] Solomon is presumably the קֹהֶלֶת; *Qoheleth*, although it is equally possible the content of Ecclesiastes represents the spirit and proverbs of Solomon through the hands of temple scribes. See Tremper Longman III, *Proverbs* (Grand Rapids: Baker Academic, 2006), "Introduction" and *idem, Song of Songs*, NICOT (Grand Rapids: Eerdmans, 2001), 2-8.

(Rom 11:34). Thus arose the "doctrine of the incomprehensibility of God"[12] in systematic theology, as well as the importance of revelation—assuming knowledge of God is possible.

Even if one limits the scope of human knowledge to less transcendent matters, it is still severely limited. "There are many things," Von Mises writes, "beyond the reach of the human mind…Man is not infallible…[and] can never become omniscient. He can never be absolutely certain that his inquiries were not misled and that what he considers as certain truth is not error."[13] This is simply because humans are not God: "In reality God, not the creature, is primary. He is the archetype (the original); the creature is the ectype (the likeness). In him everything is original, absolute, and perfect; in creatures everything is derived, relative, and limited."[14]

Ignorance also has its *disadvantages*. Chief among them is loneliness. Loneliness develops in relational isolation. Since the mere presence of other individuals is no guarantee of shared knowledge, such isolation can exist in a city of millions as much as on an uninhabited island. Conversely, intimacy grows as each party discloses what was previously unknown; this may be as literal and physical or as metaphorical and abstract as human experience allows. Thus to "know" one in the ancient world is a regular descriptor for sexual intercourse (e.g., Gen 4:1, 17, 25; 28; 38:9; 1 Sam 1:19, etc.). When Jesus showed knowledge of the deep, personal matters of the woman at the well in John 4, her description to others was that Jesus "told me *everything* I have ever done" (Jn 4:29, emphasis mine), even though he obviously didn't.

Sharing knowledge also creates a sense of self-identity, which is forged through shared experience, shared memories and ongoing story-telling.

---

12 See Herman Bavinck, *Reformed Dogmatics,* abridged (Grand Rapids: Baker, 2011), ch 1-7 (esp. ch 7); Cornelius Van Til, *An Introduction to Systematic Theology* (Phillipsburg: Presbyterian and Reformed, 2007), ch 13.

13 *Human Action,* 68.

14 Bavinck, *Reformed Dogmatics,* 178.

Knowledge of self is hardly possible without knowledge of others.[15] As social constructionists have ably shown, it is through a community—a plurality— that a sense of self is built.[16] What am "I" if not contrasted/compared with an "other"? What am I outside of the language I use to think and act—which is itself a product of community relations? Just as Von Mises argued that there are no absolute values or perfect ideal in praxeology as one can only prefer one option above another,[17] so there is no absolute sense of "me" except what "I" am in relation to others. Thus, he conceded on the topic directly: "Individual [humans are] born into a socially organized environment. In this sense alone we may accept the saying that society is—logically or historically—antecedent to the individual."[18] Indeed, "man is a social animal that can thrive only within society."[19] Opitz was even more direct:

> We have no inclination to be hermits; we are social creatures, and we achieve or full humanity only in association, in mutuality, and in community.[20]

---

[15] Or without knowledge of God, as Calvin's famously introduced his *Institutes:* "Our wisdom, in so far as it ought to be deemed true and solid Wisdom, consists almost entirely of two parts: the knowledge of God and of ourselves. But as these are connected together by many ties, it is not easy to determine which of the two precedes and gives birth to the other."

[16] See, for example, Kenneth Gergen, *Realities and Relationships* (Cambridge: Harvard University Press, 1994); Peter Berger, *The Social Construction of Reality: A Treatise in the Sociology of Knowledge* (New York: Anchor, 1967).

[17] Von Mises, *Human Action,* ch 1.1.

[18] Ibid., 143.

[19] Ibid., 184.

[20] Opitz, *The Libertarian Theology,* 140. Cf. Adam Smith, *The Theory of Moral Sentiments,* cited in David Boaz, ed., *The Libertarian Reader* (New York: Simon and Schuster, 2015), 71: "It is thus that man, who can subsist only in society, was fitted by nature to that situation for which he was made. All the members of human society stand in need of each other's assistance, and are likewise exposed to mutual injuries. Where the necessary assistance is reciprocally afforded from love, from gratitude, from friendship, and esteem, the society flourishes and is happy."

This reality is affirmed in Christian theology, primarily in theological anthropology. Human beings, as God's images, are made in, with, and for community.[21] In the renowned Genesis narrative, one person alone is specifically said to be deficient (unhappy), so there must be two for life. And there is not just two, but two of a different sort within the same basic nature, for it is through *difference within sameness* (or variety amidst uniformity) that cultivates optimal human life. Without such plurality and complementarity, there is loneliness (and, literally, no *pro-creation*), and all the unnecessary limitations associated with it. So central, in fact, is interaction for human nature that Jürgen Moltmann remarked,

> To be alive means existing in relationship with other people and things. Life is communication in communion….So if we want to understand what is real as real, and what is living as living, we have to know it in its own primal and individual community, in its relationships.[22]

Thus, YHWH calls out people from obscurity to become part of a community—a community that fell into a state of humiliation but is now called to a life of renewal and restoration. The story begins with Sarah, Hagar, and Abraham, works itself out progressively through Israel, the New Covenant community of the church, and continues to this day. Unlike atheistic economics, an economics informed by Christianity assumes that God has something to say—a claim to put on creatures—regarding what

---

[21] See Bavinck, *Reformed Dogmatics,* ch 11; Thomas Oden, *Classic Christianity* (New York: HarperOne, 1996), ch 6; Daniel Migliore, *Faith Seeking Understanding* (Grand Rapids: Eerdmans, 2014), ch 7; Stanley Grenz, *Theology for the Community of God* (Grand Rapids: Eerdmans, 1994), ch 6; Karl Rahner, *Foundations of Christian Faith* (New York: Crossroad Publishing Co., 1997), Parts II-IV.

[22] Jurgen Moltmann, *God in Creation* (Minneapolis: Fortress Press, 1993), 3.

"ought" to be the case, and how a person should live and arrange their values, and therefore their actions.[23]

(2). Obsession with Knowledge. We now turn to the second extreme. What might possibly serve as an example of an obsession of knowledge with others?

Here, identifying the boundaries is more complicated, because they are affected differently according to different, related conditions. The earth and human society are not static; aggregate populations grow (and, from what we understand, rarely shrink). This movement affects the possibility and plausibility of what knowledge can be ignored, and what knowledge can be obtained. It was not possible during first-century Rome to know how many were killed in a construction accident in China the same day the event occurred. It was equally impossible to obtain consistent historical records of such local events for many of the various societies around the globe.

Today, those impossibilities are now possible—for better or worse. And that is, indeed, the case. There is a *better* and a *worse*. Human beings are made to live within boundaries—within limits regarding reproduction, food consumption, lifespan, and memory. As it was already observed above, no one person *can* be omniscient, nor would it be desirable, for human beings are human beings; they are not God.

Entrepreneur, visionary, and corporate CEO Elon Musk recently commented during an interview that while the input capacity (e.g., vision, sound, etc.) of the average human being is incredibly large, the output capacity is terribly small.[24] Texting one letter at a time or speaking one word after another to develop a thought, for example, is very "inefficient." The solution to this "problem" is a "neural lace," a neurological interface that

---

[23] Von Mises, *Human Action,* ch 8.1-2, carelessly mocks this concept in religion. Space does not allow for a rebuttal, but, suffice to say, Von Mises simply does not understand the meaning, function, and extent of "revelation" in Christian theology. He is also unaware of the flexible and changing nature of ethical standards within covenantal relationships.

[24] The interview was held at the 2016 Recode Conference at the Terranea Resort in Ranchos Palos Verdes, California May 31-June 2.

allows the output capacity of human communication to be more direct and therefore more massive.

What Musk fails to grasp is that God designed human beings with two eyes, two ears, a whole body that feels, an impressive set of olfactory faculties, and *only one mouth* for a reason. It is not human to produce and influence as much as it is to receive and be influenced. To "enhance" the output capacity of human consciousness will result in an aggregate exponential increase in the amount of information and sensory experience that other human beings have to sort out and interpret. In the notorious "information age" where virtually no one has time to even read an entire book all the way through because of blogs, podcasts, newspapers, twitter and facebook updates, it seems fair to question whether it is desirable to have such increased information output in the first place. The so-called "problem" and "limitation" of human nature turns out to be not so problematic after all.

In a similar vein, the movies and stories of wanting too much knowledge and receiving some kind of recourse after obtaining it, are endless. The Genesis story of a forbidden tree of "knowledge" immediately comes to mind, as does the film *Indiana Jones and the Kingdom of the Crystal Skull* (2008). Consider also the roles of the ring of Gyges in Herodotus,[25] *Oedipus Rex*, the character Prometheus, and Rafael in *Paradise Lost*. The idea of toying around with more insight and awareness than human beings should have has consumed a great deal of attention throughout western literature and the arts—and not without reason.[26]

Knowledge—especially sight—is a form of power. Ocularcentrism,[27] the privileging of sight over the other senses, has a long history in the west. It was associated with masculinity as much as with power in the Greco-Roman

---

[25] Herodotus, *Histories,* I.8.4.

[26] For a contemporary exploration of this topic, see Roger Shattuck, *Forbidden Knowledge* (New York: St. Martin's Press, 1996).

[27] Or "ocular hegemony," in Stephen Tyler's words. (Thanks to Gregory Howard for this reference.)

world.[28] It was also common to draw a distinction between subordinate and superior by who is permitted to see whom. Slaves and prisoners were regularly rebuked for staring at their masters ("what are you *looking* at?"), for "the gaze" is something only the powerful and privileged should perform. Today, certain forms of gazing by men upon women are considered sexual harassment. The success of the pornography industry has exploited and monetized from the feeling of power and control associated with sight. In contrast to all of this, the loss of sight is a loss of power.[29]

In the right context, having the right knowledge can mean the difference between life and death. When tyrants and dictators want to control a population, they tend to control what the masses are allowed to *know*. Thus, the internet is filtered, certain textbooks are prohibited, schools are regulated, or in extreme cases like North Korea, virtually no books outside of a fringe few are even allowed within the borders. The "knowledge" that people have in this context is manipulated *disinformation*. Ideally, for maximal control, a people will not just lack knowledge but lack the *means for obtaining knowledge*—such as literacy. For in that case, the whole world of literature, the internet, and otherwise is largely useless even if it was available to the masses.

A people lacking knowledge, then, is a controllable people. Conversely, a people well-informed is an empowered, self-governing people. A monopoly of knowledge creates authorial hegemony, while a free market of knowledge and sight disperses (potentially dangerous) concentrations of power.

Having sketched out these preliminary remarks, we should finally answer our question: what would constitute an extreme case of excessive knowledge and awareness of others?

One might immediately point the finger at God, who traditionally has been attributed with "omniscience," the power of "all-knowing." But our

---

[28] Brittany Wilson, *Unmanly Men: Refigurations of Masculinity in Luke-Acts* (New York: Oxford, 2016), ch 5.

[29] We have not space to even talk about *in*sight or *super*vision.

question does not have to do with God,[30] it rather has to do with creatures within God's creation.

Perhaps then, the extreme end of a boundary would be whatever approaches omniscience in the creature's world. Attempts to achieve such (ultimately unattainable) omniscience should be viewed with as much contempt as those who tried to build a tower reaching God's throne (Gen 11), for the "right" thing for humans to do is to do what is fully human, not attempt to dethrone our Creator and become gods ourselves.

My central question is this: What would such an attempt look like?

The NSA, Eye of Sauron, and Concept of Privacy

In today's world, such an attempt would probably take the form of coercive, secretive, large-scale data-collection through all possible means. Other than the obvious feature of government-sponsorship, this would probably involve vast towers of hard drives downloading and monitoring the conversations, communications, associations, and whereabouts of all people. There would be systems of drones and satellites monitoring and recording every square inch of activity on the planet. There, further, would be rhetorical legitimations of these processes to appease the public—who actually do not have a choice in changing the system even if they wished.

As one might suspect, what I have just described is not far from the current state of affairs with regard to the National Security Agency (NSA) of the U.S. Federal Government. There is not omniscience, but an effort underway to achieve the closest approximation to it. Most of what I outlined above already exists with respect to the U.S. mainland, and it is, regrettably, a reality that has become "normal" for the common people.

---

[30] Only one who is also absolutely good and righteous would be fit to possess and utilize omniscience. This is, of course, the traditional theological teaching regarding God's nature— and that such "attributes" are actually essential to God's essence, being coterminous and complementary (e.g., God's goodness is wise, God's wisdom is good, God's power is wise, God's wisdom is powerful, etc.).

However, just because something approaches a theoretical extreme does not necessarily mean it is evil or somehow illegitimate. Even for how terrifying the all-seeing Eye of Sauron is in Tolkien's *The Lord of the Rings,* what is terrifying is who the Eye works for (evil forces), not merely the fact that there is an all-seeing Eye.

Or is it?

This is an important question that deserves pondering. Whether or not the Eye of Sauron is evil, I know that I myself would feel a bit intimidated by it, living from day to day under the gaze of a singular point of vision. Being watched by someone/something that you are not in communication with generally produces a feeling of being exposed, vulnerable, and insecure.

This situation was explored by the French historian Michel Foucault in his study of prisons. The Christian ethicist and theologian, Stanley Hauerwas of Duke Divinity School, concisely explains this concern:

In his extraordinary book *Discipline and Punish: The Birth of the Prison,* Michel Foucault challenges the presumption that the use of modern prisons as a mode of punishment is more humane than past uses of torture. Foucault begins his book with a horrific account of the burning and quartering in 1757 of a man named Damiens who was being punished for plotting to kill the king. Foucault does so to make clear he does not underestimate the cruelty of torture. But Foucault is intent on helping us see how the development of prisons, which are allegedly an alternative to torture, can obscure how we continue to punish bodies; the only difference is that now we do so in a manner that hides from us the cruelty involved.

In particular Foucault calls attention to the great representative of the Enlightenment, the utilitarian philosopher Jeremy Bentham, who sought to reform prisons in the hope that those imprisoned might be punished in a manner that would lead to their reform. Bentham thought the way to do this was to build prisons on the model of a Panopticon. The prison would be a circular or eight-sided building in which each prisoner would have a cell. The external wall would be solid with perhaps only a high window providing some back-lighting. The front of the cell would consist only of bars making any privacy for the prisoner impossible.

A tower would be in the middle of the prison in which a guard could constantly observe the prisoners. The genius of Bentham's prison is that the guard in the tower could not see all the prisoners at the same time, but the prisoners could not know if the guard was watching them or not. So the prisoners had to learn to live as if the guard was watching them at every moment. As a result prisoners had to internalize the gaze of the guard because they had to assume the guard was always watching them. Bentham thought the prisoner would be reformed in the process. Foucault not so subtly called attention to Bentham's Panopticon because he thought it is a metaphor for modern life.

From Foucault's perspective, the Panopticon is no less a disciplining of the body than torture. In some ways torture is less cruel because at least when you are tortured you know who has power over you. In contrast, the Panopticon is a machine in which the one whose body is subject to such an unrelenting gaze becomes the agent of his own subjection. Accordingly, the body so subjected becomes disciplined to be what the gaze of those in power desire without their power ever being made explicit.[31]

In other words, omni-vision may constitute a form of coercive control.

Whether or not that is the case, what is disturbing about the theoretical Panopticon is that it has already been surpassed by today's prison systems, which are saturated with video-cameras, archives of audio and video material, entire staff trained in "keeping track" of all who are monitored, etc. Are today's prison systems therefore any less torturous? More pertinent for our topic, are today's national surveillance systems any less torturous? Any less psychologically and sociologically damaging?

Snowden put his finger on this matter during his 2013 Christmas video:

---

[31] Stanley Hauerwas, *Without Apology* (New York: Seabury Books, 2013), 41–42.

A child born today will grow up with no conception of privacy at all. They'll never know what it means to have a private moment to themselves, an unrecorded, unanalyzed thought. And that's a problem because privacy matters, privacy is what allows us to determine who we are and who we want to be.[32]

Those who are placed in a particular role tend to play the role. Stanley Milgram's experiments vividly demonstrated this point.[33] Whether one is in front of a camera, in a position of authority at work, or behind a steering wheel, people take on different identities and act out according to the positions they are in. Expectations, responsibilities of an "office," and peer-pressure are incredibly powerful "forces." Snowden's point is particularly striking in this context, for the entire citizenry is now playing the role of the watched. There is no privacy anymore. What kind of people, society, and self-identity is this going to create long-term? We have all heard it said that a person's true identity is revealed when they're not being watched. Given that this is no longer possible, does this suggest that people's "true identity" (whatever this may be) in a society is becoming ever more elusive?

Whatever the case, it is clear that Jesus often preferred privacy. Throughout his entire earthly life, the Gospel writers regularly took note of how Jesus went away from crowds and life as usual to be alone (e.g., Mk 7:33; Mt 14:23; Lk 9:18). Whether this was to avoid the feeling of being watched and heard or to ensure a more conducive environment towards prayer is not always clear. But given his full humanity, it is not difficult for us to understand; *private* experience has always been an integrated feature of *human* experience.

---

[32] Published by Costas Pitas, "Snowden Warns of Loss of Privacy in Christmas Message." *Reuters.* (December 25, 2013). http://www.reuters.com/article/us-usa-snowden-privacy-idUSBRE9BO09020131225

[33] See the film *Experimenter* (2015) and Stanley Milgram, *Obedience to Authority* (New York: Harper Perennial Books, 2009).

Whether or not the effects of mass surveillance are psychologically harmful, the *power* of today's pseudo-omniscience is hard to overstate. One example (of countless) involves the ability to effortlessly incriminate by association, as Snowden aptly addressed:

> ...even if you're not doing anything wrong you're being watched and recorded. And the storage capability of these systems increases every year consistently by orders of magnitude to where it's getting to the point where you don't have to have done anything wrong. You simply have to eventually fall under suspicion from somebody even by a wrong call. And then they can use this system to go back in time and scrutinize every decision you've ever made, every friend you've ever discussed something with. And attack you on that basis to sort to derive suspicion from an innocent life and paint anyone in the context of a wrongdoer.[34]

No matter what amount of good can come from technological innovation, engineering, or data collection, it can always be used for evil in the wrong hands. Thus, Randy Isaac (former President of the American Scientific Affiliation) says in an essay on technological development, "Not everything that can be made should be made."[35] Perhaps in a similar vein, just because everything *can* be recorded does not mean it *should* be recorded.

There is, indeed, reason for pause when it comes to technology. Perhaps no one possessed better insight on this matter than Albert Speer, Minister of Armaments Production of the Third Reich. Speer began his career as a gifted architect but eventually fell into the hands of Hitler's political regime. He was then on track to build the greatest city since Rome. However, things took a

---

[34] Edward Snowden, interview with Glenn Greenwald. Cited from Gabriel Rodriguez, "Edward Snowden Interview Transcript FULL TEXT: Read the Guardian's Entire Interview With the Man Who Leaked PRISM." *Policy.Mic.* https://mic.com/articles/47355/edward-snowden-interview-transcript-full-text-read-the-guardian-s-entire-interview-with-the-man-who-leaked-prism#.eHU367c0Q

[35] Randy Isaac, "Creativity and the Development of Technology" in *When God and Science Meet* (National Association of Evangelicals, 2015), 48.

turn for the worse and the "god of building" became responsible for weapons development and production for the German army. After the war, trial at Nuremberg, and serving his 20-year prison sentence, Speer published memoirs recounting his experience in deeply introspective reflections.[36] Since WWII was the playground of all sorts of new—and terrifying— technologies,[37] it was only natural that he gave some attention to that area. His conclusions are powerful and grim:

> I thought of the consequences that unrestricted rule together with the power of technology—making use of it but also driven by it—might have in the future. This war, I continued, had ended with remote-controlled rockets, aircraft flying at the speed of sound, atom bombs, and a prospect of chemical warfare. In five to ten years it would be possible for an atomic rocket, perhaps serviced by ten men, to annihilate a million human beings in the center of New York within seconds. It would be possible to spread plagues and destroy harvests. "The more technological the world becomes, the greater the danger...As the former minister in charge of a highly developed armaments economy it is my last duty to state: A new great war will end with the destruction of human culture and civilization. There is nothing to stop unleashed technology and science from completing its work of destroying man which it has so terribly begun in this war...The nightmare shared by many people," I said, "that someday the nations of the world may be dominated by technology—that nightmare was very nearly made a reality under Hitler's authoritarian system. Every country in the

---

[36] For various reasons that need not be reviewed here, Jessica (my wife) and I read all 530 pages of Speer's memoirs in the spring and summer of 2016 (usually over breakfast).

[37] In his final speech at Nuremberg, Speer said, "Hitler's dictatorship was the first dictatorship of an industrial state in this age of modern technology, a dictatorship which employed to perfection the instruments of technology to dominate its own people...By means of such instruments of technology as the radio and public-address systems, eighty million persons could be made subject to the will of one individual....The means of communication alone enable [the authoritarian system] to mechanize the work of the lower leadership. Thus the type of uncritical receiver of orders is created." Albert Speer, *Inside the Third Reich*, trans. Richard and Clara Winston (New York: Galahad Books, 1970), 520-21.

world today faces the danger of being terrorized by technology; but in a modern dictatorship this seems to me to be unavoidable. Therefore, the more technological the world becomes, the more essential will be the demand for individual freedom and the self-awareness of the individual human being as a counterpoise to technology."[38]

Decades later, Orthodox philosopher David Bentley Hart reflects on the same topic in equally poignant and sinister terms:

We seem on occasion, at least a good number of us, to have embraced (often with a shocking dogmatism) the sterile superstition that mastery over the hidden causes of things is the whole of truth, while at the same time pursuing that mastery by purely material means….if the modern story of freedom is what I have said it is, then in a sense each of us is already a sorcerer, attempting to conjure a self out of the infinite vacuum of indeterminate possibility. And today's magicians possess the powers they claim: the occult energies of matter have really been unlocked, the secrets of the cosmos truly fathomed, and the realms of physics, biology, chemistry, and so on—the chief glories of the modern age—are also now places where real monsters can be bred, and real terrors summoned out of the depths of nature.[39]

Privacy: A Privilege or a Right?

Some reasoning tends to follow the idea that knowledge is neutral with respect to privacy if nothing is ultimately done with it. If a person in the suburbs has a camera on her roof that is pointed towards her neighbor's backyard, some will argue that, should the neighbor tan unclothed and this be captured on the video camera, no boundary has been crossed—even if the neighbor objected to his being recorded. No property rights have been violated. If the neighbor wanted privacy, he could have built a high enough

---

[38] Ibid., 521.
[39] David Bentley Hart, *Atheist Delusions* (New Haven: Yale University Press, 2009), 233-34.

fence to ensure it. Some would even argue that there is nothing wrong if such video material is publicly posted on the internet without permission.

There are concerns about this approach. First of all, there are already the problematic psychological issues associated with mass-surveillance (see above). Such mass-surveillance is also particularly problematic when it becomes *involuntary*—as most of it already is (no American citizen gets to choose if a surveillance drone will or will not fly over their property, or if their text messages won't be monitored by the NSA).

Second of all, the right to private property involves *enjoyment* of property. Should a noisy wind tower on my neighbor's yard cast a massive shadow on my yard and create vibrations that don't allow me to sleep, the owner of the wind tower should pay damages, or obtain (from neighbors) a kind of "permit" to continue doing this.

Judge Andrew Napolitano provides a similar case study:

> If you lived in a very crowded area, would the government be justified in preventing you from blaring extraordinarily loud music at midnight, or at least requiring you to pay 'damages' to your neighbors for doing so? Certainly, by playing obnoxious music, you are diminishing your neighbors' natural right to the use and enjoyment of their property. And over time, if you were habitually noisy, then most likely would decrease the market value of their property. Thus, although the government could not criminalize this kind of expression, it would be more than justified in making it actionable, or in other words, the basis for lawsuit.[40]

A neighbor that records your every movement with one camera or a dozen has the potential to negatively affect your right to enjoy your property. So, while there may not be a "right to privacy" that can be consistently enforced[41]

---

[40] Andrew Napolitano, *It is Dangerous to be Right When the Government is Wrong* (Nashville: Thomas Nelson, 2011), 48.

[41] "Privacy is a benefit, not a right. It is a benefit that the market, when and if it is freed, will confer on those of us who wish it." Walter Block, "There is No Right to Privacy." *LewRockwell.com.* July 13, 2013.

(especially since it is a positive right)[42], surveillance and "invasions of privacy" may, indeed, constitute a violation of property rights.

What if it is simply a given that a particular house is systematically "spied" on? Then the value of that property will correspond accordingly; the negative properties of the lot are reflected in lower costs. This already happens today. The "free-market system"[43] allocates the resource of privacy to those who desire it. Many small-town and country-folk value privacy much more than the perks of a big city and live in such rural locations for that reason. Those who prefer city life at the expense of privacy tend to gravitate toward cities. Properties near cities with greater degrees of privacy cost more, while more common, exposed properties are cheaper. In short, some people prefer more privacy than others, and in a free (non-coercive/-centrally-planned) market, these variables are accounted for to some degree.

A growing concern, however, is that as the world develops and means for data-collection increase, privacy becomes more and more scarce. It thus becomes a more valuable commodity. Whereas privacy was easy to come by for thousands of years, it will become more difficult to come by as time goes on. We can expect that the market—people's freely expressed desires—will sort out this situation in the future as it has been. Drones with cameras are

---

[42] Generally speaking, a negative right requires the *inaction* of others (e.g., the right to life simply requires that fatal violence not be committed against me), while a positive right requires the *action* of others (e.g., the right to health care, which would require people to build businesses, systems, a certain amount of wealth, and everything else required to provide me adequate health care). It is a libertarian position (and my own) that it is both theoretically and practically impossible for any entity to enforce positive rights without compromising the protection of negative rights. Thus, entities like governments should only attempt to protect negative rights and liberties and nothing more, since violence will inevitably result otherwise.

[43] I put this phrase in quotes because it is a questionable arrangement (since "system" often presupposes central planning, and that is the opposite of a free-market). I am not the first to raise questions about this phrase; other libertarians have gone as far as to say (in effect) "the free market is nothing but a series of voluntary exchanges; it is no system at all; it is not a 'thing'."

on the rise right now; drones with jamming equipment will be on the rise in the future.

Privacy today is not threatened chiefly by decreasing supply or increasing demand, however. It is threatened by the monopolies of power. What does one say about the legitimacy of the NSA's data collection systems, especially if its purpose is (allegedly) to ensure "national security"? And what about "whistle-blowers" like Edward Snowden?

Concluding Thoughts

Where can I go from your spirit? Or where can I flee from your presence? If I ascend to heaven, you are there; if I make my bed in Sheol, you are there.
—Psalm 198:7-8

As it has already been hinted at above, the NSA is more or less a modern day tower of babel. History has repeatedly shown that attempts to become God or reach God-like status not only fail, but create human suffering. Such projects cannot typically be undertaken without forcing populations to surrender resources and property to achieve the desired end. Because the NSA is part of a government that compromises the principle of non-aggression, it should be opposed for that reason alone.[44]

Second, just because mass surveillance is possible does not mean that it is desirable. In fact, there are good reasons to believe that state-run mass surveillance is *undesirable*, namely, the negative effects it has on people and the catastrophic consequences of its abuse.[45] The NSA appears to have no boundaries in its data collection systems; as long as the goal is some ideal of "security," then it is legitimized. This naïve and secular outlook ignores not

---

[44] The principle of non-aggression generally states that it is wrong/illegitimate to initiate force against a person and/or their property. This applies to governments as much as it does to businesses and individuals. A certain degree of force may only be used in response to someone or something else's initiation of force (e.g., arresting a thief).

[45] A comparison with the KGB during the Cold War may be appropriate here.

only the inherent ignorance of such an approach, but a doctrine of creation that recognizes boundaries and optimal limits for a flourishing human experience.

Snowden has been interpreted by various "conservatives" and "liberals" as both a "patriot" and a "traitor" of the American republic. Those who argue that he is a traitor suggest that he has endangered the mainland by empowering foreign enemies with knowledge of U.S. intelligence operations.

In my perspective, if Snowden's lord in his contract with the government is the U.S. Constitution, then he is fully justified in exposing the unconstitutional practices of the surveillance state,[46] regardless of any repercussions or dissent from his immediate employer. If the NSA's practices do not violate an "unreasonable search"—which includes a search of the entire citizenry, then nothing probably does. If Snowden is accountable first and foremost to his immediate employer and not the Constitution, then he is guilty of breaking the "law" (not the supreme law of the land, of course, but the law as understood by his employer) and should be prosecuted.

I want to end this essay with some questions that need to be addressed as this topic unfolds for the next several generations:

1. What are the effects of mass-surveillance on people's consciences, self-identity, and personal experience, both short-term and long-term?

2. Is mass surveillance necessary for "national security," and what evidence exists in supporting both an affirmative and a negative answer to this question?

3. What constitutes "too much information"? If democracy and American ideals recognize the need to decentralize power, how will it embody that same value in decentralizing knowledge?

4. Does it benefit the public to restrict surveillance to the state and outlaw it from the people? Who watches the watchers?

---

[46] E.g., 4th amendment: "[t]he right of the people to be secure in their persons, houses, papers, and effects, against unreasonable searches and seizures, shall not be violated…"

5.   Is it possible, either theoretically or actually, to regulate surveillance operations without initiating force? If not, what purpose does surveillance serve since violence is already being committed on the very people who are supposed to be protected?

6.   Is it possible, either theoretically or actually, for the state to successfully manage aggressions in a monopolized bureaucracy more successfully than a free-enterprise free-market public—a public who is naturally more concerned about their own personal safety than government employees? Shouldn't the people be allowed and encouraged to put as much value on privacy as they wish, and embody those values in free-exchanges and free-associations?

7

Reflections on Religious Liberty in Light of the Current Crisis

Hunter Baker

I would like to begin by extending my thanks to the leadership here at John Witherspoon College for having me and to all of you for attending this talk. Apathy is our enemy in the crisis taking shape before our eyes. I am grateful to you for caring about religious liberty.

In the fifth century before Christ, Sophocles dramatized the problem of the individual caught between faith and the law in his play *Antigone*. Two brothers, the sons of the tragic figure, Oedipus, have struck each other down in battle. Though one died as a defender and the other as a rebel, the situation was morally complex. Nevertheless, King Creon honors the one fallen brother and insists that the other remain unburied as a sign of his dishonor. Their sister, Antigone, cannot abide seeing her brother shamed in this way. Despite the king's order, Antigone fulfills the duty she feels is owed to her sibling and buries his body.

In the face of the king's outrage, Antigone confesses that she has committed the deed and that she feels no remorse for having done so. She tells the king:

For me it was not Zeus who made that order. Nor did that Justice who lives with the gods below mark out such laws to hold among mankind. Nor did I think your orders were so strong that you, a mortal man, could over-run the gods' unwritten and unfailing laws. Not now, nor yesterday's, they always live, and no one knows their origin in time. So not through fear of any man's proud spirit would I be likely to neglect these laws, draw on myself the gods' sure punishment.

Creon replies:

The man the state has put in place must have obedient hearing to his least command when it is right, and even when it's not. He who accepts this teaching I can trust, ruler, or ruled, to function in his place, to stand his ground even in the storm of spears, a mate to trust in battle at one's side. There is no greater wrong than disobedience. This ruins cities, this tears down our homes, this breaks the battle-front in panic rout.

In this dramatic interaction between king and subject, we have the fundamental tension of religious liberty perfectly illustrated. The state insists that its laws are binding regardless of the opinions of citizens or subjects. But individuals see the state as having something less than the final word. They object with Antigone that there are laws and then there are laws. The greatest and most true authority comes from God. And few who believe as much are able to easily choose the will of a secular ruler over the will of God.

Despite the instruction of Romans 13 to submit to authorities because the source of their power is God, the action of the apostles makes clear that rulers (either secular or religious) do not have *carte blanche*. See, first, Acts 4:18-20:

So they called them and ordered them not to speak or teach at all in the name of Jesus. But Peter and John answered them, "Whether it is right in God's sight to listen to you rather than to God, you must judge; for we cannot keep from speaking about what we have seen and heard." (Acts 4:18-20 NRSV)

And then we follow with Acts 5:27-29:

> When they had brought them, they had them stand before the council. The high priest questioned them, saying, "We gave you strict orders not to teach in this name, yet here you have filled Jerusalem with your teaching and you are determined to bring this man's blood on us." But Peter and the apostles answered, "We must obey God rather than any human authority. (Acts 5:27-29 NRSV)

Unless the church settles for a servile relationship with the state, conflict is virtually inevitable. We now live in a day when the likelihood of such clashes in the United States is growing, as is their intensity. This fact is a painful one because our country has been a world leader in terms of the positive nature of the relationship between our religion and politics. And we have been a beacon of religious liberty.

However, many of us realized long ago that the controversy over gay marriage was likely to result in a crisis for religious liberty. I first saw gay activists attempting to block religious liberty protections in the late 90's. The crisis that was brewing then has now arrived.

If we could examine the whole scope of human history, it is likely that we would conclude that the traditional pattern has been to combine political and religious authority. Why is that? I think the answer can be found in Aristotle's *Politics*, book III, part IX. It is there that Aristotle asks the question whether a state can be satisfied with simply protecting its people from violence and facilitating commerce. He concludes that those things are not enough for a true state (the ultimate political association, in his view). Instead, the state needed to be composed of people who pursued the good life together. This good life would be based on virtue. What I am describing is a political association that is fundamentally moral in nature.

States have traditionally been moral entities. Religion and politics are two activities that are not the same, but that definitely overlap when it comes to morality. Because people tend to see the law as something more than just a sterile set of rules, the state seeks a moral basis for law. The great difficulty that emerges in a time such as ours is to know what to do when a people lacks an agreement about what is good.

For many centuries before the birth of Christ, there was a partnership between religion and political rule. The Roman Empire had worked out its own formula for incorporating the various religious cultures living under its great tent of nations. Virtually any religion could be tolerated as long as its followers agreed to the convention of Roman emperor worship. Christians, however, insisted that, as a recent book title proclaims, "Jesus is Lord. Caesar is Not." The empire viewed itself as sharing the gift of *Romanitas* with the known world. But that gift was often imparted via conquest. Peace depended upon acceptance of the sacred canopy that Rome provided. Christians did not easily yield. That is why the history of the early church includes so much persecution and so many martyrs. It is difficult to understand how the church survived other than to remember Gamaliel's counsel to those who opposed Christ's followers.

> Then he said to them, "Fellow Israelites, consider carefully what you propose to do to these men. For some time ago Theudas rose up, claiming to be somebody, and a number of men, about four hundred, joined him; but he was killed, and all who followed him were dispersed and disappeared. After him Judas the Galilean rose up at the time of the census and got people to follow him; he also perished, and all who followed him were scattered. So in the present case, I tell you, keep away from these men and let them alone; because if this plan or this undertaking is of human origin, it will fail; but if it is of God, you will not be able to overthrow them--in that case you may even be found fighting against God!" They were convinced by him, (Acts 5:35-39 NRSV)

The church did survive and we do believe that the Pharisees did find themselves fighting against God. But it was only in the 4th century that Constantine's conversion to Christianity and his reign changed everything for the church. Looking back from the relative safety of our own era, many have decried the turn of events that resulted from Constantine's rule, but Christians of the time were delivered from great trials.

The marriage of Christianity with power, however, did change the nature of the faith. Between the experience of the Christian emperors and the need for the church to fill the void after the fall of the empire, the faith changed from being an outside system challenger to being something more like the structural backbone of western civilization. Christianity became the vessel which spread Judeo-Christian values throughout much of the world.

There is much good that resulted from the influence of Christianity upon the governments of the earth and certainly upon European Christendom. But the negative part of the story has to do with the political and bureaucratic taming of the church. It would seem that having the church in an official alliance with the nation would be a good thing, a great way to spread the blessing of faith. But in reality, it has tended to be the case that state churches are weak, uninspiring, and compromised churches. In one of my books, I argued that state churches become departments of God with largely ceremonial and meaningless responsibilities. They became props for rulers and governments.

Though the American colonies and then the United States had some experience with state churches, establishment just wasn't the same as it had been in Europe. We were too far away from the national churches located across the Atlantic Ocean. And Americans developed an independent attitude about religion due to features such as distance, much less settled conditions, a greater degree of religious pluralism, and major religious upheavals such as the First Great Awakening.

As a result, when we Americans had our revolution it was a significantly different thing than the one that would be carried out by the French. The French revolution, which followed the American one by a few years, was a rebellion designed to overthrow both throne and altar. Partisans of the revolution are said to have expressed the hope that "the last king would be strangled with the guts of the last priest." Our American revolution was aimed squarely at the throne, but not at the altar. Our complaint was not directed at Christianity. We established no temples of reason and attempted no resetting of the calendar to the year one. Americans loved their churches and largely honored Christ.

Both revolutions have cast long shadows. My favorite line about the French Revolution comes from the Chinese premier Chou en Lai. He was supposedly asked for his opinion about the French Revolution, which had occurred almost 200 years ago by the time. He replied, "Too soon to tell."

For a long time, especially with the seeming triumph of American, and yes, Christian, values after the fall of the Soviet Union and atheistic world communism, it appeared that it would be the American revolution, and not the French one, which would prove most decisive in history.

That is an opinion that I think may not be too early to reconsider, especially as it relates to religion. The French Revolution was one propelled largely by secular nationalism. Jean Jacques Rousseau was a philosopher genius in the revolution's pantheon of heroes. He praised "the general will" and argued that if a citizen found himself at odds with that will, then he would have to be "forced to be free."[1] This attitude is considerably different from the one advanced by John Locke, the Englishman who inspired many American thinkers. Locke was a champion of liberty (including religious liberty). Rather than force recalcitrant individuals to be free, he argued that we should only use force to protect freedom.[2] The difference between the two is a crucial one.

Coming to America in the mid-19th century, the young French nobleman Alexis de Tocqueville observed the American sensibility in action. He wrote that "In France, I had always seen the spirit of religion and the spirit of freedom marching in opposite directions. But in America, I found that they were intimately united and they reigned in common over the same country."[3]

---

[1] See generally Jean Jacques Rousseau, *The Social Contract*, widely available in the public domain.

[2] John Locke, *The Second Treatise of Government*, also much reprinted and in the public domain.

[3] Alexis de Tocqueville, *Democracy in America*, ch. 17.

This was in contrast to Rousseau's view. He thought that religion had to serve the state. Otherwise, you would always have the problem of two Masters and citizens caught in confusion between the two. He opted for religion tamed for the state's purposes. The only unforgivable sin, by his lights, was to accept anyone as a citizen who believed that any other citizen might be going to hell.

In reality, we have seen that the existence of strong churches can actually provide a balance to state power and therefore improve the prospects for human freedom, as Brian Tierney and other scholars have noted. Though we are often taught about the church's supposedly abysmal human rights record, the simple fact is that the Catholic church at its worst *could never hold a candle* to the atheistic totalitarians of the 20th century.[4] For that matter, I'm not sure they wouldn't compare favorably even to the more closely contemporary record of French revolutionaries such as Robespierre. It was they who made such extravagant use of the guillotine.

For a long time, the echoes of the French revolution sounded much more loudly in Europe than they did in the United States. Europe's national churches hardly needed to be tamed. They were already domesticated by state establishment.

As I have said, though, America was different. The scholar Henry May has written that there are two major idea systems critical to understanding America in the 18th century and probably any period: Calvinistic Protestantism and the Enlightenment. Around 1800 when conflict began to crystallize and sides had to be chosen, Americans chose Protestant Christianity. May observed, "This is, I think, a major fact of American history and not only of American intellectual history."[5]

For a long time, America has been special. Even with the challenges of the Civil War, the Fundamentalist-Modernist Controversy, and the Scopes

---

[4] Editor's Addition: Cf. David Bentley Hart, *Atheist Delusions* (New Haven: Yale University Press, 2009).

[5] Henry F. May, *The Enlightenment in America* (New York, Oxford University Press, 1976), xv.

Trial, American Christianity has continued to shock and confound those who predict its demise. The 1970's surprises of Chuck Colson's runaway bestseller *Born Again*, the election of Southern Baptist Sunday School teacher Jimmy Carter to the presidency, and then the later emergence of the Moral Majority stunned many observers who thought such people no longer existed and certainly not in numbers sufficient to make much of a difference.

But something has happened to us. Our uniqueness is beginning to come into question. Now, I think we are truly beginning to feel the impact of movements that advanced more deeply into the European heart long ago. Abraham Kuyper, whose life bridged the 19th and 20th centuries and who amazingly preached, ran a newspaper, founded a university, and served as the Dutch prime minister, wrote of Christianity and what he called "modernism" as "two life systems" which "are wrestling with one another in mortal combat."[6] He offered an observation more prescient than he could ever know when he stated that:

> Modernism, which denies and abolishes every difference, cannot rest until it has made woman man and man woman, and putting every distinction on a common level, kills life by placing it under the ban of uniformity. One type must answer for all, one uniform, one position and one and the same development of life; and whatever goes beyond and above it is looked upon as an insult to the common consciousness.[7]

That's over 100 years ago that he wrote those words, which he spoke at Princeton, by the way. How could he have known that we would do far more than merely suffer confusion over sex roles? What might he say if he were to see that we have literally made "woman man and man woman?"

From his European standpoint, Kuyper perfectly grasped the cultural situation. He noted that Germanic philosophical pantheism had given us the idea of the sovereignty of the state as something like a mystical conception.

---

[6] Abraham Kuyper, *Lectures on Calvinism* (Grand Rapids: Eerdmans, 1987), 11.
[7] Ibid, 27.

Accordingly, the law is right not because of any harmony with eternal principles, but simply because it is the law. Thus, the will of the state effectively becomes God. He saw the French Revolution as offering a civil liberty for every Christian only to agree with the unbelieving majority. Kuyper also realized that the government will always be inclined to invade social life, while social life will resist the authority of the government. He stated that it is the task of constitutional law to maintain a balance.[8]

And here we are. A century later we are looking more like Western Europe. The state is pushing harder to enact its programs and with little regard for religious sensibilities or ethical objections. We look to our constitution to help us maintain the crucial balance. And the constitutional value with which we concern ourselves is religious liberty.

We must remind the state that it is not divine and neither is the general will. Instead, we should embrace the traditional Christian insistence that there are some things that do not belong to the state because they are between men and women and their God. We belong to God and not to the state. Jacques Maritain has written that the state is made for man, not man for the state. It is an instrument. It should have no pretensions of either ownership or immortality.[9]

Part of what has happened is the sexual revolution. Now, that is not exactly a new insight, but let me explain a bit further. The magic of Christianity in America has been that while the faith has not been formally established and institutionalized, it has still been highly influential and greatly appreciated. Sometimes, we have thought of the U.S. as having an informal establishment of Christianity that maintains its independence. Every culture has its cult (which makes sense considering the root of the word). Christianity has been the American cult.

---

[8] Ibid, 88-94.

[9] Jacques Maritain, *Man and the State* (Washington, DC: Catholic University of America Press, 1988), 13.

Because of the sexual revolution, the values divide between the American church and the broader society has become too great to easily reconcile. Some have made the case that the church is to blame, that we have too easily accepted the dissolution of traditional marriage. I would argue that the opposite is true. Certainly, marriage is not nearly as strong as it once was. We have a culture of cohabitation, fornication, easy divorce, serial monogamy, and adultery. All of that is true. But the fact is that the Christian church has been battling the sexual revolution just about all the way. We have opposed abortion, tried to encourage virginity as the norm prior to marriage, praised lifelong marriage, and discouraged divorce. If we are guilty, it is not of failing to fight. We are guilty of losing and then not giving up. We could have followed the Protestant mainline and conformed to the culture as thoroughly as possible, but we have remained faithful. It is that faithfulness that fuels the crisis in religious liberty.

In America today, the antithesis between church and culture has become fairly clear. Christianity does not provide the "cult" in the culture. The modern cult can be found in the earnest professions of movie stars, media personalities, ambitious politicians, and corporate executives. The new American religion, while shaped by Christian ideas about the dignity of human beings and Christian benevolence, is increasingly intolerant of Christian orthodoxy. We have seen a major corporation fire one of its founders who was the CEO for having donated to a traditional marriage referendum in California. The mere act of his previously unpublicized donation was enough to establish his unsuitability, his out-of-stepness with the new American faith. He had become, in fact, a type of heretic. More recently, we have seen the mayor of Atlanta terminate his fire chief because of his expression of traditional Christian sexual morality in a book written for his Sunday school class. There is a sense in which holding ordinary Christian beliefs is now a form of heresy marking one as unfit for a position of authority.

Whether the issue is the HHS mandate regarding the provision of contraceptive products or new attitudes regarding same-sex romance and marriage, the group representing the theology of this new cult has demonstrated a willingness to push those who disagree into conforming.[10] The Christian florist or baker with objections to working on a gay wedding must be brought to heel.

When the U.S. Supreme Court handed down a narrow decision in favor of Hobby Lobby despite its heretical view of biological ethics, the members of the new community cult howled as though some peasant had failed to remove his hat in the presence of the king. The dangerous Christian sect had been granted a stay.

There is a realization among the enemies of the Christian faith that we have become something like heretics. And for those who believe that people like us have been barring the door to a future filled with progress and greater happiness for mankind, the temptation to attack and marginalize Christianity in America is irresistible. Gay marriage, specifically, has proven to be the most effective wedge issue.

The *Obergefell* decision delivered the blow many Christians have known would fall upon the church for years. With the Supreme Court's ruling, one of the last intact pieces of the Christian sexual ethic cracked.

We might ask why the fight was such a slog? Why was it so hard? Part of the answer has to do with our culture's declining respect for the Bible's authority, but there is more to it than that. If you look back at Justice Kennedy's decisions prior to *Obergefell*, he often charged opponents of homosexuality with irrationality and animus. Many critics of Christianity latched on to that idea. We were crazy. And we were hateful.

In Plato's *Republic*, Socrates is discussing justice with various persons when Thrasymachus the sophist enters the previously calm debate in an angry and aggressive way. Straight off, he insists that Socrates must not make this argument or that argument about the nature of justice. He simply rules those ideas out of court. We have been through something like that in the gay

---

[10] Editor's addition: Cf. Michael Brown, *A Queer Thing Happened to America* (Concord: Equaltime Books, 2011).

marriage debate as the other team says, in essence, "The biological and sexual complementarity of men and women is irrelevant! *Now*, give us your argument."

We must realize, by the way, that Christianity is not being overtaken by reason. Is the community cult changing? Yes. Is there a new orthodoxy being imposed? Indeed. But what has not happened is that superstitious Christians have been overwhelmed by the superior rationality of smart, scientific, modern persons. I find that it takes little discussion with people to gain their agreement that the traditional marriage argument is rational. They don't agree with it. It clashes with their own will. But it is not some bizarre position to hold.

Where do things stand today? Christians (serious Christians, anyway) are becoming marginalized. Taking a traditional stance on marriage may limit opportunities in both government and business. Institutions may be pressed to change their views or lose the ability to compete on a level playing field with their peers.

Christians know whom they love and why they love him. They will continue to follow the teachings of their God and of the Bible. The question that remains is not whether we own the American house, but whether there is room in that house for us. Will we be allowed to maintain our integrity and yet still participate fully in American life? The end result will show us how much of the American pretty talk about rights and liberties is real and how much is just marketing for U.S.A. Inc.

Religious Liberty and the Nature of Law

Given the recent election in Kentucky that was almost certainly affected by the events surrounding Kim Davis (the county clerk who was jailed for refusing to issue marriage licenses), I think it makes sense to use her story to help us think through the situation. Kim Davis— whether you find her actions to be obstinate, principled, or poorly expressed—has raised a fundamental question about the nature of law.

For almost two decades, I have been a student of and then advocate for religious liberty. I spent my summers in law school writing pamphlets and briefs and otherwise pressing the cause of free exercise. But despite my deep commitment to religious liberty, when I heard about Kim Davis' case I was less than supportive. It may have been my legal training, but what I saw was a bad case.

My ideal is something like the husband-wife team running the Sweet Cakes bakery. They were just two private citizens, trying to live their lives and provide for their family when an intrusive state came after them for their religious beliefs. That case has good facts, sympathetic clients, etc. You'd like to go to court with that one.

In Kim Davis, I saw a person who is employed within the apparatus of the state government. Her job is to process marriage licenses. The Supreme Court has ruled that the right to same-sex marriage is fundamental. She doesn't have the case I'd want to argue before a bunch of skeptical judges.

But here is the crux of the issue. Law is more than a set of rules generated by human beings working under the auspices of the government. It almost has to be more than that, despite what Justice Holmes thought. Consider a couple of examples.

When World War II ended, the German soldiers and officials who had committed or participated in various atrocities had to answer for their crimes at Nuremberg. It is simply the case that they had not violated the laws of their government. So, why were they standing before the court? They were being tried according to some higher standard than the laws of their country. Where did that standard come from? If you say it came from the Allies who won the war, then you are saying that the Allies just imposed some kind of winner's justice. But I doubt that many of us would settle for that idea. We believe the war criminals received punishment because they did wrong. Not some artificial or socially useful wrong, but real wrong, a wrong that transcends formal political rules.

Martin Luther King, Jr. addressed his *Letter from Birmingham Jail* to white ministers who thought King went too far in planning protest activities that were unlicensed and illegal. They were thinking about the Christian emphasis on submission to government authorities (Romans 13) and wondered why King did not comply and delay his protests. He famously responded by looking to the work of Christian thinkers (Augustine and Aquinas, for example) in order to distinguish between just and unjust laws. The letter is widely admired and continues to stand as an important reminder of the priority of true law over the kind that is merely man-made.

Whether you agree with her or not, Kim Davis stands in the tradition of appealing to a higher law. (I began with Antigone and here we are again.) Many fair-minded people will look to the examples I highlighted above and will say, "Yes, such a tradition exists and is indispensable, but I don't agree that Kim Davis's refusal to participate in licensing same sex marriages fits with either Nuremberg or Martin Luther King, Jr."

Does the Supreme Court's decision to expand the definition of marriage to include same-sex pairings resemble historic evils such as genocide or segregation? If we are talking about the harm done or the rights violated, then I say no.

However, I am not seeking to make a point about the scale of harms. I am making an argument about the nature of law. The Supreme Court redefined marriage. The four dissents (especially the Chief Justice's opinion) clearly highlight the nature of what has occurred. Five lawyers out of nine who serve on an unrepresentative court, imposed their own view of marriage on the nation. The word "lawyers" is important because while people who go to law school should have a greater ability to interpret laws, there is nothing about the experience that would necessarily impart knowledge of the true, the good, and the beautiful.

There is a strong case to be made that male-female marriage is actually prior to the state and that the state would not exist without marriage. Aristotle argued as much. In other words, marriage creates the state rather than the state creating marriage. Further, I would argue that the case Justice Kennedy made about the evils of coverture, miscegenation restrictions, and laws prohibiting deadbeat dads from remarrying are all examples of the states attempting to wrongly redefine the nature of marriage in line with political preferences. Seen in that light, the court actually committed the evil it purportedly deplored.

Given the short-circuiting of democracy, the fundamental redefinition of the oldest human institution, and the relationship to be made between marriage and the design of the creator (the most obvious source of any "higher" law), Kim Davis has a leg to stand upon. She may not be Gandhi or Martin Luther King, Jr., but she is a reasonable candidate to appeal to the "big L" *Law* behind the law. In addition to the question of the higher law, I think she and others can argue that the Supreme Court has delivered an unconstitutional decision. Chief Justice Roberts' opinion illustrates the problematic nature of the narrow majority's jurisprudence very effectively.

It seems to me that the least we can do as a nation in light of the debate at hand is to recognize that the logic of accommodation appears to be unusually apt. Let us say that we do not wish to relitigate the issue, but instead that we want to focus on finding a way to live together as a people with a dwindling consensus on social issues. Religious liberty takes center stage. One of the great benefits of religious liberty is that it offers us a way to deal with competing claims to moral and metaphysical authority. We can seek to accommodate the religious and conscientious objectors in such a way as to respect their right to exist and not to yield to a questionable new social orthodoxy. Though many excitable new victors on the left would like to press their advantage and view religious liberty as some kind of license for haters, they should realize that the cases which emphasized accommodation began with the old liberal Warren Court, the same one that expanded constitutional liberties and protections in a variety of areas.

The logic of accommodation allows a nation such as the United States to house members of both camps by reducing the friction between winners and losers. If we take a strong view of religious liberty, we encourage peace between citizens instead of war because we acknowledge their right to exist and to avoid crises of faith and conscience. In the same way that the just war tradition encourages fighters to limit the means they will employ in order to win so that peace will be more easily achieved when the war is over, the logic of religious liberty may allow us to live together when substantive consensus is hard to come by. The nerves of our system are exposed, but religious liberty can serve as a balm.

Conclusion

Chief Justice Roberts' compelling dissent in the *Obergefell* case argued that a right to same sex marriage could not be discovered in the text of the constitution nor in the history of our jurisprudence. However, he observed, religious liberty is actually *in* the constitution. Nevertheless, he expressed his pessimism and his concern that religious liberty would actually be respected in the wake of the decision.

He is right to be concerned. The Solicitor General of the United States openly admitted during the oral argument of the case that if his side won, then the tax exemptions and non-profit statuses of many institutions would become an issue. Immediately after the court released its opinion, a variety of commentators began calling for the elimination of such legal statuses. The implication of such an act would be to make it impossible for Christian institutions to participate on an equal legal footing with other groups involved in similar work.

In the area of higher education, for example, the loss of non-profit status would be a significant penalty, but it is far from the worst that could happen. A simple regulation issued by the Department of Education could prohibit access to federal loans and other aid for students. It would not even require an executive order.

Secularists are already laying the groundwork for reducing the size of the Christian footprint on our society and the institutional life of the country. The White House has consistently elected not to employ the language of religious liberty. Instead, the president prefers to speak of "freedom of worship." It is obvious that freedom of worship is a much smaller protection that seems to limit its scope to things that happen in church buildings rather than out in the life of the community on the other six days of the week. Others are flatly hostile. They deny that opposition to gay marriage has anything to do with religious liberty and instead refer to "religious refusals."

Part of the reason the courts are unlikely to protect us in the way we might hope is because we are not like the Amish in breaking off from the world. We are still fully engaged and working. The establishment that one is challenging is unlikely to protect you if it views you as a threat. We are engaged and we still number in the tens of millions if not more.

Another major hurdle we face is the lack of solidarity we appear to have within our own ranks. The broader culture doesn't easily distinguish between evangelicals of the type gathered here and such persons as David Gushee, Tony Campolo, and Rachel Held Evans. What the culture hears is that some Christians can easily accommodate themselves to gay marriage and the rest need to get with the program. As I look upon those whom I would call the Christian appeasers of culture, I remember H. Richard Niebuhr's classic description of the same camp in his day for whom:

> A God without wrath brought men without sin into a kingdom without judgment through the ministrations of Christ without a cross.[11]

We have an arduous path before us. We will make constitutional claims. We will seek to inspire the good faith and assistance of those who disagree with us, but who yet may believe that we still deserve to participate in the American republic as full citizens with the rights and privileges such persons deserve.

We will also find ourselves improved by the challenge. I have suggested that state sponsorship virtually ruined the churches of Europe. I believe we will find that being further pressed by the secular state and secular elites will cause us to become more intentional, more disciplined, and hopefully more devout and sincere. The classic metaphor is that of gold being refined by the

---

[11] H. Richard Niebuhr, *The Kingdom of God in America* (Middletown, CT: Wesleyan, 1988), 193.

fire surrounding the crucible. Let us be found to be genuine by enduring the fire.

Perhaps we can be inspired by Abraham Kuyper, to whom I pointed earlier for insight.

> Even yet, after a lapse of three centuries . . . you will find entire social circles into which this worldliness is never allowed to enter, but in which the richness of human life has turned, from without, inward, and in which, as the result of sound spiritual concentration, there has been developed such a deep sense of everything high, and such an energy for everything holy, as to *excite the envy even of our antagonists*. Not only has the wing of the butterfly in those circles been preserved intact, but even the golddust upon this wing shines as brilliantly as ever.[12]

This description by Kuyper is a true one. I have seen this envy of our antagonists excited before. Years ago, *Christianity Today* asked me to review a book written by a secular reporter about Patrick Henry College. She clearly felt as though she were writing about Martians, but I could also see that she was touched by the earnest courtship rituals she observed among the students there. At one point, she described a New York Magazine story about her old high school and "bi-queer, metroflexible friends." A girl from the school posed on the cover with "her lightly acned cheek on the chest of an obviously naked boy." Rosin found herself disquieted by the story and concluded, "Given a choice for my daughter, I'd take all-girl reading circles over that any day."

Finally, the trouble that is coming upon us will help us to place our trust in Christ and Christ alone. I am no theologian, but I have read 1 Samuel 8 in which God warns the Israelites against their wish for a king. And I have taken account of the miserable experience of the kings of Israel and Judah. What it says to me is that there is only one king worthy of the name in this world. And that is King Jesus. We will continue to look to him.

---

12 Kuyper, *Lectures*, 76.

8

Gay Marriage and the Fourteenth Amendment

Debra Shattuck

On June 25th 2015 the United States Supreme Court issued its long-awaited decision in the case of Obergefell *et al* versus Hodges, Director, Ohio Department of Health, *et al.* The high-profile, landmark case culminated decades of litigation by gay rights advocates who had consistently argued that it was unconstitutional for the federal government and states to limit legally-sanctioned marriages to those between one man and one woman. On June 25, 2015, they were able to convince five of nine Supreme Court justices that the U.S. Constitution (specifically the Fourteenth Amendment) not only requires states to issue marriage licenses to same-sex couples, but also requires them to recognize any same-sex marriages lawfully licensed and performed in other states.[1]

The Supreme Court's decision seemed incomprehensible and unconscionable to millions of Americans for whom the definition of

---

[1] For details on the ruling and the historical background of the case see: Supreme Court of the United States Syllabus, *Obergefell et al. v. Hodges, Director, Ohio Department of Health, et al.*, (October Term, 2014).

marriage is a *moral* issue. It had only been 43 years since the Supreme Court had refused to hear the case of two gay men in Minnesota who were appealing their state's decision to deny them a marriage license. The Supreme Court had cited "want of a substantial federal question" when it dismissed the appeal of Jack Baker and Michael McConnell in October 1972.[2] What had transpired in the ensuing four decades to elevate the issue of gay marriage to that of a "substantial federal question," and why did five of nine Supreme Court justices decide in June 2015 that the U.S. Constitution *required* them legalize same-sex marriage in the United States?

Obviously, I cannot provide a comprehensive response to this question in the brief period allotted to me for this presentation, but I can help you understand the historical context that led to the Supreme Court's decision— particularly as it relates to changing interpretations and applications of particular clauses of the U.S. Constitution. To be honest, I was not at all surprised by the Supreme Court's ruling in *Obergefell v. Hodges*. Ever since the Spring of 2011, when I took a course on Family, Gender, and Constitutional History at the University of Iowa, I fully expected that gay marriage would become the law of the land in my lifetime. During my studies of Constitutional history, I learned that, over the course of two-plus centuries, marriage in the United States evolved from a private, social arrangement between individuals, into a governmentally-managed, civil contract between citizens. I also learned the extent to which both government and private sector entities had increasingly based rights and privileges on the marital status of citizens. This latter reality, more than any other, best explains the inevitability of the Supreme Court's decision, because the Fourteenth Amendment of the U.S. Constitution forbids any state to "deny to any person within its jurisdiction the equal protection of the laws." If a state allows one

---

[2] Molly Ball, "How Gay Marriage Became a Constitutional Right: The Untold Story of the Improbable Campaign that Finally Tipped the U.S. Supreme Court," *The Atlantic* (1 Jul 2015), http://www.theatlantic.com/politics/archive/2015/07/gay-marriage-supreme-court-politics-activism/397052; Lyle Denniston, "Gay Marriage and *Baker v. Nelson*, Analysis," www.scotusblog.com/2012/07/gay-marriage-and-baker-v-nelson/.

group of citizens to enter into the civil contract of marriage, it cannot deny that same right to other groups of citizens—especially when it, and other entities within the state, are basing rights and privileges of citizenship on the marital status of individuals. During this presentation I will provide an overview of some of the case law relating to the changing nature of marriage in the United States and I will explain how same-sex marriage advocates used the U.S. Constitution—particularly the Fourteenth Amendment—to force social change on the issue of marriage.

First, however, I want to set the stage by giving you a brief overview of the history of marriage itself, because in order to understand why the Supreme Court ruled as it did in *Obergefell*, you must understand that the definition of marriage is *not* solely a religious matter. Marriage is a *cultural* and *social* arrangement that became, over time, increasingly leveraged by states (here I am speaking of governments in general) as a civic relationship that established citizens' status within the state and that conferred certain responsibilities upon married parties. As you will learn during my presentation, it was the changing relationship of marriage to Federal and state governments within the United States that rendered the Supreme Court's decision in *Obergefell* virtually inevitable.

I suspect that many of you in this room believe that marriage (or at least Christian marriage) has always been overseen by the church. Consequently, you see attacks on "traditional" marriage only through the lens of Christian morality or as an assault on First Amendment guarantees of Freedom of Religion. And there is no question that there is a religious and moral component to the legal campaign to redefine marriage in the United States. However, it is important to recognize that there are also social and legal components to marriage that have influenced recent judicial decisions. So let's look briefly at the cultural, social, and legal aspects of marriage.

For millennia, groups of individuals have made decisions about marriage based on religious beliefs, personal preferences, and cultural traditions. These cultural choices influenced not only how marriage was defined, but also how it was identified. In other words, they dictated who could marry whom and they enabled others in the community to identify who was married and who was not. These cultural practices differed tremendously through time and geographic space. I don't have time this afternoon to take you on a worldwide cultural tour of marriage throughout history but, if you do some internet queries later today, you will find evidence of widely divergent cultural practices of marriage over time and geographic space. Marriage customs in Bronze Age Africa, Asia, and South America were unique to those locations and times just as marriage customs in those locations in the twenty-first century differ substantially from their Bronze Age pre-cursors.

We in the United States generally trace our cultural heritage back through Western Europe to the Roman empire, so let's look briefly at marriage in those cultures. In ancient Rome, a couple was considered married after their families got together (usually in the bride's home), exchanged gifts, and agreed to a dowry. (The dowry was money or property that the bride's family transferred to the husband to help establish the household and to help provide a financial cushion for the daughter should the husband die before he had achieved financial solvency.) Once the fathers signed the dowry agreement, the betrothed couple kissed and were now considered married.[3] In Germanic tradition, the transfer of money and property went from the groom's family to the bride's family. The "bride price" as it was known in some cultures, was a central part of the marital transaction—officially marking the transfer of responsibility for the woman from her father to her husband. Early Germanic law also recognized marriage "by capture" (basically abduction and rape) although this was not encouraged. Another form of marriage was "by consent;" this marital form was reserved for men whose families were too poor to pay a bride price. Under this arrangement, a man and woman could be recognized as married in the community, but the

---

[3] "Weddings, Marriages & Divorce," The Roman Empire in the First Century. http://www.pbs.org/empires/romans/empire/weddings.html.

bride's family reserved *mundium* (legal power) over their daughter because they had not been compensated for her transfer to the husband.[4]

In some parts of medieval and early-modern Europe, a man and woman were considered married when they agreed to be married and shared a drink to seal the deal. European court records include numerous cases of either men or women arguing before judges that they were certain that the drink they had shared with another person was done to consummate a marriage. On March 23, 1542, for example, John Calvin and his fellow syndics in Geneva, Switzerland, heard the case of a young man named Thibaud who was shocked to learn that the young woman who handed him a drink while he was playing skittles at the local tavern considered that they had been officially married when he drank it. The young woman, Loyse Bozonet, refused the five florins that was offered to her to give up her claim to her new husband; she hauled Thibaud before the Consistory (basically an ecclesiastical court) in Geneva. John Calvin and the other judges had to weigh the testimony of the numerous witnesses who described the exact circumstances of the drink Thibaud and Loyse shared. The drink had been followed by toasts from others saying, "May you be happy." The case of disputed marriage was so complex that the syndics deferred judgment until the following week when they finally decided to declare the marriage null and void because Loyse's father had not given his consent and Thibaud's father was refusing his consent without the other father's consent.[5] Thibaud was off the hook and his now "ex-wife," Loyse, left the room disappointed—and perhaps in search of another man with whom to share a drink.

---

[4] James Brundage, "Germanic Law & Marriage," *Law, Sex & Christian Society in Medieval Europe.* Excerpt posted to "Women of History," 30 Sep 2010, http://womenofhistory.blogspot.com/2010/09/germanic-law-marriage.html. See also, Philip Lyndon Reynolds, "Germanic Law: Betrothal and Divorce," Chapter 3, *Marriage in the Western Church: The Christianization of Marriage During the Patristic & Early Medieval Periods* (New York: E.J. Brill, 1994), Google Books.
[5] Robert M. Kingdon, ed., *Registers of the Consistory of Geneva in the Time of Calvin, 1542-1544* (Grand Rapids: William B. Eerdmans Publ. Co., [English translation] 2000), 25 & 29.

The case I just recounted for you took place in the sixteenth century—almost 400 years *after* the Church (the Roman Catholic Church) began asserting its authority over marriage by declaring it one of the seven sacraments. It had taken this step at the Council of Verona in 1184.[6] It was not unheard of, prior to the twelfth century, for couples to ask monks, priests, or other holy men to witness their marriages, but the vast majority of Christian couples in medieval Europe continued to contract and consummate marriages without the involvement of clergy. After the Church declared marriage to be a sacrament in 1184, increasing numbers of Christians did go to the local priest after getting married to ask for a prayer of blessing, but the ceremony or act by which they become "officially" married continued to be done outside of the church. Evidence of the prevalence of non-church marriages during the Middle Ages is the decision of Roman Catholic officials at the Council of Trent in 1563 to decree that from that time forward: "Those who shall attempt to contract marriage otherwise than in the presence of the parish priest or of another priest authorized by the parish priest or by the ordinary and in the presence of two or three witnesses, the holy council renders absolutely incapable of thus contracting marriage and declares such contracts invalid and null, . . .?"[7]

Even before the Council of Trent's decree that only marriages conducted by or in the Church were valid, both Catholic and Protestant churches had begun requiring that before a marriage contract could be finalized, the couples' intention to marry had to be publicized in church for three successive weeks. This weekly announcement was known as "the banns"—a term meaning proclamation—and was established to allow time for

---

[6] Timothy Buckley, *What Binds Marriage: Roman Catholic Theology in Practice* (London: Continuum, 1997), 53. Google Books. The decision of Verona was confirmed at the Council of Florence in 1439 in language reminiscent of Augustine's teachings about the threefold good of marriage—to support procreation, the faithfulness of the partners to one another, and its status as a symbol of the union of Christ and the Church.

[7] "Decree Concerning the Reform of Matrimony, Chapter I," The Council of Trent, Sessions XXIV, 11 Nov 1563, https://www.ewtn.com/library/COUNCILS/TRENT24.HTM.

individuals to come forward to challenge the validity of a proposed marriage. The problem the Church was trying to address was the high number of spouses (both male and female) who were leaving privately-conducted marriages in order to marry others. The publicizing of marriage "banns" in churches was an effort to ferret out potential adulterers and bigamists before they could contract new marriages with spouses unaware of previous marriages. It was also an attempt to hold them accountable to care for the children of their current marriages. Many modern wedding ceremonies still include the pastoral pronouncement: "If anyone knows any reason why this couple should not be married, let him speak now or forever hold his peace." This statement is a holdover from an era when marriages were almost always private affairs contracted between individuals or families. When the banns were read in church, if you had knowledge that either the bride or groom had already been married to someone else in a private ceremony, you were expected to speak up.

The evolution of marriage in the West from a business contract between families or a private agreement made by individuals into a church-sanctioned, religious ceremony with spiritual ramifications, took centuries. For most of Western history, marriage was not dependent upon any act of the church (or of the state for that matter.) It remained almost exclusively a cultural and social practice conducted by individuals and their families. The term "social practice" refers to the fact that marriages are generally the basis on which groups of people organize themselves. Communities have distinctive characteristics based on their marital practices because the marital relationship of individuals determines their relationship and responsibilities within the community. The reason there was so much emphasis in Roman and Western European marriage traditions on the signing of contracts and the transfer of property from one family to another was because marriage changed the status of both the groom and the bride within the broader society. The groom became an independent head of a household and the bride moved from being under the authority of her father to being under the authority of her husband. A key reason why there are so many cases involving disputed marital status in medieval court records is because communities had a vested interest in determining who had responsibility for taking care of children born within their communities *and* they had a vested interest in determining the status of those children—legitimate or illegitimate.

As modern nation-states evolved in Europe, marriage became increasingly integral to the political and economic stability of the state; consequently, governments took steps to oversee and control marriage by requiring either civil or ecclesiastical licenses and by recording marriages in civil records. This process of licensing took centuries to be fully implemented. In the United States, for example, it was not until the mid-nineteenth century that most states began licensing and recording marriages. Even today, there are nine states (Alabama, Colorado, Kansas, Rhode Island, South Carolina, Iowa, Montana, Utah, and Texas) that recognize common-law marriages—marriages in which two individuals cohabitate for a set period of time stipulated by each state. Common law marriages are, in essence, the private marriage arrangements of the past carried forward into the present. Even before the *Obergefell* decision, the Federal government had recognized Common Law marriages as valid for tax purposes and for determining the definition of "spouse" under the Family and Medical Leave Act of 1993.[8] Thus, even in the United States, there has never been a single *method* of marriage either legally stipulated or culturally adopted. So, what transpired in the last half century to cause the issue of same-sex marriage to rise to the level of national debate and to cause both Congress and the Supreme Court to decisively act to intercede in what had been a disparate practice throughout the country for most of its history? The simplest answer (to a question that has no simple answers) is that the issue of same-sex marriage entered the

---

[8] "Common-law Marriage in the United States," Wikipedia. The decision to recognize spouses in same-sex unions and common law marriages was issued by the U.S. Department of Labor in February 2015 after the Supreme Court ruled in *United States v. Windsor* that the Defense of Marriage Act's definition of "spouse" as only applicable to heterosexual unions was a violation of the Due Process Claus of the Fifth Amendment. https://en.wikipedia.org/wiki/United_States_v._Windsor.

national stage as part of a broader struggle over the meaning of the U.S. Constitution as it relates to the questions of individual "privileges and immunities," states' rights, and federal authority.

Let me begin the final portion of my presentation by reviewing the legal ramifications of the Supreme Court's decision in *Obergefell*. The Court's decision immediately nullified the federal Defense of Marriage Act (DOMA) and rendered scores of state laws banning same-sex marriage, unconstitutional. In 1996, the 104th U.S. Congress had passed the federal Defense of Marriage Act, known as DOMA. The Act entered the statute books as Public Law 104-199 when it was signed into law by President Bill Clinton. Section 3 of DOMA stated:

> In determining the meaning of any Act of Congress, or of any ruling, regulation, or interpretation of the various administrative bureaus and agencies of the United States, the word 'marriage' means only a legal union between one man and one woman as husband and wife, and the word 'spouse' refers only to a person of the opposite sex who is a husband and wife.[9]

Note that this was a *legal* definition of marriage—created to instruct federal government officials and employees how to interpret the terms "marriage" and "spouse" in federal laws and in the rules and regulations of federal bureaus and agencies. Section 2 of the law applied to states, territories, Indian tribes, and possessions of the United States. It stipulated that none of these entities was "required to give effect to any public act, record, or judicial proceeding of any other State, territory, possession, or tribe respecting a relationship of persons of the same sex that is treated as a marriage under the laws of such other State, territory, possession, or tribe, or a right or claim arising from such relationship." In other words, no government entity had to

---

[9] The text of Sections 1, 2, and 3 of DOMA are available at:
https://www.govtrack.us/congress/bills/104/hr3396/text/rh

recognize a same-sex marriage contracted elsewhere. Between 1998 and 2012, over 30 states followed the lead of the 104th Congress and passed constitutional amendments or laws banning same-sex marriage in their states. The flurry of federal and state legislation relating to marriage was prompted by a series of legal victories won by three gay couples in Hawaiian state courts between 1993 and 1996.[10]

On May 5, 1993, the Supreme Court of Hawaii ruled that if the state wanted to discriminate against gay couples seeking marriage licenses it had to prove it had a compelling reason to do so. This first-of-its-kind ruling galvanized gay rights activists nationwide who began strategizing how to gain legal recognition of same-sex marriages. Meanwhile, back in Hawaii, a judge ruled in a follow-up case in 1996 that the state had failed to prove it had a compelling public interest in preventing same-sex marriage. This ruling sparked a flurry of legislation across the country (and in Hawaii) to create a legal definition of marriage—one stipulating that it could only include one man and one woman. The same-sex marriage rulings in Hawaii also prompted a flurry of lawsuits by gay rights advocates in multiple states to test the constitutionality of same-sex marriage bans, and they inspired a movement, beginning in 2002, to amend the U.S. Constitution to stipulate that legal marriage in the United States could only be between one man and one woman.[11] In other words, the issue of gay marriage was being addressed by both legislative and judicial branches of government at the state and federal levels.

Between 1996 and 2015 gay rights advocates and defenders of traditional marriage faced off in multiple court cases centered on the question of whether the citizens of individual states have the right to define marriage as the union of one man and one woman. The key legal argument of gay

---

[10] For details on *Baehr v. Miike* (originally *Baehr v. Lewin*), see: Ball, "How Gay Marriage Became a Constitutional Right.

[11] For a legislative summary of the Federal Marriage Amendment (Marriage Protection Amendment), see: https://en.wikipedia.org/wiki/Federal_Marriage_Amendment.

marriage advocates was that bans on gay marriage violate the "due process" clauses of the U.S. Constitution's Fifth and Fourteenth amendments. The Fifth Amendment had been passed as part of the original Bill of Rights in 1791. It contains a number of provisions. One provision states that no person can be charged with a capital or "infamous" crime unless indicted by a Grand Jury (except in cases involving naval or armed forces in time of War or "public danger.") Another provision protects citizens from being tried twice for the same offence—i.e., double jeopardy. A third provision states that individuals cannot be "compelled in any criminal case to be a witness against himself"—leading to the oft-heard phrase "I plead the fifth" in court rooms and Congressional hearings. Finally, the Fifth Amendment states that no one can be "deprived of life, liberty, or property, without due process of law; nor shall private property be taken for public use without just compensation." That last sentence actually includes two provisions, the latter of which we relate to cases of eminent domain where the government wishes to take someone's private property for the public good. But, tucked within that last sentence is the concept that gay-rights activists used to challenge bans on same-sex marriage. "Due process of law."

What, exactly does "due process of law" mean? A check of the Free Legal Dictionary states that "due process of law" is: "A fundamental, constitutional guarantee that all legal proceedings will be fair and that one will be given notice of the proceedings and an opportunity to be heard before the government acts to take away one's life, liberty, or property."[12] Many of the guarantees within the Fifth Amendment regarding Grand Juries and self-incrimination, and eminent domain relate to this definition. But the dictionary adds an additional meaning, noting that "due process of law" also refers to "a constitutional guarantee that a law shall not be unreasonable, arbitrary, or capricious." It is this latter idea that gay-rights advocates initially leveraged to attack bans on same-sex marriage; they argued that these laws were unreasonable because they served no public good.

---

[12] http://legal-dictionary.thefreedictionary.com/Due+Process+of+Law

It is somewhat ironic that gay-rights advocates were able to use the Fifth Amendment to successfully challenge state bans on same-sex marriage considering that the Fifth Amendment was part of the Bill of Rights—a collection of ten amendments to the Constitution designed to set limitations on the power of the federal government over state governments. The U.S. Constitution probably would not have been ratified in 1787 without the assurance of advocates that a Bill of Rights (of states and citizens) would soon follow. The Constitution proposed a revolutionary form of government to replace the ineffective confederation of sovereign states that had been operating under the Articles of Confederation for a decade. The confederation had been a compromise government, enacted during a political revolution to overthrow the centralized power of the British monarch over its American colonies. Concerned about replacing one autocracy with another, the states sharply curtailed the authority of the federal government in the Articles of Confederation; it had no authority to levy taxes, manage trade, or compel compliance with its directives. By 1787, many state legislators recognized that the states would have to surrender some of their political sovereignty to a federal government if the new nation was to endure and prosper. The new Constitution granted that expanded authority, but the Bill of Rights—a group of ten amendments ratified *en toto* on December 15, 1791—set limits on that newly-expanded authority.

The Tenth Amendment was particularly important. It states: "The powers not delegated to the United States by the Constitution, nor prohibited by it to the States, are reserved to the States respectively, or to the people." Much of the opposition to the Supreme Court's decision in *Obergefell* (and to other decisions with national implications, like *Roe v. Wade*), center on the belief that the Federal government is overstepping its Constitutional authority by overturning state laws on marriage and abortion. We live in an era in which debate over Federal authority versus state sovereignty is particularly heightened; harkening back to the pre- and post-Civil war arguments about whether the Federal government had the authority to stop the spread of slavery and to halt the Southern states' racist treatment of blacks. The Fourteenth Amendment—the final key to gay rights advocates' judicial successes on same-sex marriage—originated in the immediate post-Civil War era as members of Congress sought to clarify the citizenship status of millions of recently-freed black slaves and to force Southern states to recognize their civil rights.

The Fourteenth Amendment became an official part of the U.S. Constitution on July 9th 1868. The amendment was bitterly contested; it was so unpopular in the South that, in order to get it ratified, the Congress (still operating without representation from the former Confederate states) passed a law in 1867 that denied representation to Southern states until they ratified the amendment. Talk about playing political hardball! Few, if any of us in this room, would have opposed the Fourteenth Amendment when it was proposed. Its purpose was noble. Not only did it stipulate that "all persons born or naturalized in the United States, and subject to the jurisdiction thereof are citizens of the United States and of the State wherein they reside," but it forbad any State from passing laws that abridged the "privileges and immunities" of U.S. citizens. It further stipulated that no state could "deprive any person of life, liberty, or property, without due process of law; nor deny to any person within its jurisdiction the equal protection of the laws." Did you catch the repetition of the Fifth Amendments reference to "due process of law?" Who, except the most recalcitrant Southern Fire-Eater,[13] could oppose such soaring rhetoric—rhetoric that harkened back to the glory days of 1776 and that invoked the spirit of the Magna Carta?

Though initially conceived, passed, and ratified by legislators focused on how to reintegrate the Southern states back into the Federal government and how to the protect the civil (i.e. citizen) rights of freed blacks, the Fourteenth Amendment became a key tool of subsequent generations of political and social activists intent on effecting social and legal change on issues like civil rights, women's rights, immigration, abortion, contraception, and gay

---

[13] "Fire-Eaters" were the extremist pro-slavery Southern politicians who fomented the creation of the Confederate States of America.

marriage. That is because, sown within the phrases of the Fourteenth Amendment's opening clauses, was a principle that the Federal government could and *must* act to protect the privileges and immunities of U.S. citizens when those privileges and immunities were threatened by the actions of state governments. This assertion of Federal power would have been untenable in the political environment that birthed the Tenth Amendment, but, in the context of post-Civil War America, when the health and welfare and civil rights of millions of vulnerable black Americans were being threatened, it seemed absolutely necessary.

In the ensuing decades, litigators used the Fourteenth Amendment to right many social wrongs—particularly those relating to blacks, Asians, and the poor. In 1898, for example, the Supreme Court ruled that 21-year-old Chinaman, Wong Kim Ark, was a citizen of the United States even though his parents were prohibited by the Chinese Exclusion Act of 1882 from becoming U.S. citizens.[14] In 1954, the Supreme Court cited the Fourteenth Amendment when it overturned its 1896 decision in *Plessy v. Ferguson*. The *Plessy* Court had said that segregation of facilities based on race was legal if they were equal; the Court ruled in *Brown v. Board of Education* that segregation of facilities based on race was unconstitutional.[15] Thirteen years later, the Court ruled in *Loving v. Virginia* (1967) that state laws preventing interracial marriage were unconstitutional under the Fourteenth Amendment.[16] In 1963 the Supreme Court ruled in *Gideon v. Wainwright* that state courts have an obligation under the 14th Amendment to provide poor citizens with counsel in criminal cases. "You have a right to an attorney; if you cannot afford one, an attorney will be provided to you." Those of you who watch crime dramas

---

[14] *United States v. Wong Kim Ark*, https://www.law.cornell.edu/supremecourt/text/169/649. See also, Linda K. Kerber, "Can the 14th Amendment Defend Itself?" Special to CNN, 15 Feb 2011, http://www.cnn.com/2011/OPINION/02/14/kerber.14th.amendment/.

[15] NCC Staff, "10 Huge Supreme Court Cases About the 14th Amendment," http://blog.constitutioncenter.org /2015/07/10-huge-supreme-court-cases-about-the-14th-amendment/.

[16] Ibid.

on television have no doubt heard this statement which was incorporated into Miranda warnings during the 1960s.[17] All of these rulings I just mentioned grew out of the provisions of the Fourteenth Amendment that protect the "privileges and immunities" of U.S. citizens and that guarantee them "equal protection of the laws."

During the 1960s and 1970s, litigators continued to expand the application of the Fourteenth Amendment to areas many believed were moral issues best left to the states. In *Griswold v. Connecticut* (1965), the Court ruled that the Fourteenth Amendment protected the right of the director of a Planned Parenthood clinic in Connecticut to counsel a couple about birth control options. The Court found a "right to privacy" not previously invoked in decisions about the Fourteenth Amendment. This newly-identified privilege of U.S. citizenship was subsequently leveraged by litigants in *Eisenstadt v. Baird* in 1972 to successfully argue that a Massachusetts law prohibiting the distribution of contraceptives to unmarried people was unconstitutional. It was also this "right to privacy" privilege that carried the day in the Court's *Roe v. Wade* decision legalizing abortion nationwide in 1973, and in its finding in the *Lawrence v. Texas* case of 2003 that state anti-sodomy laws were unconstitutional.

The proverbial "writing was on the wall" regarding same-sex marriage in the United States as early as the *Lawrence v. Texas* case, but it became especially apparent in 2013 when the Supreme Court ruled in *United States v. Windsor* that Section 3 of the Defense of Marriage Act was unconstitutional. If you recall, this was the clause that defined marriage as between one man and one woman and that defined "spouse" as a person in this form of marriage. The case was brought by Edith Windsor, a woman who had married Thea Spyer in Ontario, Canada in 2007. The two women had subsequently moved to New York state where, in 2009, Spyer died, leaving her estate to Windsor.

---

[17] The Miranda warnings grew out of another Supreme Court case—*Miranda v. Arizona* (1966)—which stipulated that statements made by suspects are admissible in court only if an individual was made aware of his/her right to an attorney before making them.

When Windsor tried to claim the federal estate tax exemption for surviving spouses, her claim was denied on the basis of DOMA's definition of "spouse;" she was liable for $363,053 in taxes on Spyer's estate. Windsor sued the federal government claiming that DOMA unfairly treated married same-sex couples differently than "similarly situated couples." In a 5-4 ruling that presaged its *Obergefell* decision, the Court held that: "The federal statute is invalid, for no legitimate purpose overcomes the purpose and effect to disparage and to injure those whom the State, by its marriage laws, sought to protect in personhood and dignity." Though the Court based its ruling on the "due process" clause of the Fifth Amendment, rather than on the Fourteenth Amendment, the vote indicated that the Court was poised to negate all similar state laws banning same-sex marriage. This is exactly what it did in June 2015 in its *Obergefell* decision.

Why had the Supreme Court decided that it was unconstitutional for the federal government and state governments to exclude same-sex marriage from legal recognition? The primary reason is because, over time, federal and state governments had increasingly used marital status to confer benefits and obligations on citizens. As Nancy F. Cott explains in *Public Vows: A History of Marriage and the Nation*:

> The governmental apparatus in the United States has packed into marriage many benefits and obligations, spanning from immigration and citizenship to military service, tax policy, and property rules. Husbands and wives are required to care for and support each other and their children. Social Security and veterans' survivors' benefits, intestate succession rights and jail visitation privileges go to legally married spouses.[18]

Cott notes that, in 1996, the General Accounting Office of the United States "found more than *one thousand* places in the corpus of federal law where

---

[18] Nancy F. Cott, *Public Vows: A History of Marriage and the Nation* (Cambridge: Oxford University Press, 2000), 2.

legal marriage conferred a distinctive status, right, or benefit."[19] It was not just governments that were basing rights and privileges on marital status—it was businesses and non-governmental agencies as well. Hospitals stipulated that only immediate family members could visit those in Intensive Care Units or make decisions about whether to terminate life support. Businesses granted survivor benefits to legally-married spouses and sick leave to care for legal spouses. In other words, the government and private entities were withholding certain privileges from citizens based on their marital status.[20] This practice made it possible to challenge the definition of legal marriage under the Fourteenth Amendment.

Same-sex marriage is now legal in the United States. Time will tell how citizens will respond to this momentous decision which portends seismic legal, social, and cultural changes. Judicial and legislative battle lines are already forming. Gay activists have begun suing Christian business owners in multiple states who decline to provide goods and services for same-sex marriages. (Most of the business owners have lost the cases and been fined and many have decided to stop providing their services for *any* weddings.) Meanwhile, just as they did after Hawaii's early rulings on same-sex marriage, legislators in many states and locales have begun framing legislation to provide religious conscience exemptions for those opposed to same-sex marriage. Emotions are running deep and the level of verbal vitriol is, unfortunately, high. Check out any social media discussion of same-sex marriage if you don't believe me.

I hope that those of us in this room will model Christ-like behavior when we address the issue of same-sex marriage with others. From a moral perspective we stand firmly on the Word of God that same-sex marriage and sexual relations are *not* God's design for His creation, but we should articulate

---

[19] Ibid.

[20] In February 2015, the Department of Labor, revised the definition of "spouse" for purposes of the Family Medical Leave Act, in light of the Supreme Court's ruling in *United States v. Windsor.* Prior to this action, businesses could refuse to grant leave to individuals in a same-sex marriage to care for the other partner. http://www.dol.gov/whd /fmla/spouse/.

this truth in love, just as Christ addressed the woman caught in adultery. From a civic perspective, we need to remember that we are sojourners in a civil society—a society based on the rule of *man's* laws. For much of our history, laws in the United States were formulated by Christians intent on integrating God's moral laws into society. Unfortunately, many of those laws were openly racist, sexist, anti-Semitic, and discriminatory and they sparked a backlash that laid the groundwork for the hostility we are seeing toward Christianity today. Nonetheless, we should not grow weary in well-doing nor become fainthearted. The proverbial pendulum has a way of swinging back the other way in civic life. Remember that the U.S. Constitution once counted 5 slaves as the equivalent of 3 white men for purposes of determining tax levies and representation in Congress; remember that the Supreme Court once ruled that segregation based on race was legal in this country; it took decades of courageous activism by blacks and sympathetic whites (many, if not most, of whom were Christians) to overturn this onerous ruling, but it did happen.

Christians have the same civic right to govern and to shape society as any other citizen. Educate yourself on the issues—especially on the historical background of issues—and exercise your right to vote, to legislate, and to participate in the judicial process of governing your city, state, and country. Same-sex marriage became the law of the land in June 2015, but you have the right (some would argue, the obligation), thanks to the Constitution, to shape how the Supreme Court's decision plays out in the future.

Pastor and patriot John Witherspoon did not hesitate to let his voice be heard in Colonial America; will you let your voice be heard in modern America?

9

Fundamental Differences:
How the Legal Lineage of *Obergefell* Can Help
Us Frame a Response to It

Donald Roth

In many ways, it was an expected blow.

Nevertheless, the *Obergefell* decision still set conservative circles reeling, a fact which exposed a critical weakness: while the coming of the same-sex marriage ruling was predictable, its opponents haven't necessarily articulated a response which goes beyond political or theological opposition to gay relationships. For a variety of political and legal reasons, gay marriage is *fait accompli* in the United States; however, this does not mean that the cause is lost, particularly for Christians. Instead, this opens up an opportunity for the Christian view of marriage not to stand in opposition to society's liberalizing vision but in antithesis to it. That is, with the legal sword removed as an obstacle to so-called marriage equality, the Christian view of marriage becomes not an enemy but another option, and that may prove much more effective as an avenue for persuasion than it first appears.

To learn how this might be the case, we first need to understand the decision's place in the history of the court, then we can seat this within a framework of comparable cases, and, finally, we can draw some ideas from this to help frame future advocacy.

The Emerging Jurisprudence of Liberty

First, it is important to recognize that the *Obergefell* decision is part of a solidification of a growing movement on the Supreme Court to define and strengthen the concept of "liberty" as a fundamental right guaranteed by the Constitution. This is not to say that the United States was founded without a fundamental respect for liberty, but a peculiar definition of that right has become more prominent in recent jurisprudence, and it represents a move to something new that is arguably grounded in a post-modern philosophical anthropology that merits criticism. The emergence of a new "liberty" right has been largely shaped by the judicial impact of one member of the Court: Justice Anthony Kennedy.

Justice Kennedy is arguably the most influential justice on the Supreme Court of the United States at this time. This is because, with the retirement of Sandra Day O'Connor in 2006, Kennedy became the sole "swing vote" on the Court: that is, on many contentious ideological issues, the Court splits between the (formerly) four "Conservative" justices and the four "Liberal" justices, with Kennedy unanimously playing the tie-breaking role.[1] At the same time that Kennedy has taken on this key role, his vision of the nature of rights granted by the Constitution has been evolving to embody an expanded conception of the right to "liberty" granted by the Due Process

---

[1] According to SCOTUS Blog, Kennedy has been in the majority on 100% of the 5-4 decisions since the Court's 2007 term. "5-4 Cases, October Term 2013 Stat Pack" *SCOTUS Blog* (accessible via: http://sblog.s3.amazonaws.com/wp-content/uploads/2014/07/SCOTUSblog_5-4_cases_OT13.pdf)

clause of the 5th and 14th Amendments.[2] However, both this conception of liberty and its relation to precedent prove problematic.

For Kennedy, "[a]t the heart of liberty is the right to define one's own concept of existence, of meaning, of the universe, and of the mystery of human life. Beliefs about these matters could not define the attributes of personhood were they formed under compulsion of the State."[3] At first blush, this might seem like a fitting description of a libertarian freedom of conscience, but, digging deeper, issues emerge. For one, this statement makes an explicit presumption that one's beliefs define their personhood, and not beliefs only, but the ability to put these beliefs into action, which Kennedy describes as "choices central to personal dignity and autonomy."[4] This means that human dignity is not inherent, but conditional, and government restrictions which limit a freedom of choice are inherently dehumanizing.[5]

While this analysis can be helpful in identifying government overreach in some circumstances—the restriction of free choice bound up in American slavery was dehumanizing in relegating certain persons to the status of livestock—it carries with it an implicit assumption that personhood is bound up in freedom of choice, something which can be granted or denied by the government. Justice Thomas argues forcefully and persuasively in his dissent that dignity must be rooted in something other than choice for the simple reason that this means that the government cannot take it away, hence its designation as an *inalienable* right.[6]

---

[2] The Amendments state, in parallel to one another, that persons cannot be "deprived of life, liberty, or property without due process of the law." U.S. Const. amend. V; U.S. Const. amend. XIV, § 1.

[3] *Planned Parenthood v. Casey*, 505 U.S. 833 (1992) at 851.

[4] *Id.*

[5] We can see Kennedy reach essentially this conclusion in *Lawrence v. Texas*, 539 U.S. 558 (2003) at 575 (stating that the *Bowers* precedent upholding sodomy bans "demeans the lives of homosexual persons").

[6] "The corollary of that principle is that human dignity cannot be taken away by the government. Slaves did not lose their dignity (any more than they lost their humanity) because the government allowed them to be enslaved. Those held in internment camps did not lose

Essentially, Kennedy's concept of liberty is a libertarian sentiment born of the same stock that rejects the concept of "legislating morality." While this is a common modern sentiment, its implications chip away at the very foundation of a social order, as every legal prescription and proscription telling us what we can and can't do has within it an implied morality. Society favors law-abiding behavior, and setting any law legislates the morality of continuing in that vein. For this reason, we largely waste of time to quibble over whether a law legislates some "morality," since this is not only inherent to the task of law-making, but deeply rooted in our jurisprudence.[7] Our nation itself was founded on Enlightenment principles such as the social contract, wherein people sacrifice some measure of personal autonomy of choice for the greater goal of social order. If a restriction of choice or a restriction of action along the lines of majoritarian morals is to be counted dehumanizing, then the entire enterprise of government itself must be said to have this effect.

While Kennedy's philosophical anthropology stands to a degree at odds with the Enlightenment principles animating the Constitution, it raises even deeper issues for someone professing a Christian view. From this perspective, Kennedy's vision implies a philosophical anthropology which says people are persons in their most fully realized sense only when they operate as a law unto themselves, free to "be who they are" without the disapproving glares of society. At its base, then, this is a view of mankind which falls prey to the same desires that first led humanity astray in the Garden. Although made in His image, we often long not to *serve*, but to *be*

---

their dignity because the government confined them. And those denied governmental benefits certainly do not lose their dignity because the government denies them those benefits. The government cannot bestow dignity, and it cannot take it away." *Obergefell v. Hodges*, 135 S.Ct. 2584, 2639 (2015) (Thomas, J., dissenting).

[7] Indeed, the police power long recognized as belonging to the states includes the right to legislate in the interest of the general welfare, including its morality. *See, e.g. Jacobson v. Massachusetts*, 197 U.S. 11 (1905) (Upholding mandatory vaccination laws over personal objections on the basis of the state's interest in the common welfare).

God, and we chafe at the notion that anyone ultimately possesses the ability to restrict our delusion.

I will work this out at more depth later, but it is worth at this point positing what an alternative Christian philosophical anthropology might be. John Witte, in his excellent work *God's Joust, God's Justice*, traces the development of the concept of rights in the western tradition, particularly since the Reformation. In the book, Witte highlights the important and often neglected contributions of Luther and some of the early Reformers to a view of the state grounded in an essential view of persons as *simul iustus et peccator*: since mankind stands equal before the throne of God, individuals should likewise stand equal before the bar of God's delegated hand of justice in this world (that is, government). At the same time, since mankind is plagued by sin, the government should serve as a restraint on evil, and mankind's own tendency to abuse such power should be checked and balanced through the divine institutions of church, home, and state.[8] This idea would be developed further by statesman Abraham Kuyper to the concept of sphere sovereignty, a notion which he would define politically by the principle that "political authority operates alongside many other authorities that are equally absolute and sacred in the natural and spiritual world, in society and family. Every attempt by political authority to try and rule over one of those other areas is therefore a violation of God's ordinances and resistance to it is not a crime but a duty."[9]

So how might this view of human nature and the purpose of the state stand at odds with Kennedy's formulation? To start, this view affirms the notion that human dignity and equality are innate and inalienable, and the government overreaches where it seeks to restrict those things. Given the varied substantive definitions, this might not stand at odds with Kennedy's concept of dignity, but the notion that individuals are communally governed

---

[8] John Witte Jr., *God's Joust, God's Justice: Law and Religion in the Western Tradition*, 38-41 (Grand Rapids: Eerdmans 2006).

[9] Abraham Kuyper, *Our Program* 21, trans. and ed. by Harry Van Dyke (Lexham Press 2015).

by a variety of institutions serves a caution for the notion that any perceived mistreatment of an individual be remedied solely by the government. If the family is anchored in the institution of marriage, and if that entity serves as a co-regent over individuals, then the government should be exceedingly cautious about stepping in to try to redefine the boundaries under which that institution operates. Yes, because of human sin, the government may act as a check on abuses within the family, but weighing in to enforce a new definition of that entity should be a last, rather than first, resort. In the view of sphere sovereignty, the state should take a more modest role that supports the flourishing of other spheres, one which favors the enforcement of so-called negative liberties[10] over the expansion of positive liberties.[11] This is not to say that no positive liberties are recognized, but when the Court is going to mandate entitlement to them, it must be careful in doing so.

More could be said on the root issues which lie behind a postmodern concept of liberty, but the primary importance to my thesis here is to highlight this root problem and see how it has been applied so that we might begin to formulate a response to it, and, with this explanation of the definitional concern, we can turn to its application.

Progressive Fundamentals

In my discussion above, I asserted that the thrust of Kennedy's philosophical anthropology stands at odds with the very enterprise of government. This is not an assertion that Kennedy himself stands at odds with that enterprise, it is a *reductio ad absurdum* which illustrates that the capacity of choice is an inappropriate grounding for human dignity. Indeed, no Justice on the Supreme Court believes that someone's fundamental self-

---

[10] That is, the right to be free from interference in things like privacy, speech, and religious exercise.

[11] That is, the right to assert a positive entitlement to something, such as a right to healthcare, food, or a living wage.

identification as a cannibal would entitle them to fully realize their personhood by killing and eating another person. Instead, even if we were to adopt Kennedy's approach, we would see universal agreement that some line must be drawn restricting a person's liberty to fully express themselves, but deciding exactly where this line would be drawn would be difficult, and, when that line is drawn by the Supreme Court, it has a deep national impact which may have unintended consequences. For these reasons, a concern for judicial restraint has established a jurisprudence in the Court that only those "principle(s) of justice so rooted in the traditions and conscience of our people as to be ranked as fundamental."[12] The *Obergefell* majority does not completely eschew this line of analysis, but they do twist it by application of a progressive, teleological hermeneutic to history that forces precedent to dance to their tune.

In *Obergefell*, the majority seats its analysis in a mixed narrative of both continuity and change. It hangs its precedential hat on the hook that marriage has been long recognized as a fundamental right, but it emphasizes a narrative of change to argue that the substantive definition of marriage itself is an evolving concept. In doing so, the majority plays a sort of bait and switch, taking the part it most likes about the traditional right to marriage but gutting the concept of any static meaning, and this is not the first time that this sort of tactic has been applied, but before we consider other examples of this

---

[12] *See, e.g. Snyder v. Massachusetts*, 291 U.S. 97 (1934) at 105. Justice Alito also argues this point in his dissent. *Obergefell* at 2640-41 (Alito, J., dissenting) ("Our Nation was founded upon the principle that every person has the unalienable right to liberty, but liberty is a term of many meanings. For classical liberals, it may include economic rights now limited by government regulation. For social democrats, it may include the right to a variety of government benefits. For today's majority, it has a distinctively postmodern meaning.

To prevent five unelected Justices from imposing their personal vision of liberty upon the American people, the Court has held that 'liberty' under the Due Process Clause should be understood to protect only those rights that are '"deeply rooted in this Nation's history and tradition."' Washington v. Glucksberg, 521 U.S. 702, 720-721, 117 S. Ct. 2258, 138 L. Ed. 2d 772 (1997). And it is beyond dispute that the right to same-sex marriage is not among those rights.").

hermeneutic in action, we should how it operates in this case with greater precision.

A. *Obergefell relies on a Progressive, Teleological Hermeneutic*

Speaking for the majority, Justice Kennedy starts his rhetorical movement first by emphasizing the centrality of marriage: "From their beginning to their most recent page, the annals of human history reveal the transcendent importance of marriage."[13] From this point, the majority moves quickly to seat the definition of marriage within a context of evolution and change that stands parallel to an ever-mounting recognition of the rights of homosexual persons. Kennedy starts his historical review with the assertion that marriage was once a matter of parental negotiation over various political, religious, and financial concerns. This evolved into a view of marriage as a "single, male-dominated legal entity" which was abandoned when "society began to understand that women have their own equal dignity." Citing a line of legal developments seeing a similar increase in the recognition of the dignity of homosexuals, the majority sees the availability of marriage to these individuals as a logical next step. Reviewing the evolution of marriage, Kennedy asserts that "[t]hese new insights have strengthened, not weakened, the institution of marriage," and it's clear from his opinion that he sees the expansion into same-sex marriage in much the same light.[14]

After placing marriage in a context of cultural change and evolution, Kennedy reaffirms the centrality and fundamental nature of marriage within our legal system. He cites significant legal history upholding marriage as a fundamental right, saying that these were a reflection of the Fourteenth Amendment's guarantee of protection from deprivation of "life, liberty, or property, without due process of law," and he speaks of that liberty interest

---

[13] *Obergefell* at 2593-94.
[14] *Id.* at 2595-97.

in the sense discussed above.[15] He moves from this re-centering on the fundamental nature of marriage to elucidate four reasons for why marriage is fundamental, and Kennedy brings his analysis home by arguing that each of these four purposes are either equally applicable to or even furthered by same sex marriage.

First, the majority argues that "the right to personal choice regarding marriage is inherent in the concept of individual autonomy." The majority draws language directly from precedent in cases like *Loving v. Virginia*, which said the freedom to marry "resides with the individual and cannot be infringed by the State." By this line of reasoning, marriage should be available to anyone, subject only to their personal preferences and the consent of a willing spouse (or spouses).[16]

Second, the Court argues that marriage "supports a two-person union unlike any other in its importance to the committed individuals."[17] This argument is tied into the first, seeing marriage as a way for people to define their identities by reference to their commitment to another person. By the logic of the liberty interest that Kennedy favors, it is then dehumanizing to limit the self-actualization available to those who choose the avenue of marriage to craft their identities.

Kennedy carries this logic further with his third argument, that marriage "safeguards children and families and thus draws meaning from related rights of childrearing, procreation, and education."[18] While stating that same sex couples can provide loving homes, the majority makes the unstated assumption that these homes are in every way equal to mixed gender households, meaning that current marriage laws run afoul of equal protection and actually "harm and humiliate the children of same-sex couples" because they create the stigma that same sex parents are somehow less desirable.[19]

---

[15] *Id.* at 2597-98.

[16] *Id.* at 2599.

[17] *Id.* at 2599.

[18] *Id.* at 2600-01.

[19] *Id.* at 2601.

Finally, Kennedy reiterates that "[m]arriage is a keystone of our social order." Kennedy cites the 1888 decision of *Maynard v. Hill*, saying "marriage is 'the foundation of the family and of society, without which there would be neither civilization nor progress.'" He then mentions that this sentiment "has been reiterated even as the institution has evolved in substantial ways over time." However, Kennedy's primary argument on this point seems to be that marriage, as central to the social order, carries with it a wide variety of legal and material benefits, which it is unfair to deny to same-sex couples.[20]

Looking over the fabric of this argument, it becomes clear that several assumptions are at play which seriously skew the result. For one, the majority does not answer the point made by the various dissents that one consistent feature across all of the historical examples given is that marriage in all of those cases was between a man and a woman. Far from being an accidental anomaly, the majority's own acknowledgement of the family orientation of marriage points to the essential aspect of this characteristic across historic marriage practice. Secondly, other than the fact that homosexual individuals seek to marry and society has been increasingly inclined to sympathy toward the group, there's little about Kennedy's arguments on the four fundamental aspects of marriage that necessitates extending marriage to same-sex couples unless that is an *a priori* inclination. While one might recognize an equal access claim to have marriage as one would like it (addressing the first foundation), little argumentation is given to link the other foundations beyond the fact that same-sex couples can love one another and children. Again, the reasoning serves the foregone conclusion.

At the end of the day, even the majority would not contest that same-sex marriage is a new innovation; however, the majority has a vision of history marching forward from a backward past into a progressively enlightened future that somehow makes this innovation simultaneously new and rooted in tradition all at once.

---

[20] *Id.* at 2601-02.

B. This Hermeneutic is not new

Of course, this is not the first time that historical or precedential analysis has been cast in a way that skews the result. The dissents in *Obergefell* focus on comparing the majority's reasoning to the now-abandoned progeny of *Lochner v. New York*, a period in the Court's history where an invented notion of freedom of contract led the Court to invalidate a number of labor reforms.[21]   However, there are far more recent and valuable points of comparison, specifically in *Roe v. Wade*, *Planned Parenthood v. Casey*, and *Lawrence v. Texas*.

This approach reared its head notably in the somewhat convoluted reasoning underpinning the *Roe v. Wade* majority. Section VI of *Roe* is a litany of historical precedent designed to suggest that opposition to abortion is a relatively new invention. While citing some contrary precedent, the majority argues that earlier society did not treat abortion, especially before quickening – the beginning of observable fetal movement – as homicide, then it uses this analysis to suggest that society was much more accepting of abortion than recent developments.[22]   While the Court only takes its analysis so far as finding the decision to terminate a pregnancy to be a protected matter of privacy, it still fashions this fundamental seemingly on the assertion that abortion was permissible at some point through history, conveniently sidestepping the fact that quickening was long viewed as the beginning of life such that the historical consensus on opposing the termination of prenatal life was much more uniform than the majority suggested.

While *Roe* took the first step of a jurisprudence that would be embraced in *Obergefell*, it sat on shaky ground until the second step was made in *Planned Parenthood v. Casey*. In shoring up the legal case for abortion, *Casey* leaned heavily on the precedential value of *Roe* while making the important shift from defending abortion as a private decision to a matter of liberty and

---

[21] *See, e.g., Obergefell* at 2617 (Roberts, C.J., dissenting).

[22] *Roe v. Wade*, 410 U.S. 113, 129-48 (1973).

autonomy that a woman is entitled to make.[23] In doing this, *Casey* cast the scope of liberty quite broadly. In addition to the quote discussed previously regarding the anthropological underpinnings of Kennedy's approach to liberty,[24] *Casey* openly discarded any specific limitation to the scope of the liberty interest protected by the 5th and 14th Amendments, saying "[n]either the Bill of Rights nor the specific practices of States at the time of the adoption of the Fourteenth Amendment marks the outer limits of the substantive sphere of liberty which the Fourteenth Amendment protects."[25] The majority then went even further to quote Justice Harlan's dissent from *Poe v. Ullman*, where he said the right to liberty "is a rational continuum which, broadly speaking, includes a freedom from all substantial arbitrary impositions and purposeless restraints, ... and which also recognizes, what a reasonable and sensitive judgment must, that certain interests require particularly careful scrutiny of the state needs asserted to justify their abridgment."[26] The conclusion reached was that, since reasonable minds could disagree as to abortion, the government had no business banning it, at least in the early stages of pregnancy.

In *Lawrence v. Texas*, Justice Kennedy first brought these two rhetorical moves together in an opinion which invalidated Texas' anti-sodomy laws. Kennedy began the body of his analysis by tracing decisions such as *Griswold v. Connecticut* (finding prohibitions on contraceptives to married couples violated their right to privacy) and then subtly shifting the grounds of analysis away from a focus on the negative liberty of privacy, that is, keeping the government out of certain affairs, and toward grounding this right in what the majority characterizes as the broader, encompassing right to liberty.[27] In fact, Kennedy would reason his rejection of Texas' anti-sodomy statutes not as a matter of infringing on typically private relations but because it infringed

---

[23] *Planned Parenthood v. Casey*, 505 U.S. 833, 853 (1992).

[24] *See supra* n.3.

[25] *Casey* at 848.

[26] *Id.*

[27] *Lawrence v. Texas*, 539 U.S. 558, 564-68 (2003).

on an individual's choice of sexual activity, something Kennedy found to "demean the lives of homosexual persons."[28]

Again, like in *Obergefell*, Kennedy was not content simply to shift the grounds of analysis from privacy to his preferred liberty framework, he also cast a highly skewed gloss over history to suggest that social opposition to homosexual activity was of relatively recent vintage, and a vintage that was more recently being repudiated by broader society.[29] He did this to suggest that the legal reasoning in the case explicitly overturned in *Lawrence, Bowers v. Hardwick*, had been wrongly decided when it found no fundamental right to engage in sodomy. The dissent excoriates Kennedy for this move, pointing out that the Constitution only prevents states from infringing fundamental liberty rights and that Kennedy's historical analysis is selective at best, if not outright deceptive.[30] By any fair analysis, the majority's claim here that any right to same sex relationships might be deeply rooted in our Nation's history is suspect at best.

Taken as a whole, the rhetorical approach taken in *Obergefell* is troubling, but hardly new. It is a hallmark of the Court's more activist decisions, but that doesn't mean that those decisions don't have a lasting legal impact, and perhaps the legacy of *Roe* is most instructive as a point of comparison on this front.

Learning from the Past: *Roe* Advocacy

As explained above, abortion has seen historical exegesis and an eventual precedential argument that mirrors what was used to justify *Obergefell*, and, in many ways, this makes it an excellent test case for strategizing what the way forward can look like. In this regard, there are two principal messages that I

---

[28] *Id.* at 575.

[29] *Id.* at 567-572.

[30] *Id.* at 592-598 (Scalia, J., dissenting).

think are particularly important: first, this precedent is unlikely to go away, and, second, this does not mean that opposition to this holding is doomed.

With perhaps the exception of *Lochner*, the lesson of most of the more activist judicial opinions of the past century is that they stick around. In general, conservative justices are less apt than liberal ones to upset settled precedent, and, despite strong initial backlash to *Roe*, *Casey* marked what was likely the high water mark in seeking to repeal the earlier decision. While *Casey* did alter the rules of the game in ways that are yet unresolved, it upheld the essential holding of *Roe,* and, after so many years, it's unlikely that any but the most lopsidedly conservative future Supreme Court would ever disturb that. Given the moderate to significant step left that Justice Scalia's recent death likely signals for the Court, it's unlikely that there will be a coalition anytime in the near future to disturb the consensus behind *Obergefell*.[31] Given this fact, the traditional marriage movement wastes some of its valuable political capital if it pushes for an absolutist rollback of the decision. After all, even if *Obergefell* were overturned today, that would not invalidate same-sex marriage, only return the issue to the States, a significant number of whom already recognized the practice.

However, I don't think this is grounds for losing hope as to advocacy around this issue. Abortion is a good comparison case because it is, in many ways, a comparable social hot button, but one with a longer history behind it than the relatively recent successes of the gay rights movement. Also, with this issue, there are some reasons for optimism. Firstly, Gallup polling has shown not only a resurgence of the pro-life position since its low ebb in the 1990s, but this change in the wind has been led by an increasing opposition to abortion among the 18 to 29-year-old demographic.[32] This suggests that there was a period in the wake of *Roe* which saw increased support for

---

[31] Whether the Senate moves to confirm an Obama nominee or the Democratic candidate wins the presidential election, the majority of most likely scenarios see a leftward shift for the Court.

[32] Lydia Saad, *Generational Differences on Abortion Narrow*, Gallup (March 12, 2010), http://www.gallup.com/poll/126581/generational-differences-abortion-narrow.aspx.

abortion, particularly as issues came to a point near the decision of *Casey*. The data is insufficient to draw a causal link between the high water mark of efforts to repeal *Roe* and the waning support for abortion, particularly those that say it should be legal in all circumstances, but the correlation is clear. Again, while causation is unproven, it would not be inconsistent with information we have about the polarizing effects of more confrontational approaches to the issue, and a heightening of the culture war dynamic around that time might have actually done more harm than good. Regardless of why, however, polling does indicate that something about the pro-life position has been becoming more attractive, and this may have to do with a shift in approach among those who advocate for it.

One very successful approach that departed from the culture war dynamic was pioneered by the Vitae Foundation and first described in a ground-breaking essay on the website *First Things* back in April of 1998. In that essay, Paul Swope, a project director with the foundation, described a radical reimagining of pro-life advocacy around an empathetic understanding of the psychology of a woman faced with an unwanted pregnancy. In extensive research, the organization learned that women would tend to carry their children to term when "guilt wins out over shame, when they feel that the pregnancy will not end their own current and future selves, and that the unborn will be better off alive than dead."[33] Taking their research to heart, the foundation sponsored a thirteen week television campaign in the Boston area in 1997. In independent polling conducted to test the effectiveness of these advertisements, the study showed a 7% increase (308,000 people) in the population supporting the pro-life position, a shift that was explicitly linked to those who remembered the foundation's advertisements.[34] While unlikely to lead to total victory for the pro-life movement, this type of advocacy has

---

[33] Charles T. Kenney & Paul Swope, *A New Understanding of the Trauma of Abortion*, Vitae Foundation (January 2015),
http://vitaefoundation.org/wp-content/uploads/2015/01/trauma-of-abortion-long.pdf.
[34] Paul Swope, *Abortion: A Failure to Communicate*, *First Things* (April 1998),
http://www.firstthings.com/article/1998/04/004-abortion-a-failure-to-communicate.

a tremendous cumulative effect, and the traditional marriage movement can learn much from modeling this type of approach.

Leaning into the Future: Holistic Advocacy

Moving forward, I believe that my analysis shows that the root issue which brought about the *Obergefell* decision is not just an isolated political preference for the gay lobby but a fundamentally different approach to both government and, ultimately, philosophical anthropology, that favors a radically self-centered view of the person. For those locked in a worldview that sees personhood as the ability to define the rules of their own universe around their personal desires, it will be incredibly difficult to achieve persuasive traction on the issue of marriage. This becomes evident when we pursue the same empathic line of reasoning that the Vitae Foundation used to drive its pro-life advocacy.

The Pro-life Movement is faced with a much more winnable battle when advocating for unborn children. As described above, it seeks to help balance guilt over shame. Where typical culture war-type advocacy focuses on piling on the guilt, the Vitae Foundation worked to chip away at the perception of shame. Where the typical pro-life advocacy focuses on the definitional life of the unborn child, the Vitae Foundation addresses the nearer issue for women in their self-identification and supports the idea that a woman's identity/self will not be lost by carrying a child to term. The power of empathy helped to focus the movement on the parts of the balance that struck most closely to women facing the abortion decision, but, ultimately, pro-life advocacy could be successful without having to challenge the fundamental worldview of self-definition.

With traditional marriage, the task will be more difficult, because the decision involved is about resolving a personal dissonance between sexual desires and self-expression weighed against potential shame and interpersonal backlash. Furthermore, the point of decision isn't at the point of getting married. Instead, this path is largely embarked upon around the time an individual is considering whether or not to come out. At that level, the LGBT movement has been very successful in both encouraging people to be their "authentic selves" while working to minimize the social stigma of making the transition. Both the pregnant woman and the closeted person face the same perceived future of a destruction of the self in the face of an untenable status quo, but while pro-life advocates can help relieve that tension by helping women come to peace with who they perceive themselves to be (moral people), traditional marriage advocates would need to convince someone that they've had their fundamental assumptions wrong all along.

This is not to say I believe the cause to be lost, just that this line of analysis suggests that a more fundamental strategy must be taken. Drawing our cues from the pro-life movement, I don't believe that we invest our resources well if we rely on winning victory through the courts or even by Constitutional amendment, legislative workaround or any other of the typical tools in the culture warrior toolkit. Instead, we must see this as a fundamental effort to shift worldviews. We should seek to emphasize the deficiencies of a worldview centered on self-definition, recognizing that, while we do have individual characteristics, our personhood has a relational dimension to it. We are who we are because we have been endowed with certain characteristics by our Creator, and this not to pursue life, liberty, and happiness in isolation, but because our happiness is best seated in lives lived in joyful service to both our God and to one another. These ideas, that we save our lives by losing them, that we find ourselves by giving up ourselves, that we stand simultaneously individual and collective, sinner and (for those in Christ) saint, are foolishness to the world's wisdom, yet they resonate deeply for those who can hear their Savior's call. Rather than fighting in the front lines of the marriage wars (which aren't even the front lines of the persuasive fight), we should step back and see where we can offer a different way to those struggling with who they are. Authors like Debra Hirsch make a start at this sort of thing by helping to give a more holistic view of sexuality that moves past defining a person by their genital preferences. In her book, *Redeeming Sex*, she talks frankly about her own transition out of lesbianism not because someone sat her down and told her it was wrong, but because she realized that there was more to her sexuality than her sexual partners.[35] This is the type of reasoning that offers a genuine alternative to those wrestling with sexual orientation. It doesn't ask people to rewire their desires but to broaden their horizons. While desire may shift over time, a broader, more holistic, and communally integrated view of the person allows for someone to face the thought of abstaining from desired behavior without viewing that as a subversion or reduction of the self.

Of course, all of these ideas will only work if the Christian community and others in the traditional marriage camp can live them out themselves, and this may mean coming face to face with the frank realization that we all feel the seductive call of the ethos behind Kennedy's definition of "liberty," not because it's a reflection of truth, but because our sinful parents were wooed by the very same inclination in the Garden. Ultimately, we must ourselves live better and model the alternative way, allowing us to stand not primarily in opposition, but in antithesis to the way of the world. After all, the struggle with *Obergefell* is rooted in a view of who we are as persons that makes each of us a law unto ourselves, and the Christian church has been called to struggle against that worldview from the very beginning. We have not given up that struggle since, and we should not give it up now, but we should still recognize it and winsomely pursue it for what it is.

---

[35] Debra Hirsh, *Redeeming Sex: Naked Conversations about Sexuality and Spirituality* (Downers Grove: InterVarsity, 2015).

www.ingramcontent.com/pod-product-compliance
Lightning Source LLC
Chambersburg PA
CBHW060448280326
41933CB00014B/2702